HEADS OF STATE

HEADS OF STATE

Icons, Power, and Politics in the Ancient and Modern Andes

Denise Y. Arnold
Christine A. Hastorf

Left
Coast
Press
Inc.

Walnut Creek, California

LEFT COAST PRESS, INC.
1630 North Main Street, #400
Walnut Creek, CA 94596
http://www.LCoastPress.com

ISBN 978-1-59874-170-4 hardcover
ISBN 978-1-59874-171-1 paperback

Library of Congress Cataloging-in-Publication Data:

Arnold, Denise Y.

   Heads of state : icons, power, and politics in the ancient and modern Andes / Denise Y. Arnold, Christine A. Hastorf.
      p. cm.
   Includes bibliographical references and index.
   ISBN-13: 978-1-59874-170-4 (hardback : alk. paper)
   ISBN-13: 978-1-59874-171-1 (pbk. : alk. paper) 1. Indians of South America— Andes Region—Politics and government. 2. Indians of South America—Andes Region—Kings and rulers. 3. Indians of South America—Andes Region— Antiquities. 4. Kings and rulers—Andes Region—History. 5. Head—Political aspects—Andes Region. 6. Head—Religious aspects—Andes Region. 7. Andes Region—Politics and government. 8. Andes Region—Antiquities.
I. Hastorf, Christine Ann, 1950- II. Title.
   F2230.1.P65A76 2008
   323.1198—dc22   2007033242

Printed in the United States of America

♾™ The paper used in this publication meets the minimum requirements of American National Standard for Information Sciences—Permanence of Paper for Printed Library Materials, ANSI/NISO Z39.48–1992.

Printed on recycled paper

07 08 09 10 11 5 4 3 2 1

In memory of our friends and colleagues: Anne Paul and Medha Yodh

Contents

List of Illustrations   11

Acknowledgments   15

Introduction   19
  Headhunting in the Andes   20
    The Models in Play   22
    Ancestral and Enemy Heads: Interweaving Identities   26
    Heads and the Regeneration of Life   28
    The Ancestral Dead, Identity, and Andean Polities   30
  Methods and the Organization of the Book   32

PART I THE ETHNOGRAPHY OF ANDEAN HEAD TAKING AND POWER   35

1 Heads in Small-scale Polities   37
  Toward a Theory of Heads in Expanding Polities   37
  The Fetishism of Heads as Protected Things   44
  Heads and the Powers of Regeneration   47
    The Nature of These Powers of Regeneration.   50
    Transformations in Values and the Fetishism of Commodities Revisited 58
  Why a Head?   60
    Flying Heads   65

2 The Captured Fetish, the Mountain Chest, and Sacrifice   71
  The Concentration of a Head's Powers   72
  The Counting Boards Called *Yupana* and the Spirit of
    Calculation   80

3 Drinking the Power of the Dead   91
  Sucking out of a Skull   91
  The Patterns of Drinking Pathways   94
  Toward an Iconography of Drinking, Social Memory, and Warfare   96

Visual Representations on Colonial *Qirus* of the Potent Energy
of Trophy Heads   99
The Space above the Feline Head   103

4 The Nested Power of Modern Andean Hierarchies   **107**
Personal Heads   108
Initiation Rites   109
Household Heads   110
Gendered Heads and the Parallelism of Warriors and Weavers   114
Ayllu Heads   117
Heads as Holders of Power; Holders of Power as Heads   117
The Vara *Staff of Office*   121
The Geopolitical Place of Heads in the Major Ayllu Formation
and Beyond   124
The Ayllu Political Center   126
The Ritual of Expanding Power Outward: Willja   130
The Ayllu Boundaries   132
From Ayllu Limits to Ayllu Center   132
The Postwar Remaking of Regional Relations between Ayllus   133
The Major Ayllu within a Wider Andean State   137
Early State Bureaucracies and the Management of Heads   139
Weaving and Kipu *Practices at the Service of the State*   139
Conclusions   143

PART II   THE ARCHAEOLOGY OF ANDEAN HEAD TAKING AND POWER   **147**

5 Heads and the Consolidation of Andean Political Power   **149**
The Dual Political Forces that Patterned Past Community Formation   150
Heads of State   152
Heads and Ancestral Power   154
The Mallki   154
Remembered Bones   156
Heads and Rains   157
Ancestral Heads in Archaeological Settings   161
Rituals Centered around Tombs, Body Parts, and Images of the Dead   163
The Ñatitas *of Contemporary La Paz*   163
Bodily Relations in Architectonic Form   166

**6 Heads and Andean Political Change from an
Archaeological Perspective**   **169**
The South-Central Andes   169

The South Coast | 169
    Paracas | 169
    Nasca | 176
The Lake Titicaca Region | 182
    The Formative Phases | 182
The Middle Formative: Chiripa | 187
    Late Formative/Early Intermediate Period (Tiwanaku I, III): Pukara | 190
    Middle Horizon Tiwanaku | 192
Middle Horizon State Developments: Wari | 196

7 Central Andean Political Developments | **205**
Early Ceremonial Centers of the Central and North-Central Andes | 205
North-Central Peruvian Coast | 209
    The Late Intermediate Period | 211
Late Horizon | 212
    The Inka and the Colonial Period | 212

8 Conclusions | **217**
    1. Heads as Symbols of Political Power | 218
    2. Heads and Regeneration | 220
    3. Heads, Violence, and Fertility | 223
    4. The Language of Heads | 224
    5. The Body Politic | 226
    6. Heads and Political Systems | 227
    7. Heads as Constructors of Social and Cultural Identity
       and Difference | 229
    8. Heads as Part of Economic Transactions | 230
    9. The Guarding and Maintenance of Heads | 232

Appendixes | **235**
Sites and Toponyms Mentioned in the Text | 235
Andean Cultural Sequences | 239

Glossary | **241**
Notes | **247**
References | **257**
Index | **281**
About the Authors | **293**

List of Illustrations

Figures

1.1 Photo of a Nasca Ceramic Figure of a Corpulent or Pregnant Woman with the head of the Oculate Being Tattoo around Her Vagina   52

1.2 A Nasca Being with a Head Pouring Out of Its Mouth   53

1.3 An Interlaced Border with a Head Motif from an Early Horizon Coastal Textile   56

1.4 Two Early Intermediate Period Pukara Ceramic Images of the Camelid Woman Holding Living Things and the Male Associated with Heads   59

1.5 Line Drawing of the Tello Obelisk Cayman Being   62

1.6 A "Flying" Ecstatic Shaman from a Paracas Textile   68

2.1 Photo of the Platform Mound from Pampa de las Llamas–Moxeke, in the Casma Valley   74

2.2 Drawings of Moche "Mountain Chests" in Roll-outs from Two Stirrup-spout Bottles   76

2.3 Model of a "Gaming Board" Made of Wood, Found in Chán Chán   82

2.4 Checkered Counting Board with Relief Figures of Human Heads, from Chordeleg (Cuenca Prov., Ecuador)   84

2.5 The Same Board from Chordeleg with Two Platforms, Seen from above   84

2.6 The Same Checkered Counting Board, from Chordeleg. Rosettes Incised on the Base   85

2.7 Iconography of a Moche Ceramic Vessel Showing a Procession, a Large Measuring Board, and Trophy Heads on Poles   86

2.8 Guaman Poma's Drawing of an Inka Accountant with *kipu* and *yupana*   87

3.1 Colonial *qiru* Designs Showing Centrifugal and Centripetal Tendencies   97

3.2 Silver Colonial *qiru* (Qu. *akilla*) with Bodiless Heads and Flowers Enclosed by Zigzagging Lines 102

3.3 *Tocapu* Designs in the Frieze of a Colonial *qiru* 105

4.1 Photo of the Modern Ritual of *uruyaña*, where a Young Man after Military Service, Eats the Brains of a Sheep 110

4.2 Severed Heads on Poles Painted on a Nasca Ceramic Vessel 115

4.3 Diagram of the Central Plaza of *Qaqachak marka*, with Its Five Buried Skulls 129

4.4 Diagram of the Main Plaza of Qaqachaka as an Immense Loom, with the *jira mayku* Spirits Dancing in the Corners 129

4.5 Diagram of the Ritual of *willja*. The Communal Field, or *manta*, with Its Five Skulls and Their Containers 131

4.6 A *wincha* Headband from Paracas 134

4.7 Diagram of the Major Ayllu of Qaqachaka. Going to the Boundaries and Returning with Trophy Heads 136

4.8 Guaman Poma's Drawing of a Provincial Administrator Holding a Wrapped *kipu* and Another *kipu* Unwrapped 141

4.9 Guaman Poma's Drawing of an Inka Warrior Holding a Trophy Head as if It Were a *kipu* 142

5.1 Guaman Poma's Drawing of a Dead Inka Being Carried on a Litter 151

5.2 *Ñatita* Skull Decorated with Flowers and Smoking a Cigarette 164

5.3 *Ñatita* Decorated with Flowers, Laid out on a Tomb after the Mass 165

6.1 A Paracas Textile with a Figure Holding a Trophy Head 172

6.2 A Chiripa Carved Head-stone Plaque 185

6.3 A Pukara Ceramic Fragment Feline Face with Rays or Tears Coming out from the Eyes 186

6.4 Carved Middle Formative Rock from Kala Uyuni (Qala Uyuni) Enclosure, Taraco Peninsula 189

6.5 *Chachapuma* Stone Figure from Three Sides, Uncovered from the Base of Akapana, Tiwanaku 191

6.6 A Front-faced Image from Tiwanaku, the Ponce Stele 193

6.7 Gateway of the Sun Image of the Front-faced Destroyer, Tiwanaku 196

6.8 A Conchopata Face-Neck Liquid Storage Jar 199

6.9 A Tiwanaku Portrait Head Gray-ware Tumbler from Kalasasaya 200

7.1 A Moche Portrait Head 210

Maps

1.1   The Region of Qaqachaka in the South-Central Andes,
with insert a): The Ayllus Mentioned in the Study, and
insert b): The Historical Regions   39

6.1   The South-Central Andes, with Sites Mentioned in the Text   170

7.1   The Central Andes, with Sites Mentioned in the Text   206

Acknowledgments

MANY PEOPLE have helped us develop the ideas expressed here. Ongoing conversations between Denise Arnold and Christine Hastorf since 2000 served as the basis of the theories we put forward. In these conversations, we were aware of the possible pitfalls of combining both ethnographic descriptions and the approaches of interpretative anthropology with an archaeological approach grounded in material data only.

An all-too-brief collaboration between Arnold and the late Anne Paul concerning the modern-day ethnographic equivalents of the iconography of borders in Paracas weavings led to key questions that we have been able to explore more fully here. Conversations with Carlos Fausto, and a mutual sharing of books and articles in 2005, helped us understand some of the relations between Andean and Amazonian variations on common themes. A general sharing of ideas with Martha Sandra Bustillos and the students in the course "Duke in the Andes: Visual Languages," in 2005, inspired some of the debates presented here. Anita Cook and Mary Weismantel clarified some of the archaeological concepts and the examples that we use.

The book draws on anthropological fieldwork carried out since 1985 by Denise Arnold in the ayllu of Qaqachaka (Prov. Abaroa, Dept. of Oruro, Bolivia) and the surrounding region, especially in the period 2000–2001 with the aid of a Leverhulme Trust research grant (reference no. RFG/6/RFG/2000/0367). Ayllu, a term that will recur throughout this book, is an Andean community that claims descent from ancestors in common, and has common territories. We thank the ayllu authorities of those years for their hospitality, and Elvira Espejo of the pueblo of Qaqachaka for sharing her ideas on textiles and their meanings. In the neighboring ayllus, we thank Don Domingo Jiménez of ayllu Milma in the northern Potosí valleys for sharing his thoughts on many aspects of Andean ritual life.

Ideas also began to grow during the archaeological fieldwork between 1977 and 1986 in the Upper Mantaro Archaeological Project, Peru, and continued since 1992 on the Taraco Peninsula in the southern Titicaca Basin, Bolivia.

There, Hastorf has codirected the Taraco Archaeological Project that has been funded by the U.S. National Science Foundation, the National Geographic Society, the Wenner Gren Foundation, the University of California Undergraduate Research Apprenticeship Program, and the Stahl Foundation. We thank the local and national authorities in both Bolivia and Peru for their hospitality. We also thank all the members of the Taraco Archaeological Project team and the Andean archaeology seminars at the University of California, Berkeley, for inspiring a sense of Andean worldview, rigorous data collection, and historical trajectories. They have warned us of essentializing "Lo Andino."

Apart from Spanish, both Qaqachaka and the modern-day Taraco Peninsula are predominantly Aymara-speaking communities. The Qaqachakas, particularly the men, also speak Quechua; the pre-Hispanic Taraco Peninsula peoples probably spoke Pukina or Urukilla, languages that are now practically extinct. Aymara is the second-largest language group in the Andes today after Quechua. Throughout the text, we mention important Aymara and Quechua words, written in the official alphabets of these languages, and we include a "Glossary of Andean and Specialist Terms" in the Appendix for consultation.

The book collects together in English, for a wider public, some arguments already published elsewhere, mainly in articles in Spanish. Parts of Chapters 1 and 2 have been published in the article "The Social Life of a Communal Chest: Hybrid Characters and the Imagined Genealogies of Written Documents and Their Woven Ancestors," in Verónica Salles's edited volume *Remembering the Past, Retrieving the Future: New Interdisciplinary Contributions to the Study of Colonial Latin America* (2005). Some of the concepts in Chapter 4 have been published in "At the Heart of the Woven Dance-Floor: The Wayñu in Qaqachaka," in *Iberoamericana* (Frankfurt, 1992) and in an article published with Elvira Espejo: "Las cabezas de la periferia, del centro y del mundo interior: Una comparación de la dinámica bélica en la iconografía textil arqueológica de Paracas-Topará y del ayllu Qaqachaka (Bolivia) contemporáneo," in the book *Tejiendo sueños en el Cono Sur: Textiles andinos: pasado, presente, futuro*, edited by Victòria Solanilla Demestre (Grup d'Estudis Precolombins, Universitat Autònoma de Barcelona, 2004). Parts of Chapter 6 were developed in "Archaeological Andean Rituals: Their Performance and Liturgy," in *The Archaeology of Ritual* (Cotsen Institute of Archaeology, 2007), edited by Evangelos Kyriakidis, and in "Community with the Ancestors: Ceremonies and Social Memory in the Middle Formative at Chiripa, Bolivia," in the *Journal of Anthropological Archaeology* (2003).

For the maps and illustrations we thank Stacy Kozakavich, Shanti Morell-Hart, Nilton Callejas, and Roberto Espejo, who crafted the figures elegantly and efficiently. In the Instituto de Lengua y Cultura Aymara (ILCA) in La Paz, Bolivia, we thank Juan de Dios Yapita and Elvira Espejo for sharing their insights on many issues that have puzzled us for years and Dany Mena for her secretarial help of one kind and another. In La Paz, too, thanks to Alison Spedding for a spirited revision of the final draft. Finally, at Left Coast Press, we thank Mitch Allen for his comments, suggestions, and support and Carole Bernard for her editorial skills.

Denise Y. Arnold and Christine A. Hastorf
La Paz and Berkeley, May 2007

Introduction

In this book, we consider the early stages of political formation in the Andes in the light of both archaeological and ethnographic data. Our aim is to analyze how political power might have been created, organized, consolidated, and maintained by different forms of leadership and in distinct political formations. The focus of this broad topic centers on the body politic, specifically the head, and what we perceive as the key role of the political use of heads in the initial and ongoing conformation of political power throughout the history of this region. Our arguments, at times provocative, synthesize a body of previous works that the readers are referred to throughout the text.

Denise Arnold's book *The Metamorphosis of Heads* (with Yapita, 2006) set out some key arguments concerning the importance of heads in contemporary ethnographic settings, and their possible repercussions in the past. Her forthcoming book, *Warriors and Weavers* (In press), describes in more detail the warfaring practices mentioned here. Christine Hastorf's archaeological work in pre-Tiwanaku sites provided a background of archaeological data that made possible a dialogue between these two disciplinary perspectives. Drawing on both disciplines, we discuss the political models developed until now in the archaeological and anthropological literature to explain the rise of these early political formations, their means of control over populations, and the more contested levels of dispersed power implicit in more heterarchical cultural practices. Finally, we propose alternative models to understand this same data.

Apart from grounding our arguments comparatively, drawing on ideas from interpretative and political anthropology and archaeology, we use a symbolic approach to trace links between political changes and cultural practices concerned with human heads. The human head has been an important artifact as well as a key signifier of meaning throughout Andean history. This compels us to examine a broad category of "heads" in practices concerned with real human skulls, captured and trophy heads, curated crania, and stone carvings, taking into account in each case whether these are derived from ancestors or enemies.

"Curatorial practices" here include simply caring for heads, wrapping and unwrapping them, making libations to them, and offering them incense or even cigarettes.

We are also compelled to examine the more symbolic realm of imagined heads. Here we allude to the famous Andean flying heads, head imagery painted or modeled on ceramic pots, carved in stone, and head shapes (or real heads) used as the basis of serving or drinking vessels as well as the more abstract language of heads expressed in weaving designs and knotted threads. We study the cultural practices relating to all of these in examples from present-day Andean contexts, from Andean history and archaeology, and from comparative material in the Amazon basin.

One of our key interests here is the wider debate about whether specific political formations might have been more concerned with ancestral or enemy heads, in a preliminary theory of the Andean state. Alternating between the past and present, we broach the topic of social power by referring to the prominence of heads within existing models of political development, while developing new questions and offerings other models for scrutiny. Apart from the simple accumulation of heads through head taking or capture, or alternatively through keeping and curating ancestral heads, we consider the value and status of having such heads and how their significance might become transposed into other domains.

This concern with power relations leads us to reconsider some key aspects of Marxist theory, especially that of the fetishism of the commodity, from a new perspective centered in the political use of heads. It also leads us to reconsider, in a comparative way, other more general anthropological theories about value and the spirit of calculation, or keeping-while-giving (Weiner 1992). These include a rereading of Marcel Mauss's classic texts on the Maori *hau* as an aspect of "radiating yield," as a clue to the perceived power of heads held in certain hands.

Headhunting in the Andes

One of the political uses of heads is in headhunting. Headhunting in the Andean region has long fascinated both colonial chroniclers and contemporary ethnographers. In the so-called war of the ayllus of 2000, which took place on the borders between the departments of Oruro and Potosí in highland Bolivia in the region around ayllu Qaqachaka in the south-central Andes that we describe at length in this book, this fascination took hold of the national press, with all the associated ideas of cannibalism and savagery that criollo (Spanish-derived) culture still projects onto indigenous peoples. But although these images filled the national press, local populations tended to view these activities in other ways. They considered them as acts of brave warriors crazed by grief, much as the American anthropologist Renato Rosaldo has described in his book *Culture and Truth* (1989) for other parts of the world. Alternatively, local people viewed them as the acts of their culture heroes championing indigenous autonomy and defending the boundaries of traditional territories.[1]

Given this long fascination with head taking in popular thought and in other parts of the world, it is surprising that no comparative study of this theme in the Andes has been undertaken until now. A number of essays on this region highlight specific headhunting practices and their interpretations (see, for example, Mary Weismantel's provocative article of 2005), but our position is that cultural practices centered on heads cannot be understood independently from their symbolic, ritual, and political aspects. Based on extended periods of anthropological and archaeological fieldwork, each author has compared original fieldwork materials with archival documents, oral histories, ritual texts, and social memories of the past.

In taking this stance, we do not treat head taking in the Andes as a form of primitive warfare, or as part of a series of evolutionary stages leading to more complex political formations. Indeed Simon Harrison's recent "Skull Trophies of the Pacific War," in the context of Allied-Japanese relations in World War II, shows that trophy taking is clearly not an ethnological curiosity of tribal or "primitive" warfare that is "alien to the supposedly impersonal, instrumentally rational, and disenchanted warfare waged by advanced state societies" (Harrison 2006:831).

Rather, we study the relationship between early political formations and indigenous warfare to contextualize historically the phenomenon of head taking in a wider Andean regional perspective. By recognizing the changing historical circumstances of head taking, several themes emerge throughout the different chapters, including: heads as symbols of political power; heads and regeneration; heads, violence, and fertility; the language of heads; the body politic; heads and political systems; heads as constructors of social and cultural identity and difference; head taking and patterns of accumulation; head taking and political economy; the guarding and maintenance of heads; and head taking and the notion of commodity fetishism.

Given the ample colonial literature on head taking and the practices surrounding heads in the Andean region, our principal focus is on contemporary and pre-Contact examples. We are aware that this entails the danger of overlooking important associated activities such as slavery, slave raiding, and coerced trade, or even the patterns of slave trading and raiding over great distances, perhaps including the exchange of heads, that might have involved important relations between the highland, lowland, and coastal regions. We are also aware that the historical shifts from competitive raiding to the conformation of state tributary systems and incipient political hierarchy must take into account the contingent circumstances of colonial contact and regional political conditions. We leave this for a later study.

The Models in Play

To lay out the comparative basis for a study of heads in the Andes, we had to reconsider a broad range of former theories concerning political developments and the possible political uses of heads at different stages in these developments. For example, we reconsider the former "contract" theories that explained organized political power in terms of economic and property models, whereby political power was thought to derive from the control of certain forms of accumulation and dissemination.[2] This Marxist-based model focuses on certain groups within society as they gain control over the means of production, key resources and the decision-making ability of other groups or individuals.[3] With reference to these theories, we take into account the possibility that this means of control might have been expressed through the political control over heads.

A part of this "power over" model is expressed in the "predatory" theories that view the state as representing the interests of certain individuals that extract revenues from a broader group of constituents under their control. Charles Tilly explores this predatory model in his book *Coercion, Capital, and European States, AD 990–1992* (1992), as does Timothy Earle in *How Chiefs Come to Power* (1997). Among the power strategies deployed in this predatory model are some of the ideological, economic, and military aspects in certain forms of coercion and warfaring.[4] Although archaeologists have taken into account this nexus between economy and warfare in the forging of societies, historians have tended to overlook it. In *Blood Rites* (1997:196), Barbara Ehrenreich criticizes both Benedict Anderson and Eric Hobsbawm for having ignored the function of war as a vital factor in the forging of modern nation-states, although her criticism can also be directed at historians of early state formations. According to Ehrenreich, this omission can be traced to Marx himself, who in *Kapital* (1973 [1894]) overlooked this nexus between economy and warfare, probably because he was working in a historical moment when the military as a class was suffering a crisis of confidence.

In these predatory models, head taking may have been an important factor in tribute categories. Operating most prominently in such an approach is the management of resources through real military force.[5] The concept of leaders with power over others might therefore include the threat of force, or the threat of head taking, as well as the control of production and resources.[6] Associated with this kind of model is the aspect of power derived out of the symbolic nature of heads. These orientations suggest a sense of control and "power over" people and resources, where the role of heads in image and in reality seems to hold sway as the symbolic force controlling people's actions.

Our discussion also includes other approaches put forward for early state formation. One of these is centered in the "environmental and social circumscription theories" that attempt to explain the intensification of production and population expansion in terms of internecine warfare. Columbia University–based scholar Roberto L. Carneiro, in particular in a 1970 article, applied this theory to early state formation on what is now the Peruvian coast. Another approach to early state formation is framed in "world systems theory" applied to understanding precapitalist systems. This tendency, first discussed by Wallerstein in the 1980s, has been taken up by a new generation of scholars who apply world systems theory to archaeological questions.[7] For example, from the Institute for Research on World Systems at the University of California, Riverside, Chase-Dunn and Jorgenson (2001) view state formation in terms of the implementation of strategies that develop power concentrations based on the dynamics between core and peripheral polities. Both these approaches tend to appeal to a "power to coerce" idea of political hegemony as a principal of state formation, through varying strategies. Some "power over" models are directed more toward centralizing functions, whereas others are less so; some promote stratification, whereas others suggest increasingly specialized institutions, such as environmental management systems.[8] Tensions between the core polity as "head taker" and peripheral polities as "head givers" would be of interest here.

This "power over" model draws on the work by the French philosopher, Michel Foucault (1980) concerning modern states and their forms of social and physical control over populations. However, another approach to power that we include in our discussion of Andean polities, and that also draws on Foucault, is his notion of social power as an enabling or generating power, a "power to" complete things.[9] This aspect of power, present in all social life and integral to every social relation, is often perceived as an invisible energy that drives activity. Here, we agree with Foucault that both of these aspects of power, the element of capability as well as of control or channeling, are always present within political developments, although their dominance shifts in different political settings. But in this book, we specifically argue that a "power over" model is derived from an accumulation of heads, whereas a "generative power model" is often derived from having taken or accumulated heads and then curated them to appropriate their powers and apply their generative functions to one's own domain.

The point here is that what we might perceive archaeologically as increased political power, or as forms of centralization that could be associated with statecraft, does not necessarily derive from a *planned* strategy of social control. Even Carneiro (1970) made this case for the Amazonian Xingo groups. Rather, such political developments can come about as an unintended consequence of other escalating social interactions.[10] This more *internally generated* change is less clear cut within the model-building literature, but we consider it equally important.[11]

Certain similarities emerge here with former debates concerning head taking in other parts of the world, summarized in Janet Hoskins's edited volume *Headhunting and the Social Imagination in Southeast Asia* (1996a). There, Hoskins cites the work of the Swedish anthropologist Jonathan Friedman regarding tribal societies in Burma. Using a structuralist approach, Friedman compared headhunting with slave-taking societies in Burma as two sides of the same coin. Friedman argues that headhunting societies that practiced competitive feasting and continual warfare, and with tendencies toward reciprocal exchange, were, in fact, "structural transformations of societies based on large scale politically expansive theocratic chiefdoms, that took slaves instead of heads, maintained a system of strictly asymmetrical marriage and tended via the extension of tributary relations toward state forms of organization" (Friedman 1985:123, cited in Hoskins 1996b:9).

To illustrate these two poles, Friedman draws on Edmund Leach's earlier work in Burma to identify at one pole the Kachin who tried to expand production and to convert the goods produced into rank through feasting. The slaves they accumulated were assimilated into "grandchildren," who became part of the labor force. At the other pole are the Naga, who took heads instead of slaves and converted the heads into "ancestors," who were supposed to maintain fertility and bring good crops. In this case, ancestral force is siphoned off from one group to another in a struggle to maintain (or restore) declining fertility (Friedman 1985:125). Friedman thus opposed slave-taking systems, which he says emphasize "an accumulation of labor," to head-taking systems, which emphasize an "accumulation of soul force" (1979, 1985, cited in Hoskins 1996b:9). We ask if these kinds of distinctions can be made in the Andes.

As part of an array of models that focus on statecraft, the tendency has been to see "hierarchy" increasing in any diachronic political development. Yet archaeologists such as Ehrenreich, Crumley, and Levy (1995) also realize the importance of "heterarchy," a term whose social dimension has been explored by the Greek sociologist Kyriakis Kontopoulos in his book *The Logic of Social Structures* (1993). Heterarchy explores the multiple places of power within the growth of larger polities. Moreover, in the vying heterogeneous structures of "heterarchy," subjectivity and social imagination are not simply derivative; they actually constitute the structures of the wider system. These two trajectories—hierarchy and heterarchy—are not the traditional opposing tendencies of centralized versus decentralized polities, rather they can add a more nuanced dimension to this axis of political development and power. This issue of the level of political centralization will be part of the discussion when we turn to archaeological examples.

On the basis of our reading of these various theories, we built a theoretical bridge between highland and lowland studies by combining work on the dynamics of economic systems developed in a highland setting, with those of political systems developed in a lowland one. We take as our point of departure the work on the formation and dynamics of "economic spaces" by Argentine historian Carlos Sempat Assadourian (drawn originally from the French economist François Perroux), which he develops in his book *Sistema de la economía colonial: Mercado interno, regiones y espacio económico* (1982). Assadourian conceptualized these economic spaces as a "field of forces" composed of specific focal points (Perroux's "poles of growth") from which centrifugal forces derive or emanate, and to which in turn centripetal ones are attracted. In his use of these economic concepts, derived in part from world systems theory, Assadourian was wrestling with the nature of complex colonial economic systems, but the general scheme that he develops of epicenters of production and distribution has certain resonances in an archaeological setting too, as the recent studies of La Lone (2000) and Chase-Dunn and May (1997) confirm.

The specific question that interests us here is the relationship between this dynamic economic scheme and its associated political formations. Although little work has been done to date in modern-day highland settings on this association, we take certain clues from lowland studies. For example, the Brazilian lowland specialist Carlos Fausto (2001) has developed a homologous model of centripetal and centrifugal tendencies at play in the dynamics of social and political formations among Tupi-Guaraní groups. Fausto developed this model in a lowland context, but it is just as applicable in a highland one, and, as we shall see, there are certain historical relations between these two areas that make the comparison even more relevant. Basically, Fausto argues that lowland societies can be categorized as either more centrifugal and expansive in nature or more centripetal and inward looking, with more limited relations. The first category would be characterized by more offensive interethnic relations, and the second by less offensive and more pacific interethnic relations (Fausto 2001:399, 466, 533).

Fausto's categories have consequences for the political use of heads in early Andean settings and the build-up of power and economic relations that might have accompanied this use of heads. For example, in a more centripetal and inward-looking model, there would be more interest in the vertical perpetuation of identities in kin-like systems, with closed cycles of transmission between the ancestral dead and the living of the same group and less interest in the renewed acquisition of forces from the dead or the living from other groups. In this case, ancestral and initiation rituals concerning heads would be of primary importance. On the other hand, in a centrifugal and more expansive model, the renewed acquisition and appropriation of alien forces from outside the group would be of primary interest. In this case, rituals concerning the appropriation of captured heads from enemy groups would be the center of attention. This said, both dynamics would be present in either system, but to a greater or lesser degree. And equally, the way that the potency and life-giving nature of heads is perceived might be similar in each case but skewed toward one or other pole of the two models.

Regarding the articulation between political and economic developments, the centripetal models might relate to either long-lived, relatively independent settlements, or else groups that are becoming incorporated into emerging poles of growth and accumulation. By contrast, the centrifugal models might relate to the expansive phase of a new pole of growth or else characterize a contracting or disintegrating phase of one of these former centers of growth.

Ancestral and Enemy Heads: Interweaving Identities

Bearing in mind these different approaches, and both the material and symbolic aspects of political power, we focus on how political developments might have been centered in different practices concerning the "head," in their distinct manifestations and meanings throughout Andean history. At the same time, we are aware that, despite these differences (whether more ancestor based or more concerned with head capture), some consistent underlying themes link these cultural practices concerned with heads and their association with political power through time, right up to the present.

This possibility is suggested by an emerging literature on the importance of trophy heads, head taking, and human sacrifice in the Andes, both in an archaeological context[12] and an ethnographic one.[13] The problem is that until now these studies have not related these practices to political developments in the region. We develop this relation here, while also expanding on the existing literature relating the use of ancestral heads and bodies with political agency in both archaeological[14] and ethnographic writing.[15]

We resolve these lacunae, in part, by comparing these themes from an Andean perspective with similar issues in the Amazonian region. An ample literature on the Amazon region already discusses head taking, human sacrifice, and cannibalism as a part of ongoing political relations between groups.[16] The greater frequency in the Amazonian region of head taking in recent memory, as well as in historical accounts, has also meant that richer theoretical models have been developed in lowland studies, concerning, for example, the changes in status of the head taker, and the political consequences of this. Fausto has written about this in *Inimigos fiéis. História, guerra e xamanismo na Amazônia* (2001). Only a few studies of the Andean region have taken these theoretical insights into account.[17]

This wider contextualization of head taking within the political interrelations between groups is not entirely absent in an Andean context. For example, ethnohistorical writers, such as Dennis Ogburn in his article, "Human Trophies in the Late Prehispanic Andes" (2007), elaborated on the intimate use of the body and body parts, especially the head, within the crafting of the Inka state. However, the demise of political anthropology over the last decades, and its revival only in the last few years, as well as the absence of contemporary ethnographic data on head taking in an Andean context, have contributed to the long delay in making these vital interregional or interperiod connections. Added to this, practitioners in the social sciences and humanities still tend to work on relatively autonomous regions without making connections further afield, while disciplinary boundaries have also limited the scope for such comparisons.

This disciplinary predisposition toward splendid isolationism has meant that scholars have tended to miss vital connections between Andean and Amazonian warfaring practices at both theoretical and practical levels. One question at issue is how to account for these regional warfaring practices in common, including the taking of heads and their curation: by diffusion, historical contact, or the wider circuits of trading and political relations? The historical evidence for ongoing relations between these regions certainly demands serious attention. Pioneering studies by Renard-Casevitz, Saignes, and Taylor, in their book *Al este de los Andes* (1988; see also 1985, by the same authors), and by Thierry Saignes, in *Los Andes orientales* (1985) concerning these historical relations, have revealed mutual influences between highland and lowland societies in sociopolitical and economic relations and in institutional practices and their representations, including warfaring practices and headtaking. As a result, these authors prefer to study these interrelations rather than the separate domains (highlands, lowlands) of which they were composed.[18]

One consequence of this fragmentation in academic work has been that although heads have figured prominently in archaeological discussions of early Andean settlement and polity formation, in the Nasca region, for example, until now archaeologists have not explored sufficiently the role and symbolism of head taking in political formations, or drawn on lowland examples that might have illustrated another side of these historical sequences. More surprisingly, Darrell La Lone (2000:86) dismisses this possibility out of hand, seeing head taking and raiding as just localized village activities, as opposed to what he views as the larger issues of war and statecraft, in ideology and practice.

Our own thesis is that many of the cultural practices centered on heads, whether ancestral or enemy ones, have a political aspect concerned with the appropriation of the power generated through these practices for the use of certain groups. We argue that the political aspects of these practices concerning heads underlie both the practices of ancestor worship and the early accumulation of heads that served certain groups as well as those of expanding economies that participated in larger polity formations throughout the Andean region.

In both kinds of head management, whether tending toward more ancestral or more alien tendencies, and with more accumulative or more expansive preoccupations, the political use of the head seems to be reinforced by shamanistic practices that engage with supernatural powers. It is intriguing that some of these activities and their associated principles still underlie the political nature of Andean society today, in its symbols of office and forms of control over territories and populations.

By presenting the mounting evidence of practices concerning heads in the Andean past, and in a series of ethnographic settings, we put forward models of political organization centered on heads that allow us to reconsider Andean societies from a symbolic point of view, where ideology combines with praxis in the dynamic processes of ongoing political development.

Heads and the Regeneration of Life

At a more symbolic level, a central facet of the power of heads in these ongoing political developments, whether in more inward-looking or more expansive outward-looking systems, is the way that heads articulate death with the regeneration of life. Both the anthropological and archaeological literature includes discussions of the place of the dead within human societies that provide clues to the kinds of power held to reside in heads.[19]

In our view, the provocative article "Skulls and Causality" (1976), by Rodney Needham, put an early damper on the discussions around this theme. His article rightly questioned the way that some early ethnographers (see, for example,

Kruyt in 1906, concerning Toraja headhunting in Sulawesi in Southeast Asia) seemed to confuse *local* explanations of the power of heads with *science-like* theories of causation, based on the potency of accumulated substance inside heads, which drew on the metaphors of modern physics. However, mounting evidence from many parts of the world reveals a common basis to the ideas in these local descriptions, above all those concerning the connections between fertility and violence (cf. Hoskins 1996b:9). Perhaps even the metaphors of modern physics about potency, power, and generation, cited by Needham, had common origins in the headhunting practices of the past.

In this same context, Bloch and Parry, in the introduction to their edited volume *Death and the Regeneration of Life* (1982), laid out a master plan that rejects the same totalizing relation between all heads and generative potency that Needham complained about. Bloch and Parry favored linking certain deaths, and not others, to the regeneration of life. Here, they identify two dyads. First, they oppose *good deaths*, such as those of sacrifice or natural death, with *bad deaths*, such as those of suicide and unnatural death, as distinct categories of death that make a difference to the powers that such heads and bodies are held to contain. The second dyad that they identify is that of *dead enemies* versus *dead kinsmen*, and how these two categories of death also shape the meanings and powers associated with the body parts, including the heads of such dead.

Although the regeneration of life from certain categories of the dead—where Bloch and Parry's dyads may be useful—is a long-lived belief universally, we have the comparative advantage in the Andes that the manifestations of this process, unlike many other regions, are still accessible for study, both materially and ritually. Comparative clues from historians such as Connerton (1989) suggest how cultural practices centered on the curation of heads of the recently dead could have played a key role in enculturating people in the past, aiding memory as well as channeling ceremony in the process of socializing people into groups, just as they do today. These practices could also have contributed to the formation of political groupings.

This focus on the recent dead provides an immediacy linking the past to the present, and on into the future, that provides a sense of continuity as well as of imminent potency. In this sense, memorialization would have been important in the reconfiguration of each new generation, as old energies were recharged into new life. The contemporary language of "memory pathways," described by Thomas Abercrombie in reference to ayllu K'ulta, a neighbor of Qaqachaka in the south-central Andes (1998), seems to be a way of channeling such energies for individual and group use in a political sense.

Comparative clues about the way that the living continually draw on the power and experience of the dead to make decisions in the present are also useful here. Again, Connerton's argument that each new event would have demanded a response that combined past actions with new reactions tailored to actual circumstances, so linking memory to the future, is suggestive. In this way, the energy brought to bear to initiate this new cycle derived from the power of the dead. Although Barrett (2000) puts forward the idea that the agency or impulse to do this is constructed socially, and within a determined history directed by the desires and meanings of certain people, we argue that this sense of agency, while based on the accumulating power derived from past accomplishments, is more specifically related to the appropriation of the powers of the dead according to the political interests of certain groups.

Judith Butler, too, in *Bodies that Matter* (1993:15), confirms that each action is only an imperfect citation of the norm, created through past practices and the memories of the way to do things. However, we locate the potency of such events in the way they draw on the powers of the dead to channel increasing energies of life and increased fecundity for the use of distinct groups. In this way, outcomes occur not simply when a new situation with its imperfect knowledge arises. They are also charged through a considered reproduction of the wider social, cultural, and political contexts of events, which includes the place of the dead in all potential outcomes.[20]

Thus, we argue that the way people evoke the dead and the potential that the dead hold to harness this power and convert it to life essences is partly political in nature.[21] Many ethnographers of the Andes have described contexts in which regional concepts of just such a life force (*sami, inqa*) are still called on and channeled today in ceremonies carried out by particular families, kin groups, ayllus, and larger political units.[22]

The Ancestral Dead, Identity, and Andean Polities

This discussion leads to the questions: How do Andean people think about the dead compared to the living and how might such ideas about the deceased help us understand their wider political practices? More specifically, how might these ideas about the deceased relate to the theories about heads we have put forward?

Regional ideas today about these matters tend to be multifaceted and embedded in various levels of social organization, rather than hierarchically structured. This is supported by contemporary cosmological ideas that also tend to oppose a strongly centralized and hierarchical system. Even the idea that there was once an all-powerful monotheistic creator god in the past, such as Viracocha among the Inka, is much disputed.[23]

Instead, as Catherine Allen (1982:179) notes from the modern ethnographic context of Sonqo (Peru), there is often a more ubiquitous sense that all material things partake of life's powers or energy; she identifies *sami* in Quechua as one concept of this life force. For Allen, the dead, too, can hold this essence of life, as long as their material remains are still present. This is why Andean categories of the dead include not only past humans, but also harvested and stored plants and animals, even wooden tools. When the tool is in use it is considered "alive," and when it is not, it is "dead"; so things can be categorically dead but still exist among humans and still contain a life force. For Allen (1982:186), these elements are thought to continue to exist and create energy when they are dead, although they operate in a less immediate state. Ever present, these Andean dead participate in the ongoing decisions of the living. For example, it is still customary to consult the ancestors, burn a candle, and offer them incense on every Monday, the "day of the dead" (*alma uru* in Aymara).

Allen (1982) also reports on certain ongoing transformations between the living and the dead, for example, how one can feed the dead by force-feeding one's body, the idea being that some of these nutrients pass into the bodies of the dead. Living persons who do this are thus able to open the channels of communication between the living and the dead. This force-feeding, as well as force-drinking or intoxication, opens up channels of communication between the living and the dead that allows for the merging of these different beings in a common flow of energy. Such openings allow the passing of food to the dead who, in return, give potency to the living. This communication is considered necessary because the dead might resent having left the world of the living, and they can become angry and cause harm. Such activity allows the dead elders to continue on with their influence, as the ultimate elders in the cycle of power relationships within a community, an idea that Hastorf (2003) has developed in an archaeological context in the Titicaca Basin.

Another clue to the way that heads were treated, whether from warfare or in relation to the ancestors, is the manner in which meaning was and still is created and maintained in the region. In common with many other areas of the world, we argue that identity in the Andes is essentially *relational* and *partible* (what Marilyn Strathern has called the "dividual"[24]) rather than focused on the individual in a modern Western sense, and that meaning, too, is distributed throughout a social group and constructed through common practices, not by any individual.

Western scholars today often tend to project into the past social actions centered in individuals, in our own likeness. But in a study of other cultures, particularly ancient ones, it is necessary to expand this current notion of individual agency to include a wider radius of action and social forces; this means considering a person in relation to both their living and deceased kin. People live relationally among others, thus defining their concept of self through family and neighbors. They also live relationally through time, altering their interactions and attitudes to those around them as they grow, learn, and remember. In the past, as well as today, people gain meaning from their "roots," whether real or imagined. This includes the collective practices of telling family stories of ancestral homes, natal communities, past family members, and so on. It might also have included rituals where ancestral heads were handled.

In non-Western, small-scale societies, identity was and still is relational, constructed through a specific kin group and one's part in a wider life cycle, through routine and often naturalized practices of social styles of interaction. Here, choices of action were not infinite; rather, an individual's identity derived from his or her temporal and relational place within a family or ayllu structure. The sense of self in a specific family or ayllu would have been central to a person's lived experience as well as their survival. At the same time, this sense of self and identity was defined in relation to the Other, outside the limits of the family and ayllu. So, this sense of self might have been defined and nurtured through the cultural practices of handling ancestral heads as well as the handling of enemy heads and their conversion into one's own.

Methods and the Organization of the Book

In an ethnographic context, the multiple ways of drawing on and transforming the power of the head are illustrated within a gamut of cultural practices, from rituals and ceremonies to overtly political settings as well as in daily practices, in speech, and the verbal arts. In this sense, our examination of the place of heads in the Andean present sheds light on the possible origins of many of these cultural practices, while illustrating the ways that they still channel such powers for creative purposes in the interests of certain groups.

In Part I, rather than illustrating a wide variety of examples of these practices, we develop a logical argument that emerges out of locating this gamut of practices in preliminary theoretical models. At times, these fall within what Arnold and Yapita (2000:22) have called an "Andean textual-ontological theory," one that defines creative practice as emerging from the appropriation of certain aspects of the enemy other, and making them your own. This attempt to present a working hypothesis, supported by examples from a local matrix of practices, sayings, and interpretations, is situated within the methodology of grounded theory (developed originally by Glasser and Strauss in 1967). In the contemporary context, many examples from the case study of highland Qaqachaka are presented here.

In this ethnographic setting, in terms of the "contract theories" that concern changing political formations, we focus in Chapter 1 on those debates concerning the nature of possessions as commodities, the control of value, and the ways in which restricted distribution might have served elite control in the past.

In terms of "predatory theories," we focus on the critical nexus between specifically economic aspects and warfare in developing political complexity.[25] In Chapters 2 and 3, we examine the possibility that war and head taking, even cannibalism, have formed a vital part of the exchange relations between groups as one of the ramifications of Fausto's dynamic model of centrifugal and centripetal tendencies in political systems. Although the exchange of objects has been amply considered in the literature, the kind of exchanges made in warfare, of body parts including heads, captives and slaves, souls, and names have been studied much less.[26] Chapter 2 focuses on heads and their perceived powers of regeneration in a sacrificial context; Chapter 3 examines the possible iconographic significance of heads in drinking vessels made from the skulls of victims taken in warfare. Finally, Chapter 4 traces what has conventionally been viewed as the "nested hierarchy" of modern political settings, where heads figure, and describes some ritual practices that reinforce and so reproduce these levels of hierarchy. This detailed level of analysis also allows us to question the conventional view of nested hierarchies and suggest a more multi-locational (heterarchical) reading of this same material.

In Part II, which mainly traces the archaeological record, we consider the common and striking patterns that emerge from mortuary data in three distinct regions of the Andes. Chapter 5 discusses the general contribution of archaeological evidence for the importance of heads as well as the practical limitations that this evidence poses. Chapter 6 turns to regional case studies from the south-central and Lake Titicaca regions, whereas Chapter 7 focuses on the central and north-central Andes. In each regional study, we examine the evidence for the use of human body parts, whether as offerings or as objects of ceremonies concerned with memory, group formation, and eventually political formation.

From a methodological approach toward the archaeological data, we focus not on the absence of the complete body, as does DeLeonardis (1997, 2000), but on the presence of head with all its potent meanings, as Weismantel (2005) has done in her recent and fascinating article on the subject. We then read this archaeological data from the perspective of political models at smaller and larger scales as well as in terms of Fausto's model of centripetal and centrifugal forces, to outline the various ways that practices and ideas surrounding the human head have construed political endeavors. The approximate time-lines of these various regions and political dynamics is presented in a "Chart of Archaeo-logical Cultural Sequences" in the Appendixes, for constant reference.

In Chapter 8, in a series of conclusions, we examine both the formative role of heads in political processes of the past as well as the more detailed uses of heads in the political configurations of the present. In this manner, we illustrate not only the significant place of heads in conforming past political formations but also the dynamic use of them today in forging emerging political situations.

Part I

The Ethnography of Andean Head Taking and Power

In THIS first section, we draw on reflections from contemporary Andean ethnography to reconsider key anthropological and archaeological debates concerning the conformation of political power. We focus on a region in the south-central Andes characterized by ayllu communities that claim descent from putative ancestors in common, and have common territories.[1] There, the recent practices of ayllu warfare and the taking of enemy heads as trophies, as well as other customs concerning the treatment of the heads of one's own ancestors, suggest powerful analogies to what might have happened in the past. This also allows us to take up the point that curated heads come from enemies and from kin, each type evoking power and energy but from different sources and with distinct outcomes.

There are *two* axes to our approach. In the first, we seek ways of understanding practices centered on heads as the point of reference in defining forms of accumulation and exchange that can be applied to decentralized and early state societies. We do not intend to treat these practices as timeless and essentialist, but rather to ground them in specific societies, historical situations, and territorial domains. We are acutely aware that problems such as disjunction (the historical process whereby form and content separate over large spans of time) limit our ability to project back into decentralized or early state societies some of the practices we see today. We are also aware that Christian ideas about heads as hierarchical religious symbols have also transformed local practices concerning heads in many ways over the centuries (see, for example, Arnold and Yapita 1999). Even so, in the second axis of our approach, we examine ideas about the power of heads, especially trophy (captured) heads, in contemporary settings, to clarify how heads, once captured, are thought to have the power of regeneration and growth. We find resonances in the past for both axes of this approach.

In both trajectories, we draw on Fausto's model of centripetal and centrifugal tendencies to distinguish more pacific political systems, whose wider relations rely on pacific reciprocal exchange (of names, souls, persons, and things), from more warfaring political systems whose wider relations draw on the violent exchange of people and notions of vengeance and body parts, including heads (Fausto 2001:323). Implicit in this model are *two* other notions that we shall describe in more detail later. One is Viveiros de Castro's notion of "ontological depredation" as the tendency of expanding systems to appropriate external forces for their own use (1992). The other is Fausto's own notion of "productive consumption" to describe the materials and energy spent on producing objects or people (2001:327). This is evident in warfare generally, and more specifically in trophy head curation. However, it is equally evident in relation to ancestral heads, for example in the feeding and ritual attendance on ancestral heads to reproduce the kin group.

Heads in Small-scale Polities

Toward a Theory of Heads in Expanding Polities

THE ETHNOGRAPHIC context of head taking, and practices around heads, that we examine in this chapter derive from contemporary fights over land. Ample ethnographic literature on the Andean region as a whole already discusses these land fights when heads might be taken, and then curated, with a view to the future regeneration and fecundity of the victorious ayllu.[1] We pay particular attention here to the case study of ayllu Qaqachaka (Prov. Abaroa, Dept. of Oruro, Bolivia), where a serious fight over land broke out in 2000.

Qaqachaka is located some 100 km east of Lake Poopó in the Cordillera de los Frailes in the south-central Andes. In a highland territory ranging from 4,500 to 3,500 m above sea level in elevation, the Qaqachakas today produce Andean tubers, broad beans, wheat and barley, and a small quantity of quinua (*Chenopodium* spp.); they also herd llamas and sheep and a few alpacas. In the recent past, the Qaqachakas traded for maize, journeying with llama trains to the warm valley lands in Chuquisaca to the east; nowadays they tend to go by truck to trade for maize from the region of Aiquile (Cochabamba). With economic globalization, this rural economy is fraught with serious problems, and Qaqachaka youth have joined the massive outmigration of Bolivian workers to neighboring countries (Argentina and Chile) and even further afield, to the United States and Spain. Although this part of Oruro is on the periphery of much recent archaeological research in the altiplano to the north, the ethnographic details it offers provide many clues to wider practices across the highlands (see Map 1.1 and insert a).

Map 1.1: The Region of Qaqachaka in the South-Central Andes, with insert a): The Ayllus Mentioned in the Study, and insert b): The Historical Regions
Maps courtesy of ILCA, La Paz.

Historically, Qaqachaka was a former ecclesiastical annex of the colonial collative parish of Condocondo in the south-central Andes and had past ties to two great Aymara confederations: Charkas-Qharaqhara and Killakas-Asanaqi (see Map 1.1, insert b). Oral history recounts how Qaqachaka once provided pasturing lands for neighboring Pukwata ayllu, when Killakas-Asanaqi was still integrated into the larger federation of Charkas-Qharaqhara. Later on, the Killakas-Asanaqi federation separated from Charkas-Qharaqhara, and Qaqachaka became affiliated to the Toledan reduction town of Condocondo. These former relationships are in the process of being reconstituted today, as Qaqachaka sends representatives to the Jatun Killakas-Asanaqi council (JAKISA) that forms an integral part of the larger National Council of Ayllus and Markas of Qollasuyo (CONAMAQ).

Appealing to these former ties, a key social memory of the Qaqachakas is of their historical role as "warriors of the Inka." Arnold, in various studies of Qaqachaka ayllu (1988, 1993), has described how they appeal to these warfaring ties when they talk about certain items of their war dress: for example, the checkered belts with their red bobbles, said to represent the victims taken in warfare, or of the genealogical lines of local caciques in the region that were descended from Inka bloodlines. How far are such claims historical facts, and what are the possible consequences of such ties in relation to headhunting?

Documentary evidence sheds light on these claims, from both ancestral lines of Qaqachaka history, of their role in the Killakas-Asanaqi confederation as well as in Charkas-Qharaqhara. The 1575 *Información* by Juan Colque Guarache, a cacique of Killakas-Asanaqi in colonial times, records how from the very moment of the Inka Tupaq Yupanki's invasion of this territory, warriors of this Aymara nation were recruited to the Inka army in its campaign to conquer the Chichas and Diaguitas in frontier zones to the south. Colque Guarache emphasizes how the valor of his ancestor who led these troops was such that he was made an Inka by privilege.[2] Other documents describe how groups of warriors from Qharaqhara (as part of the Charkas confederation) were also involved in constant campaigns and skirmishes against the Guaraní-speaking "Chiriguanos" to the east, not only in Inka times but also long before the integration of Tawantinsuyu. French scholars Renard-Casevitz, Saignes, and Taylor, in *L'Inca, l'Espagnol et les sauvages* (1985:124), observe how these waves of Chiriguano expansion against the southeastern Andean flanks, probably in search of precious metals controlled by the Qharaqhara, seemed to accelerate during Inka times, although the Finnish archaeologists Martti Pärsinnen and Antti Korpisaari (2003) date their origins to some thousand years earlier.

In a colonial *Probanza* of 1637, a cacique of neighboring Pukuwata recounted how his ancestor, another Qharaqhara lord called Ayra Kanchi (who lived in the former times of the Inka Pachakuti, *ca.* 1438), with 20,000 of his own men, constructed a series of forts along the eastern flanks of the Andes, along headwaters of the rivers Guapay and Pilcomayo, to guard against the constant pressures from the east by Tupi-Guaraní groups.[3] Whenever these forts were attacked, the reigning Inka (from the times of Wayna Qhapaq *ca.* 1497–1527, to Manco Inka *ca.* 1500–1544) raised a local army that might have included warriors from Qharaqhara to push back the Chiriguano incursion, in dangerous expeditions, some of whom never returned.[4] These same pressures might also account for the final subordination of Charkas and Qharaqhara to Inka domination, as protectors of their territorial integration, and, in the face of Chiriguano attack, the lesser of two evils.[5]

In *The Metamorphosis of Heads* (2006), Arnold and Yapita describe Qaqachaka oral history relating to the Colonial Period, which recounts how their troops fought for years with some remaining Inka warriors to defend the region against the Spanish. These histories of their status as warriors of one kind and another came under close scrutiny centuries ago when the colonial authorities decided on the new tributary payments to be made to the colonial state. In their monumental history of the wider Qharaqhara-Charkas federation, Platt, Bouysse-Cassagne, and Harris (2006:64, 80) describe how, on such occasions, the historical memory of the component ayllus of Qharaqhara (such as Qaqachaka) of having been "soldiers of the Inka," and therefore of having accomplished the vital former tributary obligations of Tawantinsuyu to the Inka in terms of personal services, justified their valor as "warlike people" (*gente belicosa valerosa*) and their higher status as "gentlemen and peoples, soldiers of war" (*señores y gentes soldados de guerra*) in relation to other groups designated as just "shepherds" (*ovejeros*). These historical experiences were also important precursors in the new colonial processes of tax reckoning and for claiming their exemption from the heavy tax obligations of the period. These points were vehemently argued by the Mallkus of Qharaqhara and Charkas in another important colonial document, the *Memorial de Charcas* of 1582, against the tax tribute demanded by Spanish Crown, when they claimed as precedent their participation as "soldiers from the time of the Inkas called Inka Yupanki and Topa Inka Yupanki and Wayna Qapaq and Waska Inka."[6]

We argue here that these historical precedents of having fought against the lowland Tupi-Guaraní over centuries had an important influence on the Qaqachaka warriors, possibly affecting their own warfaring practices, including those of head taking. We also suggest that this social memory continues to drive the bellicose economy in the region. In turn, this bellicose economy seems to derive from an expansive political system of a centrifugal order, perhaps deriving from Inka times, that seeks to appropriate alien enemy forces and incorporate them into a reworked local identity. In the colonial record, there are accounts of ongoing violence in the region over certain boundaries going back to the 17th century and possibly earlier (Arnold, In press).

Still today, these disputes erupt periodically, generally over boundaries in conflict since colonial times. These disputes were exacerbated in the early republican cartographies of the region, with its overlaying of new boundaries on former ethnic ones. They continued to erupt at key historical moments, for example in the 1920s with the general uprisings in the region. These were about the taking by regional elites of new hacienda large landholdings in the valley lands that were traditionally frequented by the *llameros* of ayllus such as Qaqachaka. And they erupted again with the need to draw up defined territories with the Bolivian Popular Participation Law of 1994.

In the region of Qaqachaka, although head taking is a thing of the past, this practice came under public scrutiny in 2000, during some violent episodes in what became known as the "war of the ayllus." This outbreak of violence between Qaqachaka and its neighbors, principally Jukumani, Laymi, North Condo, and Aguas Calientes, mainly over territorial boundaries, was the immediate result of a long history of ecological degradation and the general shortage of arable and pasturing land in the region.[7]

A great deal of debate at this time among intellectuals and government officials in Bolivia centered on whether the fighting was inter- or intraethnic, although again the social actors of the ayllus in conflict perceived matters differently. In most cases, the ayllus in conflict had a history and culture in common, having perhaps served together as "soldiers of the Inka" in past historical alliances. In the 16th century, together with Qaqachaka, Jukumani and Laymi were both part of the larger Aymara federations of Charkas and Qharaqhara and would have shared this status. In more recent centuries, as we have seen, Norte Condo, together with Qaqachaka, formed part of the wider Aymara-Urukilla federation of Killakas-Asanaqi. In times of peace, these ayllus were trading partners and each provided sites for mutual visits in the round of feasts and religious pilgrimages that characterize the region as a whole. In this sense, these cycles of war and commerce seem to coexist, and the traditional networks of exchange are preserved in spite of these intense episodes of warfare. As in the lowlands, the exchange of death, trophy heads, souls, names, and perhaps even captive labor in the past would seem to form an essential part of the ongoing tensions between a play for autonomy or of wider political and exchange relations.[8]

We believe that these ongoing tensions are centuries if not millennia old. In historical terms, there seems to be a dynamic ferment in which political communities, such as the ayllus of the region, struggled with *two* equally compelling forces: integration and disintegration. The *first* dynamic, that of integration into larger diarchic federations such as Charkas-Qharaqhara or Killakas-Asanaqi, might have occurred initially under the threat of Chiriguano attack, and been consolidated under the influence of Inka occupation, and later under colonial administration. These diarchic federations would have been characterized by the centripetal and unifying effect of mass ceremony under one cacique or another.

As hierarchically nested political systems, they would have achieved their coherence in part through the cultural patterns of a particular diarchic political order, represented through systems of conceptually female and male functions (for example, conceptually female wife givers and conceptually male wife takers, political and ritual practitioners that tended the earth as a female element or the rains as a male element, and so on) that overlay a series of more unstable and shifting alliances. The *second* dynamic is that of dispersal and disintegration of larger political entities into multiple semiautonomous ones. This began in the colony, continued in the republic, and has resulted finally in the ayllus that exist today.

We contend that warfare, head taking, and the ritual management of ceremonial violence, perhaps forged in historical encounters with the lowland Tupi-Guaraní groups, played a key dynamic in the formation and transformation of these political units.[9] In the case of Qaqachaka, both real and ritualized violence, as well as the practice of head taking, have formed an integral part of its history of territorial expansion, at least since colonial times (Arnold 1993, In press).

This theme was particularly difficult for us to examine ethnographically. Only during the "war of the ayllus" (in 2000) could we ask questions more openly about head taking and even cannibalism, both in the present and the recent past, than we had done in all our previous years of fieldwork put together (Arnold, In press). This kind of war over ayllu boundaries, called *nuwasi* in Aymara or *ch'axwa* in Quechua, although having much in common with the so-called ritual battles, or *tinku*, are qualitatively different in scale, intensity, and ferociousness.[10] While it is common for a *tinku* in Qaqachaka to announce the opening gambits of a more aggressive confrontation between local ayllus, the *nuwasi* is a more general belligerent attitude between ethnic groups that lasts for months, and the number of casualties is generally higher. In the "war of the ayllus," there were some twenty deaths before the Bolivian state stepped in with military control.

Even so, the argument of Fausto and Viveiros de Castro still holds: instead of the number of deaths being at issue, the regional political economy derives from the symbolic power extracted from each single death. The issue is quality and not quantity. This seems to confirm that head taking was a symbolic act to weaken the enemy and not a matter of gathering life-giving substance for the conquering group, as has been noted already in other parts of the world.[11]

The Fetishism of Heads as Protected Things

Now let us turn to the wider aspects of head taking, including their economic dimensions. Head taking has often been explained through indigenous notions of exchange, including the wider economic circuits and patterns of labor and trading of which these form a part. In this context, head taking often presents an idealized vision of exchange relations that is put into a conscious and creative tension against the real order of things.[12] In this sense, the tension between the victor's and victim's perspectives on head taking might have raised the stakes from local reciprocal relations to a reconstruction of the wider regional configurations of power.

From this perspective, the ways in which trophy heads were taken in Qaqachaka during these *nuwasi* encounters in the past, and then curated in a particular household, implies that these are things to be "protected," "guarded," and capitalized on, long after the original head taking. Many studies of such protected things (that also include raided textiles) suggest they were restricted from circulation (enclaved or curated) in this way to protect them from commoditization, and so increase their value. With such a limited supply, there would be an increasing demand as well as increased value for, say, each severed head.

In his path-breaking book *The Social Life of Things*, Arjun Appadurai goes further to propose that such "enclaved commodities" (locked into what Douglas 1967 has called "controlled distribution") were the very precondition for reproducing wider exchange networks (Appadurai 2000 [1986]:24). That is, the hoarding of such objects, rationed outside real exchange circuits, would have permitted the build-up of their associated powers while conforming the values at issue in the wider exchange networks. We suggest that this restricted flow, at the service of the reproduction of certain social and political systems, such as the perpetuation of ayllu elites through the creation of difference and so the marking of power, has much in common with what Gluckman (1983) calls "kingly things" or "royal monopolies" (cited in Appadurai 2000 [1986]:22). In archaeological terms, as argued by Hendon (2000) and Joyce (2000), this restricted flow would constitute a form of social memory and identify building.[13]

Some key ideas about the wider exchange relations of which headhunting forms a part are provided by Annette Weiner, who delves into the nature of these overlapping accumulation and exchange functions in her book *Inalienable Possessions* (1992), which concerns similar kinds of controlled circulation in Melanesia. Weiner argues that closely "guarded 'inalienable possessions'" motivate the dynamics of exchange as a measure of "keeping-while-giving" by authenticating subjective value above exchange value. She relocates Marx's arguments about the "fetishism of the commodity," whereby the commodity becomes a substitute for the social relations behind it, to the wider anthropological debate about the nature of the Maori *hau* as a measure of the radiating "yield" of guarded valuable possessions. She also rescues Hubert and Mauss's definition of the pan-Pacific notion of *mana* as the "idea of difference in potential," that which extends its *aura* to other possessions (Weiner 1992:10, 51–52). We suggest that heads captured in the modern *nuwasi* incursions of Qaqachaka into neighboring ayllus, and then enclaved and curated by the head taker and his family, embody this potential yield, like *mana* in the Polynesian sense, and that through this process, the head taker and his family gain the benefit of this radiating power in other domains beyond that of the original interaction.

In this sense, it seems that trophy heads, especially those guarded in the households of some contemporary rural Andean communities, such as Qaqachaka, do not belong to the immediate category of "gifts" or "commodities." Rather, their quality of power and taboo has to do with their nature as instruments of expedience, as enclaved heirlooms, and as a part of a regional political economy in which heads gain political power through the rationing systems that control political claims to land and other possessions, even those of other ayllus (see Weiner 1992:32). It appears that through their access to and possession of heads, certain ayllu groups might institutionalize these political claims, in the kind of way that Weiner describes for the political economy of specific parts of Melanesia (1992:60). In this case, the possession of certain heads would literally give "title" to certain privileged descent lines, shaping their land claims within defined boundaries, and allowing them to speak to, and for a larger political grouping (1992:62).

In this genealogical context, the family house with its collection of heads becomes a key site where these shared values are incarnated and occasionally debated. There, heads, particularly of one's own ancestors, form part of an ancestral display in sites of shared values incarnated as group identity symbols that embody memories and life-giving power. This modern Andean form of curating and displaying heads has much in common with Weiner's account of the Maori ancestral *taonga* cloaks, with the *tapu* (tabú) removed, stored in large carved wooden boxes "to be brought out later and cried over" in certain ceremonial circumstances (Weiner 1992:61). Evidently, these kinds of practices concerning the dead were widespread. Echoes can even be found in Meredith Chesson's (1999) discussion of the curation (keeping and tending) of the dead in Bronze Age Jordan.

There is a further point to consider concerning the place and power of heads in the Andes. Taking into account the widespread interest in the nature of the exchange of commodities and gifts in Amerindian societies, Viveiros de Castro (1998), Fausto (1999), and others have argued that these societies are primarily oriented toward the reproduction of *persons* rather than *things*. According to their model of "ontological depredation," many centrifugal Amerindian societies tend to conduct their relations with neighboring groups through *depredation* rather than reciprocity, accruing their debts and credits through warfaring means. The aim here is to appropriate other subjectivities, adopt them, and convert them into kin. For example, the enemy Other destroyed in warfare, and captured as a trophy head, will later be converted into kin.

As Fausto argues, the focus here is not on accumulating a *number* of deaths but on extracting as much as possible from a single death, through symbolic efficacy, to produce new subjectivities (Fausto 1999:948, 2001:268). This implies that the historical roots of territorial claims in the Andes, too, might be grounded in such regional notions of corporeality where the head plays a vital part. Again, the vitality of the accumulated heads would radiate first into the domain of an immediate group of kin and then outward into extended kin networks, and hence into wider political alliances.

Ideas about the vitality of the head, widespread in the Amazonian region,[14] are also evident in highland Qaqachaka. In an essay on ritual battles in the region, Arnold and Yapita (1996) have argued that fundamental ideas in Qaqachaka about memory, vocal power, and the genealogy and continuity of life center on the head, especially the gray matter, as the gendered seat of male power and strength. In other works on the region of Qaqachaka, they explore how this power is disseminated by men, in part though their political oratory. In a parallel gendered domain, the heart is considered the seat of female memory and inspiration, and so of female power, and women express this female power in song and in cloth (Arnold and Yapita 2001:Chap. 2). Going a step further, they argue that male political power is derived from head taking and its subsequent curation. In parallel, female reproductive power is expressed in the associated cultural development of weaving, which seems to have been practiced originally with the pendant hair of the taken head (Arnold 2000:22). In this sense, the fetishism of accumulated "things," such as weavings, would derive directly from their historical origins in the trophy heads of enemies and from their vital links to persons.

By making these associations that express the gendered norms of Qaqachaka society, we do not necessarily mean to imply that there are deterministic gendered norms relating to heads and head taking throughout the Andes, in both the past and the present. Evidently, not all heads taken are those of men, in the ethnographic or the archaeological record. In this sense, there are some important exceptions to the rule, which we shall discuss later. Nevertheless, these associations are useful guides to wider social and political patterns in the region.

For instance, these kinds of association lead Arnold (2005) to speculate that, in an Andean context, head taking and the related cultural development of using the pendant hair to form early versions of the knotted threads, called *kipu* in Quechua or *chinu* in Aymara, might be at the heart of early developments in bureaucratic accounting systems associated with early political formations. Corroborating evidence for this idea might be that, still in the Inka period, each of the red, knotted threads that the Topa Inka wore on his headdress was associated with a head that had been taken by the Inka state.[15]

Arnold and Yapita (2006:Chap. 9) also argue that the symbolic power of taken and curated heads inherent in woven cloth and *kipu* knotted threads was later transposed to the written texts of the Colonial Period, and that this sense of appropriating an alien textuality is still present today in Qaqachaka, for example, in schooling. As a result, regional interpretations of voice, textiles, and writing are all rooted in a common theory of textuality whereby Andean societies reproduce themselves—their people, land, and other resources, even communal texts and textual practices—by appropriating the strength of the other, and then in revivifying the other, but now as a part of the self (Arnold and Yapita 2006:161–22; cf. Fausto 1999). The fact that these materials are imbued with the symbolic powers of the person, above all the head, facilitates the transmission of this power in other settings.

Heads and the Powers of Regeneration

Let us turn now to the second axis of our argument, which concerns the nature of the processes of transformation and the regeneration of life, stimulated by the initial taking of a head. Arguments about whether the head might or might not embody generative seed-like substance, and the degree to which this idea might actually have motivated head taking, have been themes debated at length in the ethnographic and historical literature of many cultures,[16] including the Andes.[17]

Many examples in the Amazonian literature would seem to confirm this idea, the most well known being the complex of ideas around the *tsantsa* head of the Shuar (or Jívaro) of the Ecuadorian lowlands (described by Descola 1993a, 1993b and Taylor 1993). There, head taking is part of a wider ceremonial and ritual process about transforming the spirit of an enemy other into an off-spring of one's own group, as a part of a gendered process in which women play a vital part.

Trophy-head taking in modern Andean societies seems to confirm certain aspects of this complex of ideas. For example, in Qaqachaka, the head is considered to be seed-like, with the potential to help generate a harvest of new "babies" for the household of its taker. Here, "baby" or *wawa* in both Aymara and Quechua is a generic term for "offspring" in the broadest sense; it includes humans, animals, and plants, mainly as food crops (Arnold 2004:148–51). In other words, we are talking about potential household production.

To initiate this process of transferring power, and then stimulate regeneration for household use, we consider a number of questions. In what context were heads taken in warfaring practices? Who took them? What parts of the head were most valued in warfaring practices? In the following pages, we shall set out a reply to these questions that derives from both the corporeal and spiritual aspects of head taking.

Many older people in ayllu Qaqachaka remember the importance of head taking and other forms of attention to the head during warfare: eating the brains, the ears, tongue, and so on in examples of exo-cannibalistic practices that sought to gain control over the powers thought to reside in the head. As a corollary to this attention to the head, there was also frequently the cutting of the sexual parts, whether the breasts of women or the penis of men. Sometimes these male parts were then stuffed into the mouth of the cadaver to confuse its powers and frighten away its kin (Arnold and Yapita 1996:350).

Historical accounts confirm the existence of these kinds of activities in the region, for example where the raw brains would be eaten with the freeze-dried potatoes called *chuño*.[18] Looking further back in the past, Mary Weismantel (2005) has called our attention to the themes of cranial contents and their vitality in Early Intermediate Period Moche ceramic imagery. Here, Moche warfare iconography seems to depict sequences where the heads of male captives seem to be losing this vital force, with blood pouring out of the nose, eyes being torn or plucked out, or captives pulling loosened hair. The earlier stone carvings at Cerro Sechín in the Casma Valley seem to illustrate historical precedents to this phenomenon.

Older people in Qaqachaka also remember how a particular goal of inter-ethnic wars was the capture, on the part of a married man, of an enemy trophy head. This married man (now as head giver) would then surrender the head to his wife (now as head taker), who was charged with wrapping it in a finely woven black cloth, frequently decorated with woven skull designs, with the aim of transforming the spirit embodied in the head into a child of her own group (Arnold and Espejo 2004:351, 356). This same black mourning cloth (*lutu awayu*) is used to take special "medicines" used in a kind of witchcraft to defend the ayllu boundaries in bellicose episodes, and with the aim of killing the enemy. After use, they are kept guarded in the household. The cloth used is always of raw wool (*ch'uqi*) that is not dyed in any way (*qhati*). This act of wrapping is considered to be a particularly female activity in and of itself, and has to do with the female gendered creative counterpart to male warfare that entails rebirthing an enemy spirit (or perhaps an animal) into the family domain (Arnold and Yapita 2001:166, 178, 239).

These kinds of practices are widespread beyond the Andes. For example, Ruth Barnes (1997) describes similar practices among some Naga groups of northeast India (bordering on Burma), where participation in a successful headhunting raid is an essential prerequisite for a young man who wants to marry.[19] She also notes how women make the textiles associated with male success in headhunting and how the making of textiles by women is comparable to the headhunting carried out by men (Barnes 1997:39). And she points out the important link between the head taken by a man and the child born to his wife in the months afterward, although she does not detail the elements of this process (Barnes 1997:41).

In this female complex of wrapping and unwrapping in Qaqachaka, and its accompanying rituals, libations making, and incense burning, as in the *tsantsa* rituals of the Shuar (or Jívaro) described by Taylor (1985, 1993) and Descola (1993a), an enemy head is gradually converted into a head of your own group. This point is important. In the Shuar context, there is a certain caveat concerned with whose head is taken that we should take into account and that might be relevant to the Andean case. It has to do with the difference between "warfare" and "feuds." In the case of Shuar warfare, the aim is to kill all members of the household under attack and take their heads to make *tsantsa* (shrunken heads). Feuds, on the other hand, are hostilities between members of the same groups, often as a result of sorcery or other misdeeds. In cases of feuds, no heads are taken and no *tsantsa* celebration takes place. In essence, this difference between warfare and feuding, according to various ethnographers of the region, concerns the status of the potential heads. In practice, fully fledged Shuar headtaking raids are only launched against groups that speak differently, enemy Others with whom the head takers do not reckon a blood relationship.[20]

This suggests that any continuum in the practices concerned with enemy heads or with ancestral heads would first demand this prerequisite—that through this kind of ritual activity, the two are made to become interchangeable. This ritual activity concerns the "metamorphosis of heads" that Arnold and Yapita discuss at length in the book of that title (2006) and that we shall explain gradually here.

These female-centered wrapping rituals are common and occur in multiple domains. When the women of Qaqachaka sing to their animals today (for example, their llamas), they say that their songs act as placental-like wrappings, which serve to rebirth the creatures (*wawas*) born wild in the hills, into the more domestic house space (Arnold and Yapita 2001:166). In the Andes, llamas are not viewed as domesticated animals, but simply as animals reared in this house space.[21]

Archaeologically, the way that people wrapped their dead in the early Chinchorro burials in the Atacama Desert, or in the Paracas Peninsula mummy bundles, might have sought to create this same sense of placental-like wrappings. In this case, the wrapped mummy bundles might have been perceived as seed-like, waiting to be reborn, as Duviols implies for the mummies called *mallki* of the ayllus of central Peru, well into the Colonial Period (Duviols 1971:380–83).

The Nature of These Powers of Regeneration

More specifically, the capture of an enemy head, and the following female ritual actions concerned with its care through wrapping, libation making, and the offering of incense, are thought to help provide for the family in question over a three-year period. (As we shall see, this three-year period is common in the rituals for the dead in general.) This sequence of curation practices, then, capitalizes on the spiritual powers present in the captured head to radiate a more generalized power capable of producing a series of generic "babies" under the head-taker's control (human, animal, and vegetable). In this sense, the generative spirit of the seed-like head is transferable, with the power to proliferate offspring for its new keeper. Arnold (2000) proposes that these ideas could be compared to the Maori notion of *hau* as the spirit of the original gift (which, in the Andean case, passes from husband to wife) that drives the subsequent exchange relations that the original gift has generated.

Throughout the three-year period after the capture of a head, the male strength derived from having captured the head, and perhaps of having imbibed the spirit thought to reside in the gray matter within the cranium, seems to be transferred implicitly to the belly of the wife. The ambiguity in Andean languages for the term "belly" (Qu. *wijsa*; Aym. *puraka*) for both the digestive and reproductive tracts (stomach and womb) seems to express this curious articulation between both, whereby a warrior who has eaten brain matter could pass on the spirit contained therein, through sexual activity, to his spouse.[22] The associated female practice of weaving, too, takes up these overlapping semantic fields, with the textile considered as both belly and womb, in a woven homologue that echoes the physiological process thought to take place as the taken head is converted into manifold babies (Arnold 2000:11, 17–20).

Again, these ideas have much in common with the process of metamorphosis that Beth Conklin describes in the case of the lowland Wari of Western Brazil (1993, 1995). There, a head-taking male would consume ample sweet maize beer that his wife had produced, to become fat and "pregnant." Through sexual activity, he then passed on the captured spirit of the enemy head he had taken to his wife's belly, from whence it was reborn into their own group.

This sequence of events is not explicit in contemporary Andean examples, nevertheless there is much iconographic evidence to support this process of metamorphosis and transference in the archaeological material. For example, many ceramics from Paracas and Nasca illustrate head images in the genital area of a corpulent woman. In a recent publication on Nasca iconography, Proulx (2006:129) suggests that these kinds of female figurines are associated with fecundity in a broad sense, including trophy heads but also plants, rayed faces, and serpents, which we would expect.[23] The alimentary aspect of this configuration of ideas also seems to be expressed in the frequent images of heads resting on the long tongues of stylized beings, although these might equally suggest another type of potency, such as other voices or essences being absorbed into the body (see Figures 1.1 and 1.2).

The possibility that a head taken in warfare later undergoes a parallel and female-gendered series of transformations in its conversion into the new babies of a household is supported by a variety of associated ideas. For example, a great deal of ethnographic literature in the Andes and other parts of the Americas would suggest that childbirth for women is comparable to warfare for men. Historical sources also suggest that the birth of new offspring was documented by the state both in Middle America and in the Andes under the Inka, as a part of the tributary obligations of groups under their dominion, just as, based on their demographic scale, labor tax was extracted.[24] In the Andes, both birth and tributary cycles are measured in *tercios*, or six-month cycles. This suggests that the family and immediate group cycles of death and regeneration, derived originally from head taking, became integrated at some stage into wider state patterns of tribute and recompense, where the state served as the ultimate head taker from groups under its dominion. The evidence suggests that the pre-Hispanic practices viewed this tribution in terms of childbirth labor on the part of women, and as the potential contribution of individual persons as tribute contributors toward the state once they had developed and grown. Later colonial practices seem to have reinterpreted this form of tribution in more material terms, with taxation in goods rather than in productive labor.

The ambiguous status of the new babies, as part descendants of taken enemy heads, is confirmed in many cultural practices in the region to the present day. For example, in many regional childbirth practices there is an implicit idea

Figure 1.1: Photo of a Nasca Ceramic Figure of a Corpulent or Pregnant Woman with the head of the Oculate Being Tattoo around Her Vagina

Image published in Proulx (1999:286), "Nasca headhunting and the ritual use of trophy heads." Originally published in German in *Nasca, Geheimnisvolle Zeichen im Alten Peru*. Ed. Judith Rickenbach (Zurich: Museum Rietberg Zürich, 1999). Courtesy of the Linden-Museum, Stuttgart, Germany (Collection No. M32258).

that a new baby is considered a foreigner in the group and that birth giving is infused with a particular sense of danger for the mother, deriving from the enemy nature of the fetus. Tristan Platt, in a 2001 article, develops this idea to the point of suggesting that the baby is perceived an enemy to its own mother! These reflections are affirmed by the still pervasive cultural idea in the Andes that a new baby is a warrior that must not be mollycoddled with instant breastfeeding or instant attention to its demands. It must become

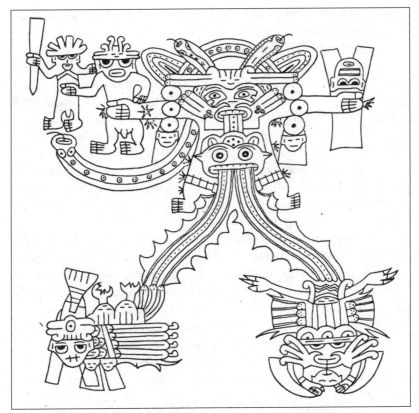

Figure 1.2: A Nasca Being with a Head Pouring out of Its Mouth

Image from Zuidema (1972:36), "Meaning in Nasca art. Iconographic relationships between Inca-, Huari-, and Nazca cultures in southern Peru." In *Annual Report for 1971, Goteborgs Ethnografiska Museum*, pp. 35–54 (Arstryck, Sweden: Goteborg Ethnografiska Museum, 1972). Courtesy of Goteborg Etnografiska Museum, Sweden.

strong and defend itself and the honor of its kinfolk, an idea that has thwarted the attempts of many development projects to change these practices.[25] In this context, the practices of child rearing are directed toward domesticating this enemy spirit, to incorporate the child fully into your own ancestral group. The same ideas are found in many lowland societies.[26]

According to older people in Qaqachaka, children taken in warfare in the past suffered the same consequences of having to be tamed into the ancestral group and at times "being bound like dogs" so that they did not escape. Similarly, women taken in battle were prevented from leaving the new group until they had become accustomed to the place. Other innuendos in these accounts of the past infer that males taken as prisoners were treated as slaves until their deaths. These modern Andean examples do not seem to confirm the polarized differences between "head takers" and "slave takers" that Friedman posits for the case of Burma.

In relation to the woven homologue of this process, many ethnographers of textiles in the Andes observe that, like babies, weavings are considered living beings, although the precise nature of this living being varies in distinct regions (see, for example, Cereceda 1978; Desrosiers 1982; Torrico 1989; Arnold 2000). Further evidence suggests that weaving itself is the mode of transformation of the new being. For example, in "Essay on the Origins of Andean Cloth," Arnold (2000) proposes that the distant origins of weaving that women recount today have to do with the female power of transforming the hair of a dead enemy head into a new baby of her own group (again, a *wawa* in Aymara and Quechua). In turn, her weaving activity gradually transforms this baby into a person (Aym. *jaqi*; Qu. *runa*).

In this process of transformation, Arnold (2000) proposes that the loom space doubles as the ontological site for trapping the captured enemy, and for appropriating its strength and knowledge. She shows how the terminology of many details of the activity of weaving, such as warping up, setting out the first foundational weft threads and tying them back to the loom poles, beating down on the weft with a weaving bone, or the reinforcing punching action of tightening the warp threads, all seem to refer to the forced restraint of this captured being during the weaving period, so that its energy provides sustenance for the emerging baby created in cloth (see also Arnold and Yapita 2006:Chap. 3).

This weaving space seems homologous to other creative spaces, where generic "babies" are born and then reared (for example, the family fields under cultivation). In another essay, the weaver Cipriana Apaza described how, in her own community of Santiago de Huata, on the shores of Lake Titicaca, the weaving terminology for the center and the borders of a textile is often homologous to the agricultural terminology of field centers and field borders. In a language of analogies or similitudes, just as child rearing involves the discipline of calling attention to a child's bad traits to better form their personalities, so the weeding and removing of excess stones in agricultural tasks is considered to attend the new plant babies under cultivation, molding their potential (Arnold, Yapita, and Apaza 1996:384–85).

How, then, do weavers perceive the potential of the weaving space created on the loom, or the cultivated space contained within the field borders that the captured enemy generates? In the region of Qaqachaka, these sites inside either woven or agricultural borders are imagined to be animated by trapped spirits. These are held to be the *jira mayku*, or "spiraling warrior beings," thought to frequent the ayllu during the rainy season to stimulate plant growth.[27]

The *jira mayku* are thought to be tiny beings dressed in the colors of the new vegetation, and their spiraling movement seeks to direct a similar movement in the sprouting plants as they push out of the ground. These tiny beings are associated with the rains (they are said to come out of the center of the rain clouds and to come down from the hills to abide on the swollen river banks of the rainy season). Sometimes these beings are associated with troops of white llamas. Arnold and Yapita examine their nature at length in *River of Fleece, River of Song* (2001).

The *jira mayku* spiraling beings seem to embody the spirits of warriors who died the previous year, and if you should see them this will announce your death in the coming year; in this sense, they are similar to the Valkyries of Nordic mythology. Also, importantly, the presence of these beings is said to inspire women in weaving, as they dance on the loom threads during weaving activity, only to escape before the weaving borders are finished.[28] Again, the weaver appropriates the creative energy of these beings as she contains them in an enclosed space (Arnold and Espejo 2004:351; Arnold and Yapita 2006:249–50).

Archaeological evidence for similar ideas concerning the woven containment of captured heads in the past to appropriate the spiritual energies therein and redirect them toward a more beneficial regenerative growth is found in some pre-Colombian examples. For example, Anne Paul, in an article on "Protective Perimeters" (2000b), calls attention to the use of images of twisted and interlaced threads, associated with trophy heads, in the iconography of various sacred sectors within the archaeological complex of Chavín de Huántar, whether on ceramics, stone, or cloth. The twisted hair of the front-faced deity of the Raimundi stone is an obvious example. She asks if these same textile images might have had a sacred power that would impart spirituality to the images and objects in which they appear. More specifically, she suspects that these twisted images might have provided the very mechanism of border containment of the spirit thought to dwell in the head, as if to appropriate its energy for particular purposes, just as a head is bordered by hair (see Figure 1.3).

In her article, Paul asks whether this ancient visual expression might refer to a preoccupation with tapping the same kind of head-derived energy or power as that contained by modern day textile (and agricultural) borders. If so, then for Paul this woven iconography in the Chavín style seems to be concerned with trapping this spirit within the confines of the sacred precincts to appropriate its power to impart spirituality to certain objects or places.

Mary Frame (1991) illustrates this ontological primacy of heads in slightly earlier coastal Paracas textiles, where headgear designs (of the headbands called *wincha*) act as templates for all the other garments a person wore, or was

Figure 1.3: An Interlaced Border with a Head Motif from an Early Horizon Coastal Textile

Detail of a painted design on a Carhua textile, showing an image of three-strand oblique interlacing around the edge of a circle. After Wallace 1991:Fig. 3.16. Reprinted from Anne Paul, *Paracas Art and Architecture: Object and Context in South Coastal Peru* (Iowa City: University of Iowa Press, 1991). Courtesy of University of Iowa Press.

wrapped in, that is, as the primary generators of subsidiary sequences. Another modern example that reiterates the rules of the regenerative sequences made possible from having trapped the energies of a captured head is when the *yatiri* or shaman, Don Domingo Jiménez (from ayllu Milma in the Aymaya valleys of northern Potosí), says, "you should not loosen the threads on a woman's weaving borders," but rather pay attention to making effective the respective warp and weft borders. He is referring to the symbolic import- ance of *closed* borders on female garments, as opposed to the cloth with *open* borders made by men, the same point developed by Sophie Desrosiers in her 1997 article.

This complex of ideas and associated cultural and political actions concerned with appropriating the masculine powers of taken enemy heads and converting these, whether by ritual means or though the containment facilitated by borders, into a more beneficial regenerative energy for your own group, led Arnold and Yapita to postulate an Andean textual theory (2000:420–25; see also Arnold and Yapita 2006:107–09, 274–76). This theory emphasizes how the creative and aesthetic appropriation of outside forces (the enemy spirit of a taken head) is made possible by revivifying something dead, and transforming its potential into one of *regeneration*, that which drives through time the generation of new beings, and their interchange between groups. It is a theory that traces a warrior-weaver aesthetic, where deconstruction gives rise to reconstruction, as an Andean variant on the theory of "ontological depredation" put forward by Viveiros de Castro and others in a lowland setting.

The sequence of transformations that is generated by having taken a trophy head reminds us of the ethnographic literature concerning the Maori *hau*, with its own particular regenerative powers. In an Andean context, the striking semantic connection between *aya*, for a cadaver, and *ayni* for these wider processes of exchange perhaps generated from an original death, merits a study in itself (Arnold 1988:302–03).

Others authors have described these kinds of processes of transubstantiation of the dead as a part of "Andean seminal thought" (perhaps reinforced in the early colonial era by Augustinian thought), whose key idea is that a captured seed will sprout into another life.[29] Cultural activity here would nourish this capacity for growth and maturation. In this process of transformation, in the Andes as elsewhere, the creative role of a woman weaver is complementary to the destructive role of men in warfare. Just as men destroy life, weavers are charged with its revivification into new beings (see Arnold 2004; Arnold and Yapita 2006:249).[30]

From an archaeological perspective, we suggest that an illustration of these ideas from another Andean context occurs in the Early Intermediate Period Pukara ceramics that Sergio Chávez has written about (1992, 2002). On these polychrome ceramics, there are two main images (see Figure 1.4). The first is a male sacrificer with a knife, surrounded by severed heads; the second is a front-faced woman who holds a live camelid tethered in one hand and a flower-staff in the other. While her objects suggest fecundity, life, and rejuvenation, the male images are destructive. Rather than viewing these two images simply as polar opposites, Hastorf proposes that these two kinds of pots might have been used together in certain ceremonies (or a cycle of ceremonies), so that the combined and complementary forces they illustrated could complete the ritual transference of death to regeneration, a point we develop later in Chapter 3.

Transformations in Values and the Fetishism of Commodities Revisited

We suggest that this play of transferences between death and life through ideas, energies, images, and the human act of materialization, drawing on the power of heads taken in warfare, is pertinent to the way that Marx, in the first volume of *Kapital*, originally used the term "fetish" in relation to early capitalism. There, Marx used "fetish" to explain an alienated attachment to objects when the consumer was not the real producer, and when, as a result, the object became more valuable or "enhanced" in a related "mystical" way even at some distance from the source (Marx 1973 [1894], Vol. 1:86–96). For Marx, the fetishism of the commodity disguised the potential gain to be made in production from the use of this particular form of capital, depending on the cycles of supply and demand in question. Taking up the ideas we have developed so far, we would say that the fetishism of the commodity, for Marx, disguised a wider cycle of implicit economic transactions concerning the stages of transformation of the original commodity. Although this has been used to explain why Westerners love to shop, it might also help explain the power of Weiner's inalienable possessions (1992) as well as that of trophy heads.

In a capitalist context, Marx proposes that for mercantile capital, capital (as money) would first be transformed (or metamorphized) into the commodity it bought, then this merchandise would in turn become retransformed into the money from its sale ($M_1 - C - M_2$; where M = money and C = commodity), although the overall fetishized impression would be just of "money that engenders money." For the producers, on the other hand, a commodity for sale would first metamorphize into currency (money), and this in turn would become transformed again into other new commodities bought ($C_1 - M - C_2$)

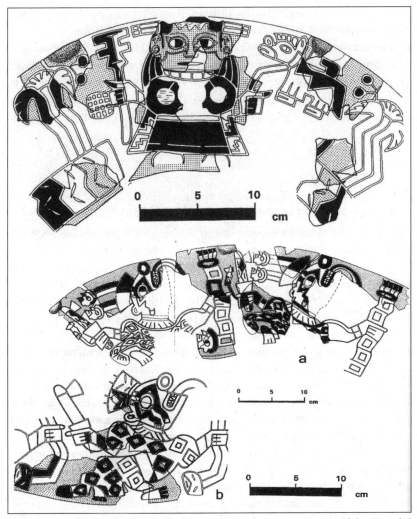

Figure 1.4: Two Early Intermediate Period Pukara Ceramic Images of the Camelid Woman Holding Living Things and the Male Associated with Heads

Identification of the camelid woman and feline man themes, motifs, and designs in Pucara-style pottery. In *Andean Archaeology II*, pp. 35–69. Eds. Helaine Silverman and William H. Isbell (New York: Kluwer Academic/Plenum Publishers, 2002). Courtesy of Sergio Chávez. From Sergio Chávez (2002:41).

(Marx 1973 [1894], Vol. 3:337–38). So, for Marx, fetishism would seem to do with the way that the "subjective or use value" of a commodity is appropriated and its potential (or productive yield) converted into exchange value through this metamorphosis-like process.

If we apply Marx's logic to the modern cycling of a trophy head (and perhaps ancestral heads, too), still in the immediate domestic and communal sphere, it is clear that the original consumer or head taker did not actually produce the trophy object, which has only a death-like quality in his hands. Therefore, to release its potential subjective value and convert this into exchange value, it is necessary for his wife to "bring it back to life" ritually, and so seem to produce related objects, the new proliferation of "babies," for the use of her own group ($H_1 - B$; where H = head, B = babies).

In this process, viewed as an economic transaction from the male point of view, the capital-like head, obtained for a household through a particular form of male labor (head taking), to release its value potential or yield, must first be transformed by female ritual labor into the new harvest of "babies" or agricultural produce, that can then circulate and be exchanged more widely between households. Then the more generalized demand for these product "babies" would, in turn, generate the necessity for more heads to reinitiate the cycle ($H_1 - B - H_2$). From the female point of view, too, the constant production of the various forms of "babies" through female labor, and their immediate circulation in spheres of exchange, would generate a demand for the periodic production of more trophy heads on the part of her husband ($B_1 - H - B_2$).

Within this broader theory about the transformation of values and returns, it warrants mentioning that the common impression of heads on more formal kinds of metal and paper currency, as they emerge in society, seem to confirm the power of this logic in other parts of the world. How far can we push this theory of transformations back into the past? And to what degree might it have to do with heads? Recent ideas about the development of writing and numerical systems at least imply a similar relation between the beginnings of the bureaucratic state apparatus and the death of the Other, which, in turn, helped generate the proliferation of one's own objects to be counted and deposited (Urton 1997:31; Arnold and Yapita 2006:224). In other words, death and its transformation through fruitful regeneration seem to underlie not only the political documentation of early economic transactions but also their very nature.

Why a Head?

Let us turn to the role of the head in these ritual and economic transactions. A number of theories have examined the particular importance of the head over other body parts, whether as a trophy object or as the key remains of revered ancestors. They do so in the contexts of ancient Andean cultures, contemporary Andean ethnography, and that of other parts of the world.[31] Like the dyads put forward by Bloch and Parry mentioned earlier, many of these theories associated ancestral heads with fertility and enemy heads with destructive relations.

However, the actual evidence from ethnographic and archaeological settings implies that cultural practice is more nuanced. For example, from an Amazonian perspective, Harner (1972) warns that head taking, viewed exclusively as a practice of warfare or conquest, is only a partial explanation for many other activities directed at the head. From a highland viewpoint, Carmichael (1994:84) confirms these kinds of doubts, seeing little difference today between these two skull types in the context of fertility, as *all* kinds of heads can watch over the fields and protect the harvests.

Likewise, in the archaeological record, Donald Proulx (1999), among others, does not perceive a substantive difference between community ancestral heads and enemy heads. For Proulx, ample evidence suggests that the ceremonialism of Early Intermediate Period Nasca, as in earlier Ica/Paracas Peninsula societies, was centered in agricultural fertility, above all the constant need for water to render soils productive in a desert environment. Proulx associates many of the mythic beings found on textiles and ceramics, as well as the ordinary animals and birds seen in the more general iconography of these ancient coastal cultures, as having to do with agriculture, water, and land. And he relates trophy heads captured in warfare to this same preoccupation.

For Proulx, the most convincing evidence that relates trophy heads to agricultural fertility are the so-called sprouting heads, trophy-head figures from which sprout plants of one kind and another that are found on Nasca ceramics.[32] Sawyer (1979), too, has examined painted Nasca textiles that illustrate masked beings with sprouting heads. Farther to the north at contemporaneous Chavín de Huántar, stone-etched iconography (on the Tello Obelisk) displays plants growing out of supernatural beings (see Figure 1.5), a point raised by Donald Lathrap (1977) to support his idea of the Amazonian origins of some agricultural crops, in his classic article "Our Father the Cayman, Our Mother the Gourd." Each of these studies reiterates the agricultural potential of heads, whether captured, engraved on stone, or in the realm of the supernatural.

In a contemporary setting, as we shall see, not only the sprouting of seeds but the whole sequence of productive activity seems to derive from bellicose influence. The breaking up of hard terrain, the digging of fields, or the building of houses in a new settlement are still considered to be like going to war in Aymara and Quechua terminology, and the capture of trophy heads is compared to bringing back seeds to sprout on that land. In modern warfare, then, the captured head perceived as a potential seed is the essence of fertility.

By contrast, in an ancestral context rather than a bellicose one, heads would perhaps represent the ancestral family line in a more benign way. What does this benignness imply? And could it be identified in an ethnographic or

Figure 1.5: Line Drawing of the Tello Obelisk Cayman Being

Note the plants growing out of the cayman's head at the bottom of the image. From John H. Rowe (1967:99, Fig. 6), "Form and meaning in Chavin art." In *Readings in Peruvian Archaeology*, pp. 72–104. Eds. John Howland Rowe and Dorothy Menzel (Palo Alto, CA: Peek Publishers, 1967).

Permission courtesy of John Rowe's estate.

archaeological context and differentiated from more aggressive relations? Evidently, both ancestral and enemy would sprout their "babies" from the eye sockets or fontanel indentation as key nodal points, much like potato tubers sprout new potatoes from their "eyes." In a society that considers power as coming from the ancestors, calling up the ancestors, like calling up the spirits of enemies, would help with the propagation of anything planted or nurtured. Because the ancestors are made manifest through their remains, their bones as well as their wrappings are an important element for ritual attention, to remember the dead. We know that Andean people have curated bones for a long time and they continue to do so. They have also curated heads expressly to help nurture children, crops, and animals, as a material manifestation of the spirit of life. So, in practice, the treatment of both ancestral and enemy remains need not be so different.

The territorial and spatial consequences of this need to appeal continually to ancestral remains meant living close to them, just as warriors kept their trophy heads close by in the very recent past. Throughout the Andes, especially during the Late Intermediate Period, the dead and the living were not always separated spatially. As we shall see, the dead were often buried under living floors and within structure walls.[33] Also, at the time when most communities moved upslope to the crest of knolls, they lived near the caves and crevasses where the dead were buried; many Late Intermediate Period sites are located just above these crevasses, which implied living just above one's ancestors.[34]

In this same period, fields were often located below the residences, meaning that people would pass the caves of the dead on their way to the fields each day. One difference might be, then, that in an ancestral setting, the *wider* haemodynamic cycle we identified above, with its destructive male-dominated phase of warfare followed by a more regenerative and creative female-dominated phase, could be more restricted, to just death and regeneration. Again, the heart of this difference, unlike trophy heads, is not necessary to ensure that ancestral heads are reborn into your own group; they are already a part of it. In more general terms, male-dominated warfare followed by the more female-dominated creative phase seems to have been an active principle up and down the Andean intermontane valleys where many high Pukara settlements were associated with internecine warfare at that time.

Proulx (1999:6) allows for this kind of ambiguity when he perceives a direct link between the two complexes of "death/decapitation/blood" and "regeneration/rebirth/agricultural fertility." He proposes that the principal uses of trophy heads in Nasca were "magical" in nature, to assure the continuing abundance of harvests. He also argues that the people of Nasca gave importance to the head as a source of power, and that the burials of groups of heads (in Cerro Carapo, Estaqueria, Chaviña, and Tambo Viejo) would therefore represent "a concentration of ritual power." For Proulx, the iconographic representations of germinating beans that take the form of trophy heads, or of corn cobs that have a trophy head face, seem to confirm the existence of a process of metamorphosis in which heads transform into plants and vice versa in alternating cycles of death and regeneration, just like the annual crops planted in irrigated fields. This notion seemed to have been widespread, given that images of the kinds of sequences found in the central Andes are also illustrated in Moche ceramics, and suggested at Pukara and Chavín de Huántar. Citing the *yatiri* Don Domingo Jiménez, this same kind of notion leads Arnold and Yapita to describe the same kinds of metamorphosis in a contemporary context (2006:242–43).

Similar notions are prevalent in sites widely separate in time. For example, Proulx's key comparison between a head and a seed operating in the ancient Nasca worldview is still evident in Qaqachaka today, especially in a warfaring context (Arnold and Yapita 2006:242–43). There, it is common to compare a trophy head with a seed that regenerates in the earth so as to augment the agricultural production of the victors in a war. They say in Aymara: "It is as if this whole head could produce like a seed" (*uka p'iqix lij similljamachispaya*). This cycle is considered to be under the control of the local mountain guardians, so they add: "It is as if the mountain guardians of the place wanted all of this" (*ukjay lij uywiris munchispa jall ukhamjamawa*).

The comments by Don Domingo Jiménez, who is from the Aymaya valleys to the east, are particularly pertinent as these valleys are outliers of the neighboring ayllu of Jukumani, the traditional enemies of Qaqachaka. As a practicing *yatiri*, or shaman, Don Domingo has another more spiritual explanation behind the reasons for head taking in warfare. He holds that when we think with the head, it is actually the spirit that dwells therein that inspires our thoughts (Aym. *amta*). "The body in and of itself does not think." This human spirit "resides in the brains, that think profoundly" (*p'iqi p'iqix llixwixay wal pinsixa*). For him, eating brains has the effect of making one's self "more intelligent," by "having more head" (*p'iq p'iq churañapataki*). This is why it is particularly important to take the heads of enemy leaders, "as they think the best."

Comparative material from modern Peru reiterates that brains are eaten to achieve greater intelligence. There are also ample studies of the generative capacity not only of the head but all of its excretions: saliva, tears, eye and nose mucus, and so on.[35] In the case of Qaqachaka's fierce neighbors, Don Domingo holds that the spirit that dwells in the head is, in turn, inspired by breath from the mouth. In this physiological process, breath mixes with blood flow and then this mixture (which he calls "the testament of the heart") flows to the head (to nourish the spirit there) and it is finally exteriorized through the voice.

Don Domingo's comparison between the brains and generative seed (*muju/jatha*) is also implicit in the reasons given by the people of Qaqachaka for eating the brains of animals (or of enemies in war), when they say that the brains contain in and of themselves the future growth of the herds. People eat the brains of animals (sheep or llamas) "so that these particular animals procreate."

An implicit comparison here between the brains and masculine generative substance suggests that just as the male penis inserts seed from the testicles into females to form people, consumed brains regenerate more of the species of which they form a part. In this sense, the brains contain in and of themselves the additional possibility of regenerating all the other body parts, especially in the context of war and pending agricultural production.

During libation making, Qakachaka men make toasts so that the young men are born strong and robust and with the strength to "put good seed inside." Here, the transformation of a trophy head into a baby of the same group is essential, so that you procreate more people of your own group as well as having success in planting and harvests (see also Arnold, In press).

It merits comment that both Don Domingo and the Qaqachaka men often call the generative force or "spirit," thought to reside in the brains, particularly of humans, simply *ispiritu*, after the Spanish. Don Domingo associates this particular spirit with the breath and suggests that the skulls under the charge of women learn to "breathe" before they create their new batch of offspring. The same kinds of Spanish borrowings occur frequently in this context, since at other times the spirit that dwells in a trophy head is called *kawisa* (from *cabeza*, the Spanish for "head"), *animu* (from *ánimo*, the Spanish for "animus," as the soul that continues after death) and *kaprichu* (from *capricho*: as a more "capricious" soul). However, in other circumstances this spirit is called *qamaqi*, a term having the broad sense of the courage, bravery, or pluck you must call on when faced, for example, by a predatory fox (see also Arnold and Yapita 1996:357–58). This Andean term *qamaqi* might possibly be equivalent to the Jívaro (Shuar) use of *arutam wakani* that Proulx (1999) has called our attention to, which describes the additional soul acquired from head taking that protects the head taker against sorcery, disease, and death.[36] In this context, perhaps the soul called *kaprichu* is more like the Shuar *muisak*, in the sense of the avenging spirit of the dead person.

Flying Heads

The psychosexual issues at play in these regional ideas concerning heads and their associated substances ensure that head capture and curation are not taken lightly. The phenomenon of "flying heads," in particular, would imply that head taking is a highly dangerous activity, often restricted to the domain of shamans. Even so, tales of flying heads are extremely widespread. Typically, a disembodied head, with its hair loose and disheveled, or, in the case of females, with its braids flapping to each side as wings, or else with hands where the neck should be, flies through the air or crawls on the ground, seeking the body of which it was once a part. The origins of these ideas seem to derive from the cultural practices related to head taking, particularly their shamanic dimensions, which people comment about on many occasions.

For example, people say that the heads of great enemy leaders, after being buried and defleshed on one's own land to tame them, are passed on to the shamans (*yatiri*) in an ayllu community such as Qaqachaka. The crania are then used for both protective and defensive purposes, as well as for more aggressive and belligerent uses. A great shaman may have a whole cache of such heads under his control. Here the *yatiri* would seem to act in the more female role of "trophy-head taker" rather than "trophy-head giver."

In these situations, the *yatiri*'s control over the power and strength of an enemy head is at stake. Because a *yatiri* is usually selected by being struck by lightning, he (or she) is considered to have the additional power of lightning to help control the potential of the trophy head in the coming period. He or she will also offer incense, make libations, and burn candles before the head in regular rituals, three times a week, to keep control of its powers.

It is mainly the specialist shamans who are able to speak to both the upper and lower worlds and able to control both the powers of the day and the night who curate heads in this way. These shamans, called *ch'amakani* in Aymara or *aysiri* in Quechua, also cultivate the ability to speak to the trophy heads, and so keep these heads and their regenerative powers under their charge. A shaman of this kind will want to know the territorial jurisdiction of the head in question to appropriate its powers and thus expand his or her own power domain.

It is interesting to note that historically, the Inka imperial leaders (Topa Inka) had similar traits to the *yatiris* of today. Many colonial chroniclers recount how these Inka leaders collected both their enemies' heads as well as curating their ancestors' bodies in special places where offerings were regularly made to them (Murúa 1946 [1590]; Betanzos 1996 [1557]). By placing both of these poles in the recycling spectrum of heads, it seems possible that the Topa Inka, as the highest representative of the Inka state, might have been perceived to be both masculine, in charge of the military, as well as feminine, curating heads and recharging the empire with regenerative growth, thus controlling the whole energy cycle of heads in favor of their own polity. His very power and status might have derived from this combined ability.

Another element to consider in relation to the power of heads is the importance attributed to the hair of a trophy head to think and act.[37] As the hair continues to grow after death, it is also attributed with the power to re-create the whole body of which it was part. This idea, which Anne Paul (1982:46–48) dates back to at least coastal Paracas Initial times, exists today throughout the Andes in the messianic idea that the Inka emperor, Inkarriy, is not really dead but that his head is simply buried in the ground, the hair growing like roots to generate the food crops in the coming harvests, and that in the future, the hair will reconstitute the whole body in a kind of second coming.[38] In the hands of women, this regeneration sequence figures in many Andean textiles styles, for example in the communities of Qeros and Choquecancha, in the region of Cusco.[39]

For shamans in the region of Qaqachaka, the power of the hair of a trophy head is related to its propensity to fly back at times to the body of which it was a part. The shaman takes advantage of this characteristic to be able to accompany the head on its spiritual flights and so dominate the upper world that looks over the enemy territory. It is this practice that has possibly given rise to the many contemporary tales of "flying heads" (Sp. *cabezas voladoras*), called by different names depending on the region (*qati qati, jururu*, etc.). Alison Spedding (1993) has collected such Andean tales, as part of a literary genre that she calls "American Gothic."

We shall consider in Chapter 6 whether these kinds of practices might also have given rise to the images that decorate the textiles of Paracas and Nasca and that Paul and Turpin (1986) interpret as "flying shamans." In this case, the shamans would be encarnating the flying head as it travels through the upper world (see Figure 1.6). Could the wild and exaggerated hair and headdress of the Raimundo Stela from Chavín de Huántar or the Late Formative heads held by stone *chacha* (man)-pumas in the Titicaca Basin also echo these shamanic practices of flying to gain power over enemy territories?

Perhaps so, but contemporary practice also cautions us to remember that there is a double-edged danger in having power over trophy heads. If the head is not buried initially within the soil of one's own territory, and dominated by a woman who contains and controls it by wrapping it up, acknowledging the head by curating it and taking it out regularly from its wrappings to make offerings of incense, reinforced possibly by the dominating techniques of a local shaman, then the head is thought to have the power to take vengeance on its new owner and even of causing his (or her) death. Hence, those who collect crania from cemeteries today, though keen to have this power, are always tentative about the dangerous potential to be gained.

* * * *

To conclude, let us return to some more general points concerning the wider politics of which trophy heads are at the center. We have argued here that in the region of ayllu Qaqachaka, contacts and influences in the distant past from

Figure 1.6: A "Flying" Ecstatic Shaman from a Paracas Textile
In Anne Paul and Solveig A. Turpin (1986:26), "The ecstatic shaman theme of Paracas textiles." *Archaeology* 39(5):20–27. Courtesy of the Paul estate.

bellicose skirmishes with lowland groups, above all the Tupi-Guaraní, in the Inka period and before, might have influenced regional warfaring practices, especially those of head taking. Drawing on Fausto (2001), we proposed that one consequence of this historical experience is the modern-day expansive and centrifugal political system (limited by the administrative competencies of the modern Bolivian state) that still erupts at times, converting a wider network of commerce between ayllus with a common history into a region dominated by the exchanges of warfare, including the taking of trophy heads. Considering the work of Douglas (1967), we suggested that the cultural practices centered on these heads seek to control (or ration) the wider circulation of these commodities and extract the maximum symbolic value from them, to generate and harness a wider radiating yield from these valuable possessions but limit its potential to the immediate ayllu group. This Andean form of "ontological depredation," centered on the taking of trophy heads by men, is focused on persons and the appropriation of alien subjectivities rather than things, and their conversion into kin. At issue for us, at a local level, and in local symbolic terms, is the appropriation of the spirits or souls thought to reside in the head, personified as the *jira mayku* or turning ones, and the cultural management of their powers of regeneration. This must have been an issue in the past as well, when people or groups attempted to harness such powers.

We have shown how the brutal male activities of warfare are complemented in a parallel gendered domain of female activities concerned with the consequences of warfare: of wrapping and curating the head and then converting it into kin through the associated nurturing activities of childbirth and childrearing. These gendered activities are not always sex-specific, as shamans and even the Inka himself seem to have been involved in nurturing activities. But the appropriation of this additional female capacity is what seems to define the extraordinary power of such individuals and their spheres of control. At a more everyday level, we argued that historically this gendered division of ritual labor is what gave rise to many associated cultural developments in female hands, such as weaving, or certain aspects of agriculture. In all of these activities, we propose that the symbolic power of the person, above all the head, facilitates the transmission of this power into other domains.

The Captured Fetish, the Mountain Chest, and Sacrifice

LET US turn now to consider how heads, whether as war trophies or from ancestors, were guarded in a household or in a community, taking our principal point of reference from contemporary ethnographic settings, but again drawing on the archaeological and historic literature. Here, we scrutinize the more general curation practices involved in keeping heads around, as well as the more specifically vengeful aspects of appropriating the powers of a captured head. In the latter case, we shall reiterate, but at another level, how the captured head must be contained in some way for its spiritual powers to be appropriated, much as we described earlier the spiritual powers appropriated from heads that are captured within the borders of weavings or fields.

Ample archaeological evidence shows that both ancestral and enemy heads were guarded in niched containers as well as cached in pits in the earth.[1] For example, Hastorf in her article "Community with the Ancestors" (2003) has identified such a niche, about 90 cm in length, on the eastern side in a Middle Formative enclosure, dating to between 1000 and 800 BC, situated on the Taraco Peninsula on the southern shores of Lake Titicaca in Bolivia. She associates this niche found in a wall with an early form of ancestral worship of the human remains contained therein. She proposes that this configuration is then elaborated at the same site of Chiripa in the later ceremonial buildings—called "Upper Houses" by Bennett (1936)—whose interiors are encircled with niches both large and small. As a container, these wall niches echo other kinds of niches found in the earth, leading Hastorf to compare them to the later niches in the sunken enclosures at Pukara around 200 BC in the northern

Titicaca Basin, where Kidder found a human mandible.[2] Another example of niches for the dead and related icons was uncovered at Pukara in the small niches of a rectangular structure (in sector BG). There, two interior niches near the doorway were empty, but on the opposite wall one niche held a painted stone head, while a second niche held a stone figure of a human body, dating to around 300 BC.[3]

Variations on this contained head-or-burial/niche complex are widespread and long-lived, beginning with the humble five niches found in the Early Formative structure 3-A at La Barca, in the southern altiplano Oruro department of Bolivia (as described by Rose 2001), two of which had complete human burials in them. Despite their early date, the cultural importance of these Formative niches are reiterated later in those at Middle Horizon Wari's ceremonial enclosures where children's burials were found,[4] as well as in the better known niches of the Inka mummy bundles housed in Coricancha (Qurikancha) in Cusco, documented in the Colonial Period.

Even today, apart from being wrapped in the ritual bundles that we already mentioned, heads are sometimes kept under the bed platform in houses or in niches within the walls of house structures (Aym. *t'uxu*). Even in urban settings, heads are often curated in wooden chests, called *baúl*. In the region of Qaqachaka, it was common in the recent past for captured heads to be displayed for a short period in caches on special piles of stones (Aym. *taqawa*), just outside the community's limits, before they were buried to become defleshed. Nowadays, these burials often take place under a rosemary bush in a household garden (Arnold and Yapita 1999, 2006:105).

The Concentration of a Head's Powers

In her article "The Social Life of a Communal Chest" (2005), Arnold proposes that these different forms of architectural niches were homologous to a series of similar enclosures that concentrated the power of the items contained therein. These include the woven bundles we described earlier, the colonial boxes made of rawhide (Sp. *petaca*) or wood (the *baúl*), where knotted *kipu* threads and later on written documents came to be guarded, as were other forms of containment. If we apply this insight to an archaeological context, then these early niches might have been key sites for the emerging social practices of focusing value, through the containment of captured enemy beings, the guarding, curating, remembering, and attendance of one's own ancestors and other things that held power, along with the associated ceremonial worship of all of these.[5]

In a bellicose context, an important link can be made between these manifold contained niche-like spaces as the sites of the suffering and sacrifice of captured humans, the gradual appropriation of their powers, and a wider interest in the power to stimulate rain. This would have been the case especially in a highland context, where rains are so unreliable, and on the coast, where rains are absent and rainwater only arrives indirectly, in rivers from the mountains. There are numerous indications that many Inka rituals involving the sacrifice and burial of humans as well as animals such as llamas, in niches or burial pits on high mountaintops, were concerned precisely with the state control of rain-making rituals in an uncertain environment, directed toward a transference of powers that would contribute to adequate rainfall in the coming year.[6] The multiple llama sacrifice on the top of Tiwanaku's Akapana pyramid, too, has been associated with the desperate need for rain at a time when a long drought had been underway (Kolata 1996:180–82).

In this context, Arnold (2005) finds key similarities between the common archaeological and historical practices of keeping heads and other objects in niches and the "mountain chests" used in the past and still used to house sacrificial offerings. These sacred pits, located on the sides of the important "guardian" mountains of contemporary Andean communities (those usually called *uywiri* or *apu*), contain the bones of sacrifice. In the contemporary setting of Qaqachaka, they are called *t'uxu*, "hole," and *samanchi*, "air sender," or *samiri*, "that which breathes." In Carangas (Oruro, Bolivia), some 100 km to the east of Qaqachaka, Ulpián R. López García (1999) describes them as *marka qullu*: "town, or pueblo mountain." The Spanish borrowed word *caja* is also often used.

Nowadays, these pits, like many caves, constitute an important part of the sacred sites of regional *wak'a*. Sacrifices are made there for plentiful sheep, llamas, and other animals, as well as for ample agricultural and herding production, and most importantly, for rain.[7] In Carangas, López García has studied how the ceremonial actions that take place at these sites are directed toward a vital process of metamorphosis, whereby the putrifying carcass of the sacrificed animal is thought to metamorphose into rain clouds (López García 1999:32, 60; Arnold 2005:119).

In this broader context of diverse containment practices, especially the siting of "burial chests" on the side of sacred mountains, we argue that the earliest platform mounds in the Andean region derived from an attempt to materialize in a more controlled way the principles still at issue in the mountain offering sites of today. We also argue that such sites served the political intention of certain groups of gaining rainmaking powers from the containment practices associated with the populations whose body parts are contained therein (see Figure 2.1).

Figure 2.1: Photo of a Platform Mound from Pampa de las Llamas–Moxeke, in the Casma Valley
Photograph by Christine Hastorf.

The illustrations of such mountain chests in Moche iconography, around what Donnan and McClelland (1979) call more generally the "burial theme," reveal that this tradition was at least as old as the Early Intermediate coastal Moche culture.[8] The large cache of heads that Browne, Silverman, and García (1993) report for Cerro Carapo and Drusini and Baraybar (1991) for Cahuachi, in the southern coastal Nasca Early Intermediate Period, were possibly more instances of this kind of storage place for containment practices, as was the cache of crania uncovered by Robert Feldman (1980) at the even earlier Initial Phase Áspero. At Chiripa, too, during the Middle Formative Period, besides the sunken enclosures with niches, there are the beginnings of raised stepped platform mounds that came to exist throughout the Titicaca Basin (Stanish 2003). Within these sites there is clear evidence for niche curation and presentation, best illustrated in the Late Chiripa "Upper Houses" (as described by Bennett 1936; Mohr Chávez 1988; Hastorf 2003). These structures are associated with a range of water-related stone-carved images (as we shall see later in Figure 6.4, on p. 189), further suggesting that the practices that took place at these sites concerned water control, or at least the concern to guarantee sufficient water for farming.

The recent discovery on top of the Huaca de la Luna, overlooking the Moche River Valley, of the remains of several young males, thought to be warriors— tied down on an upper patio room and exposed to the skies, rains, and carrion birds—seems to appeal strongly to this dynamic of metamorphosis, not only between sacrifice and rain clouds, but also of life force in general into rain and agricultural fertility. It seems pertinent that some of these bodies were headless; this might imply that the Moche curated the severed heads for future agricultural rituals, while exposing their powerful bodies to rain (Bourget 1998, 2005; Verano 2001). Figure 2.2 shows a burial scene from phase V Moche associated with the movement of conch shells and probably related to the supplication for water (Donnan and McClelland 1979; Hocquenghem 1987:80). Might the dark blotches emerging from the burial hole in the upper image be a representation of the dangerous emanations still thought to arise from the putrifying carcasses interred therein, to finally metamorphose into rain clouds?

This generalized pattern of constructing ceremonial centers as mounds echoing mountain forms—around key burials in their inner depths, and with lots of niches containing human remains in the surrounding architectural details—was practiced over a period of thousands of years. This makes it probable that the containment practices exercised at such sites would have shaped more general patterns of cultural and political activity, providing a powerful lure to concentrate human activity. This seems to be the case from early sites such as Áspero (2500 BC) on the coast, to Chiripa and Pukara in the Titicaca Basin, as well as La Galgada, Cahuachi, Cerro Sechín, and Kotosh, on until the Inka Qurikancha (Coricancha).

These kinds of practices today in the region of Qaqachaka are displaced from a wider political context. However, the ethnographic evidence provides a point of comparison with what might have happened in the past. Here, the interment of offerings on mountainsides is preceded by the sacrifice of the animal in question, often a white llama. This happens in the house of the ritual sponsors, and the meat is stripped off the bones, cooked, and eaten. Later on, the bones and other body parts that were set aside (penis and testicles) are taken to the family ritual site (*liwaña*) on the mountainside by the men of the family, accompanied by a ritual specialist. Once there, the ritual specialist reconstructs carefully all of the bones, reconstituting them exactly in their original animal form on offering plates. They are then deposited in the mountain chest, together with other kinds of "mountain food" (llama fat, llama fetuses, white and yellow maize, sweet cakes, cinnamon, sugar lumps, and a yellow dye) and an assortment of straw and twigs (called *ch'iwu*). In some rituals, small containers of clear water are also suspended in the hole. The entire carcass is covered with flowers, each animal having its special flower. The offering as a whole is called *ch'iwu*, "shadow," while that of the reconstituted bone carcass is called *qarw katuri* ("the one who grasps llamas") or *qarw uywirpa* ("the llamas' carer").

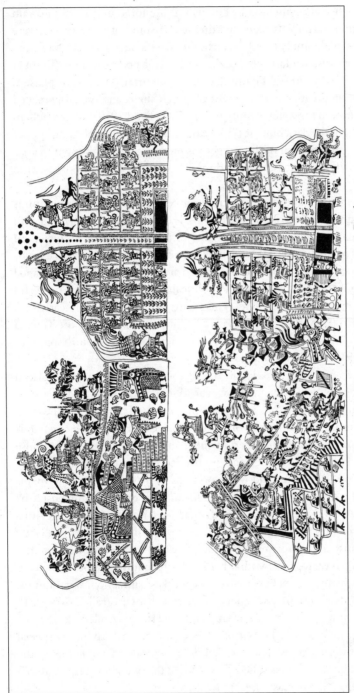

Figure 2.2: Drawings from Moche "Mountain Chests" in Roll-outs from Two Stirrup-spout Bottles
From Donnan and McClelland (1979: upper image: Fig. 6, p. 20; lower image: Fig. 2, p. 16).

a) The upper image is a drawing by P. Perlman and Donna McClelland from a roll-out of a stirrup-spout bottle, in the collection of the Museum of Art, Rhode Island School of Design, Providence.

b) The lower image is a drawing by Donna McClelland of a roll-out of a stirrup-spout bottle in a private collection in Trujillo, Peru. (These images also appear in Hocquenghem 1989:Figs. 33a and 33b): Courtesy of Don McClelland.

At the base of the square-shaped modern mountain chest, some 2–3 m deep (sometimes with stepped offering platforms inside), is a foundation stone on which each set of new offerings is placed. In Qaqachaka, these are never removed, and each new offering is just stacked on top of the previous ones, and finally covered with another flat stone, called "value," *walura*, and earth. This terminology implies that the social actors themselves acknowledge that the ritual activity of feeding the pit seeks to augment the subjective value of any particular offering into a wider exchange cycle of added value.

In ritual language, the whole carcass deposited inside the chest is said to act as an *illa* or "essence" of the animal in question, helping to reproduce its young (*aptasiña*) the following year by "breathing" (*samaña*) more animals. Other terminology for this location implies that the mountain chest actually embodies the offerings of the heads placed there to watch over and protect the territorial domain under their charge. For example, in the region of Carangas (Oruro), a ritual practitioner described to Ulpián R. López García how the "mouth" of the mountain chest (*lakap qullu*) "opens" when the offerings are placed inside: "It opens its entrails and listens to the population under its command" (1999:32). The hoarse voice held to issue from the mountain mouth is imitated by these ritual specialists in acts of ventriloquism, usually in a form of dialogue centered on the sacrifice. Here, as a part of the processes of metamorphosis in play, the spiritual power of the interred heads becomes transferred to the mountain site through the particularly male power of oratory, managed by these ritual specialists.

In practice, the offerings in the chest gradually decompose, giving off what are held to be dangerous emanations, and then the site is said to "breathe out" mist (*sama*), considered to be the "offspring" (*wawa*) of the hills. This mist gradually accumulates into small clouds (called *ch'iwu qallu, urpu qallu*) during a kind of chrysalis phase, then these metamorphose finally into rain, brought to the community in recompense by the *wak'a* or *uywiri* in return for the offerings given (cf. López García 1999:32ff., 60). It seems pertinent here how this ritual effort to bring the rains reiterates the need for aggregating units in the process of decomposition—reconstituting a whole animal carcass after sacrifice, accumulating decomposing emanations to form mists, and then aggregating mists to form clouds—to achieve efficacy.

There is evidence for such periodic additions to piled offering places in the past. For example, at the Formative site of Chiripa, beginning around 1000 BC, Hastorf has found that the locations of human burials have been periodically opened and additions made, both with objects and parts of other bodies, many covered again by large stones similar to the modern *walura* (Hastorf 2003). The Lanzón-bearing chamber at Chavín de Huántar on the eastern slopes was another offering site of this kind, with associated oracular power. Later, after the Spanish conquest, the functioning of such offering sites within mounds, with their associated vocal powers, was reported, for example, at the long-lived oracle site of Pachaqamaq (Pachacamac) on the Pacific coast.

Other instances of the ritual language used by the social actors for these practices reiterate the idea that the wider economic context of making offerings to a site is a way of adding value to it. For example, in this wider haemodynamic cycle of blood and body offerings and their recompense, community members today in Qaqachaka consider that they are upholding their *part of a contract*.[9] In a similar set of processes of change to those that occur in the aftermath of taking a trophy head, the decomposed blood and bone offerings, after rotting, are thought to help regenerate ayllu production with a new generation of generic "babies" (*wawa*). If the community members were to fail on their side of the contract, then there would only be punishments and debts (*jucha*).[10] This regional complex of ideas would seem to draw, then, on a wider "contract" or exchange model of organized political power that perhaps harkens back to the brief Inka incursion into the region, where political and economic power had to do with the organized control of forms of accumulation and their dissemination. Here is a clear example of material evidence for the ongoing articulation between human agency and exchange, discussed in the Introduction.

In essence, the rituals enacted on these sites are directed toward the "forces" (*ch'ama*) and "luck" (*surti*) necessary for generating greater ayllu production. López García (1999:54ff.) describes how in Carangas, the layered textuality of the different elements used in these rituals contributes to the wider cycles of metamorphosis of the sacrificial offering into new offspring. Textile gifts to the *wak'a* echo the ayllu parcels of land. Participants use textiles of certain colors to help renovate the animal fleece, grasses, and other vegetative coverings; gold and silver offerings stimulate greater mineral wealth; dance movements stimulate plant growth; even the children's presence in the ritual is held to stimulate the generation of new offspring of one kind and another. In the case of Carangas, the ayllu members often complete the visit to this ritual site with a round of the ayllu boundary stones (*mujuna*), recorded later in the *kipu*-like mental maps of the libations they make, when these *kipu*-like mnemonics mention the colonial title documents to lands. In the recent past of Qaqachaka, Arnold was told by the *comunarios* of the place how *kipus* were taken to such sites to count and record ritually the number of animals that had been reproduced in any year, just as they were taken to similar kinds of offering places in the middle of the large communal fields.

Historically, it is pertinent that these regional offering sites called *wak'a*, generally found on the guardian mountains of the region, defined the territorial jurisdiction under their command. Jan Szemiński defines this territorial jurisdiction as the political and administrative domain called *marka* in Aymara (1987:89–94). During the Inka occupation, these sites came under Inka military control, and the Inka state defined which of the *wak'as* were to be destroyed or brought within the state's hierarchy.[11] At this time, the *wak'a* priest would have been a military commander, active for specifically rainmaking functions or in the ordering of wider social relations through marriage, military service, and so on (cf. Ziólkowski 1996; López García 1999:51). With reference to the important regional *wak'a* called Qachaja, in Carangas, itself protected by a stone tower, López García mentions how the offering pits at this regional *wak'a* are still thought to be connected by underground tunnels to Cusco, and hence to a wider regional power network with historical importance (1999:51–53).

In the Colonial Period, this complex of ideas became transformed, although many of the underlying notions continued. During this time, Arnold (2005) perceives a transference of the ideas concerning the mountain chests on the guardian mountains, by the social actors involved, to other kinds of chests, for example those held by communities for record keeping or those used in the ayllu church to house the local saints (and even the golden *ostensario* that houses the host). These latter chests must be well painted so that they are attractive to the saints who are said to be "sleeping" inside them. Such comments suggest that these colonial and republican saints, wrapped in layers of textiles and accompanied by their particular attributes, have much in common with the former mummy bundles of the ayllu ancestors, described by the colonial chroniclers, which were also guarded in niches and only brought out on certain festive occasions, when they were amply fed and given clean clothing to wear and maize beer (*chicha*) to drink.[12] As in the case of trophy or ancestral heads, these seed-like bundles are thought to help generate the production and well being of those that serve them. The early and long-lived focus on the niche within community buildings in the distant past affirms that similar kinds of practices took place, whether in La Galgada, Chiripa, or Wari.

In each of these examples, the function of the different kinds of chest seems to reinforce the textual interface contained within them (whether sacrificed offerings, curated heads, weavings, *kipus*, written documents, or ayllu saints); they serve to guard captured beings and restrict their movement while they carry out some important function in the reproduction and regeneration of ayllu land, herds, and populations.[13] If this is the case, then the chests themselves, like the architectural niches, would act as concentrators of the essence (*illa*) or "seed substance" of the items contained within them, first containing its "spirit" and then contributing to radiating its potential power of yield in a given territorial jurisdiction.

The Counting Boards Called *Yupana* and the
Spirit of Calculation

Until this point, we have emphasized the qualitative transformations that take place in the ritual transactions centered on heads, and other forms of sacrifice, in nested layers: at the level of the household, the community, or the region under the domain of a local *wak'a*. It is now necessary to consider the *quantitative* aspect of these transformations. Here, the transactions seem to draw on the spiritual power of taken or curated heads to augment the embodied power available to the living, whether the participants in a ritual, the residents of a certain ritual and political jurisdiction, or the leaders of this polity. In this context, the quantifying aspects of these transactions illustrate the cultural practices of what we have called "power to," or "enabling power," when people become agents of change in their own right.

As we already mentioned, in many of the contemporary rituals performed in Qaqachaka that serve to raise the potential productive yields of cultivated fields or augment the radiating productive yields generated by the offering places on the guardian mountains, older members of the community record how knotted *kipu* (called *chinu* in Aymara) were formerly guarded in these places. The aim was to take note on the threads of the yield generated in past years from similar ceremonies, for comparative measuring purposes.

To facilitate these functions, Salomon (2004) and others have shown that the structuring of *kipus* in general often follows the same logic of territorial division, administration and the organization of production (see also Arnold and Yapita 2000:339–40). But there is another point that has been overlooked. The practical use of these threads also focused on the flow of energy or power that motivated these productive cycles and that drew, in turn, on the metamorphosis of sacrifice (of a victim taken and contained within certain limits), where the sacrificial seed element par excellence was a trophy head, with its potential for later regeneration. This potential for generating a radiating yield occurred within certain territorial limits, often those based on the jurisdiction of a certain guardian mountain. This is why the main cord of the *kipu* is often compared to a head or a mountain and its pendant threads compared to the rainfall, hence the agricultural production generated by the mountain (Arnold and Yapita 2006:212, 218–19, 225–27). In addition, we propose that the counting boards, called *yupana* in Quechua, that were read in conjunction with *kipus*, derived from this same logic of containment boxes, as did a series of regional games that count concave areas in the way of numbers (in dice, for example).

Here, Marx's theory regarding the "fetishism of the commodity" seems frustratingly incomplete, as it does not begin to explain the significance of the "spirit of calculation" at the heart of these quantifying transactions. These actions would have been directed at both the measurement of this potential productive yield, and the raising of the stakes in its overall value. The problem was that Marx (1973 [1894]) did not take into account the precise setting of those transactions concerned with former practices of conquest, for example, as the consequence of warfare and the calculations of recompense in its aftermath. For instance, this means of calculating the production from ayllu lands or herds would formerly have had the added objective of controlling the periodic calculations of ayllu tribute payments, say to the Inka or the later colonial state.

In this context of negotiating the spoils of conquest, the "spirit of calculation" that was engaged, while shying away from any direct allusion to its origins in sacrifice and fearful spirits, would have entailed the use of "number games" and the game-like talk of a "tournament economy" to generate the multiplying function that originally derived from captured heads.[14] Within this sphere of activity, the movement of quantities or values (like the later movement of prices) becomes an autonomous substitute for the flow of the commodities themselves. All of this would have arisen in a symbolic economy centered in the political interests of victors in warfare, in the production and forms of circulation of territories brought under their jurisdiction, when the value equivalence of commodities (produce) becomes a measure in and of itself.

In the context of this symbolic economy, the knotted *kipus* formed just part of a wider repertoire of counting and recording instruments. These included the incised *qilqa* designs and colored lines, often on wooden staffs,[15] and the use of the counting boards called *yupana*, and gaming boards called *taptana*. A number of scholars have pointed to the key relation between *kipus* and these boards with their checkered form, especially in reference to the famous drawing by Guaman Poma de Ayala (*ca.* 1615:f.360) of a *kipu* reader or *kipukamayuq* holding a *kipu*, with a *yupana* board drawn in the lower corner (see Figure 2.3). However, many of these authors, with the exception of Salomon (2002a:310),[16] have tended to limit the discussion to the way that *kipus* were really instruments of recording, whereas the arithmetical operations of counting were carried out previously using these boards (see, for example, Ascher and Ascher 1981; Urton 1997:139). There has been also a long debate as to whether the counting boards were preceded or not historically by the boards used for games of chance (Radicati di Primeglio 1990:231). We argue here that the structure of these counting boards would appear to be homologous with the demands of the wider economy, where mountain domains and the potential yields of

Figure 2.3: Model of a "Gaming Board" Made of Wood, Found in Chán Chán
In the collection of the Världskulturmuseet, Goteborg, Sweden. Originally published in an
article by Izikowitz (1967:78–79), and then in Radicati (1979:14, Fig. 2). Photograph Ferenc
Schwetz. Courtesy of the Museum of World Culture (Världskulturmuseet), Goteborg,
Sweden (Item No. 1966-41-0001).

sacrificial offerings under their jurisdiction held sway and where games of
chance sought to influence favorable outcomes.

The use of these checkered boards was widespread; they are found in
Ecuador (Prov. Cuenca), Peru (Prov. Ancash, Prov. Pisco, Callejón de Huaylas),
and Bolivia. These boards have been described by both colonial chroniclers and
modern researchers,[17] and often compared to the Chinese abacus. Formed in
wood, stone, clay, sandstone, granite, and cachelot bone, the boards are made
up of concave box or chest-like units, and many have raised platforms (that
different scholars compare to "towers" or "mountains") at the two opposing
corners. Radicati di Primeglio (1979, 1990:231), in some key works on these
checkered boards, describes how counting was done by placing grains or small
stones in their different boxes (see Figure 2.3).

In general, the boxed or checkered form as a design feature on material
objects is commonly associated with warfare, territorial extensions, and their
administration (Radicati di Primeglio 1990:230ff.).[18] For example, Inka and
Moche warriors used checkered designs in their dress for battles of territorial
expansion, as do Qaqachaka warriors today,[19] so such checkered patterning
has been in use in the Andes since at least AD 400.

An extensive literature already associates the pyramidical form of many of these counting boards, together with the games played on them, with a sphere of power and dominion, especially in the context of Tawantinsuyu expansion.[20] In practice, playing with these gaming boards might have conformed part of the well-known Inka preoccupation with numbers to impose order on all spheres of reality. As Castro Rochas and Uribe Rodríguez (2004) point out, these games, in and of themselves, might have served the Inka to gain lands, while they gave other lands as gifts or spoils.[21] They affirm that these games concerned forms of dominion, with the transference of local power to the Inka state apparatus, and hence of the relation between the victor and the vanquished.

Another series of studies reinforce the idea that Andean games with dice (*pichka, chunka, wayru*) or with gaming boards of one form or another were used to have dialogues with the *wak'as* in oracular practices, in such a way that the fall of the dice indicated its reply.[22] In a detailed study of a range of archaeological and modern sites where games of dice and games with counting boards were played, Margarita Gentile (1998:87) notes another factor to take into account in these quantitative negotiations: that is, that the *wak'as* were frequently found in "strategic sites in relation to basic natural resources (water, and cultivated land)." From the viewpoint of conquering groups, such sites "supported populations governed by caciques whose friendship or capture assured access to local labour" (Gentile 1998:113). In this case, many consultations to the *wak'as* would have been directed toward knowing, precisely, the climatic conditions for production in the coming year.

These different descriptions of gaming board use affirm how they were often used in counting practices concerned with territorial control and the quantification of booty as a result of warfare, where the boards and their iconography would reinforce the victor's claim over the vanquished. Other studies describe the use of symbolic heads in the iconography of the gaming board layout or in contemporary illustrations of the game, although they do not make the connection to the wider economic and political cycles at issue. For example, one of the boards found in 1869 near Chordeleg (in Cuenca Province, Ecuador) has incised human heads, and an animal, described by Uhle as a "crocodile," around the sides of the base, with rosettes underneath.[23] Arnold (2005) proposes that this image is, in fact, a chrysalis, and that the board illustrates the stages of metamorphosis of the "trophy head-seed chrysalis-food produce" complex that is still acknowledged in rural communities, such as Carangas and Qaqachaka (in Bolivia) (see Figures 2.4, 2.5, and 2.6).

The iconography of a Moche vase in the Museo de Arqueología in Lima, Peru, described some time ago by Lieselotte and Theo Engl,[24] suggests that the same kind of associations were operating in Moche society. The scene consists

Figure 2.4: Checkered Counting Board with Relief Figures of Human Heads, from Chordeleg (Cuenca Prov., Ecuador)

The original specimen has been lost, but there are exact reproductions in the Ethnographic Museums in Berlin and Santiago de Chile. In Radicati di Primeglio (1990:221, Fig. 1.3), "Tableros de escaques en el antiguo Perú." In *Quipu y yupana. Colección de escritos*, pp. 219–34. Eds. Carol Mackey et al. (Lima: Concytec, 1990). Courtesy of Concytec, Lima, with permission from Carol Mackey.

Figure 2.5: The Same Board from Chordeleg with Two Platforms, Seen from above

In Radicati di Primeglio (1990:221, Fig. 1.5), "Tableros de escaques en el antiguo Perú." In *Quipu y yupana. Colección de escritos*, pp. 219–34. Eds. Carol Mackey et al. (Lima: Concytec, 1990). Courtesy of Concytec, Lima, with permission from Carol Mackey.

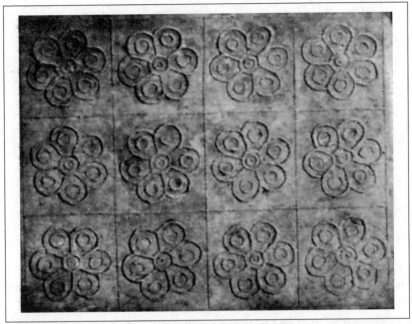

Figure 2.6: The Same Checkered Counting Board, from Chordeleg. Rosettes Incised on the Base
In Radicati di Primeglio (1990:221, Fig. 1.6), "Tableros de escaques en el antiguo Perú." In *Quipu y yupana. Colección de escritos*, pp. 219–34. Eds. Carol Mackey et al. (Lima: Concytec, 1990). Courtesy of Concytec, Lima, with permission from Carol Mackey.

of a procession of persons solemnly carrying a large counting board, the surface of which is divided into twenty box-chests (5 × 4), the majority of which have two points in the upper part. The person carrying the board is preceded by two richly dressed warriors, followed by musicians and bearers of trophy heads, impaled onto long stakes. The drawing of this particular counting board is very similar to that by Guaman Poma of the Inka counting board called *yupana* used to accompany counting on *kipus* by the readers or interpreters called *kipukamayuq* (*ca.* 1615:f.360) (see Figures 2.7 and 2.8).

In his study of these counting boards, Radicati di Primeglio (1990:231–32) describes how the 19th-century French traveler, Charles Wiener found two boards similar to that of Chordeleg in his trip to the department of Ancash (Peru), in the pre-Hispanic ruins of Chucana, and in the ancient *apacheta*, or mountain shrine, of Mount Huauyan. In *Pérou et Bolivie*, written in 1879, Wiener mentions a traditional tale, much told in the locality and probably recorded from the lips of the priest of Huandobal, which implied that these boards served for reckoning the tribute paid by the ayllus of the region. "According to the legend, they say, the contributions of all the inhabitants of

Figure 2.7: Iconography of a Moche Ceramic Vessel Showing a Procession, a Large Measuring Board, and Trophy Heads on Poles

The original vessel from the Chicama valle, in northern Peru, is painted with red on a marbled background. The drawing of the vessel iconography is in Radicati di Primeglio (1990:226, Fig. 11), "Tableros de escaques en el antiguo Perú." In *Quipu y yupana. Colección de escritos*, pp. 219–34. Eds. Carol Mackey et al. (Lima: Concytec, 1990). With permission of Carol Mackey. The original vessel is in the Museo Nacional Arqueológico, Antropológico e Historia de Perú, Lima.

Huamachuco were recorded on them in former times, by means of grains of different colors, each grain representing a particular tribe" (Radicati di Primeglio 1990:231).

As for the manner of doing the reckoning, Charles Wiener (1879) believes that "the different levels of these boards had the characteristic of raising tenfold the value of the grain found there, so that a grain in one division showed the contribution value that might be tenfold or a hundredfold that of another division" (cited in Radicati di Primeglio 1990:231–32). Wiener concluded: "in ancient Peru, there was a certain order of things that was reflected in this main ledger with the exact relation of things owed and received" (Radicati di Primeglio 1990:231; our translation). This idea would also explain the dual layout of the boxes and platforms on the boards—one form representing the quantity of tribute owed, the other registering the quantity of work as the tribute was received. Wiener's view seems to confirm our point about a "spirit of calculation" centered on high places that operated in a calculated play of forces concerning the measurement of war booty now reconceived as tribute, with the added possibility of raising the stakes.

Figure 2.8: Guaman Poma's Drawing of an Inka Accountant with *kipu* and *yupana*
In Guaman Poma de Ayala, *Nueva corónica y buen gobierno* (*ca.* 1615:f.360).
Courtesy of Fondo de Cultura Económica, Lima, Peru, p. 272, (from GKS 2232 4to).

In a modern context, Frank Salomon (2002b) mentions another facet of Andean dualism that supports Weiner's economic interpretation, in a variant of the game of *pichca* or "fives" played with wooden dice (called in Spanish *troncos*, in the sense of "tree trunks") that still takes place as part of the annual rites of augury in the pueblo of Pacota (a part of Huarochirí, in Lima Department, Peru). In this case, the game forms part of the annual community meeting, called Huarona, that takes place at New Year and on the following days. During this meeting, the authorities, both those entering and those leaving office, play *pichca* in the area outside the meeting house, which doubles as a storehouse (called *collca*), after having presented their accounts for the past year while those taking office lay out their plans for the coming period. According to Salomon, a part of the power of this modern-day oracular game is that it articulates various interrelated dual structures: in the division of space, of time, and between the political authorities, in the two moieties of the social-political organization. At the same time, no one wins and no one loses; the auguries for the coming year, as a way of planning where to focus productive energies and the respective use of resources, serve the whole community.

Another point of comparative interest regarding Salomon's description of the modern game is that the invocations for the coming year are directed at one moment toward a pair of deities called "the water owners," who are thought to send waters down from the mountains for the crops. It is pertinent to our argument that the physical form of the water guardians is as sacred skulls, kept in a secret place; again, in this modern context, there is the same semantic association between games of chance, the luck of destiny and ancestral skulls. Arellano Hoffmann (2003), in a study of similar games, this time in the Bolivian Chaco, finds the same semantic relations in a gaming board that illustrates the world of the dead, where the game is played during a feast of spirits. In this case, each end of the gaming board includes an engraved jaguar holding in its claws a human head, as if to echo the more distant origins of the game, in addition to being similar to the chachapuma Middle Horizon image (Arellano Hoffmann 2003:326, Figs. 9 and 10).

These recent descriptions all support Wiener's wider economy theory of the gaming boards. However, in its day, Wiener's theory was abandoned in favor of one centered on the gaming board called *taptana* in Quechua, now perceived as just a game of chance between two opposed players. *Taptana* was played with a pyramid-shaped dice of wood, clay, or bone (usually a llama carpal or toe bone). The players moved grains, generally the red-and-black-colored *wayruru* seeds or beans, around the gaming board, depending on the value of the throw. Even, so, descriptions of this game of chance insist on its relationship to the dead. For example, González Holguín (1952[1608]) relates in his colonial dictionary how *taptana* is played "above all in wakes for the dead" prior to burial, a fact confirmed by other chroniclers.[25] The game in this instance is not only focused on the wake of someone but also often in the questions of the inheritance of their belongings. That is, it still deals with economic issues. This game is practiced to this day in these circumstances in the

Mantaro Valley of Peru[26] and has been documented among Quichua speakers in Ecuador.[27]

In Qaqachaka, this game of *taptana* is still played by the ayllu women at funeral wakes, using maize grains of different colors (white, red, gray, orangish, brown, and speckled). The grains are grouped in odd clusters of threes, "as the aim is the reproduction of similar grains" in the coming year of ayllu agricultural production. The winner of the game is the one to gradually place their grains higher and higher on the raised tower or platform, as if to respond with an offering there that will open another round of production.

A similar game related to the dead is played at the Feast of the Dead in early November, on the night when the visiting souls are finally sent away. In this case, it is called *qanchi* and it is played with a llama huckle bone (which is the ankle bone or astralagus). The aunts of the deceased called *ipala* (the sisters on the male side) play this game with the deceased's brothers, or in their absence, the sisters. The luck of the game is about whether the *ipala* will receive her dowry or not the following year, or whether her brother will receive it instead. The dice-like bones are cast in threes—two larger pieces and a smaller one considered to be their "offspring." The luckiest fall of the dice is when the two larger pieces fall close together, with the smaller one on top. In both examples, the game has to do with the dead and the luck of destiny, in the first with pending production and in the second with inheritance.

At its most basic level, this game simply relates the recent dead to future regeneration, as Bloch and Parry suggested (1982). However, the precise dynamics of the spirit of calculation seem to involve a more complex cycle of death and regeneration that draws, in part, on the power of trophy heads. Radicati di Primilegio mentions the interesting relationship noted by Max Uhle (1922) between the magic-religious contents of the *wayruru* seed game and the decorated motifs on the Chordeleg board. Uhle suggested that the drawing of human heads distributed around the base of the board represented those of prisoners, beheaded for not being fortunate enough to win the ceremonial *wayru* game that generally *preceded sacrifices*. It is a significant fact that there are fourteen heads drawn on the board, coinciding with the sum of the two sets of squares (7 + 7), placed at either side of the board (Radicati di Primilegio 1990:233). Uhle's opinion is reinforced in the scene on the Moche clay vase and the reflections by Lieselotte and Theo Engl that it represents a procession returning triumphantly from battle and carrying the counting board that served to reckon and settle war booty and tribute received (Engl and Engl 1967:Plate 15).

In this case, the transformation and consolidation of power thought to take place during the counting of tributary payments, territorial reorganization, and the new administration of territory are illustrated in a detailed iconography of conquest. We would go a step further and propose that the trophy heads and the chrysalis on the *yupana* from Chordeleg (Cuenca, Peru) illustrate a similar sequence. These kinds of ways of consolidating power are discussed by the archaeologist Steven Bourget, with reference to the excavations in the Moche Pyramid of the Moon (*Huaca de la Luna*). He proposes that the trophy head victim was thought to metamorphose into a chrysalis and then a butterfly, in his journey into the other world (Bourget 2001b, 2005).

At issue would seem to be the conversion, through a ritualized means of counting, of the trophy head booty claimed in warfare into the new seeds for conquered fields, annotated and enumerated on the *yupana* tablets. Again, these have echoes of the trophy heads of Inka imperial expansion that were reckoned in the colored pendant *kipu* threads as visual and tactile expressions of the new vegetative covering of conquered lands. Likewise, the modern dead, and their creative potential, are still remembered through the seed grains of the *taptana* games.

* * * *

We must reiterate how the complexity of these cycles of transformation is underestimated in Marx's view of the fetishism of the commodity as a mere disguise for the potential productive gain to be made from an early form of capital. For Marx, the basic capital would become metamorphized into money and back into capital ($C - M - C$, where C = commodity and M = money), or vice versa ($M - C - M$), as the productive yield converts subjective value into exchange value.

We propose rather that the metamorphosis of heads, at least in a situation of opposed players, implies a much wider range of exchange transactions, having to do with raising the stakes in calculated play for political and personal power and with real material changes in the redistribution of territories and labor. In this sense, these transformations work not only at multiple levels, but with the added possibility of introducing a dynamic and radiating scheme fed continually by the spirit of regeneration, beyond just the banking of seeds for a new agricultural season. All of these interactions are also reflected in the material record in boards, *kipus*, storage boxes, and heads.

Drinking the Power of the Dead

ANOTHER TYPICALLY Andean way of gaining power over an enemy by controlling his (or her) head, and so channel the flow of energy embodied by the enemy head for one's own use, is by the victorious using heads as drinking vessels. On these occasions, to admit defeat, the vanquished merely had to receive and consume the beverage served by the victor, in deference to his superior status. What interests us here is that both victor and vanquished drank from special, highly significant vessels. Evidence for these characteristic drinking customs and the associated symbolism of the serving vessels comes from the distant past, the historical past, and the present.

Sucking out of a Skull

In the archaeological record, clearly from the Middle Horizon onward but also earlier, some of the drinking vessels or tumblers called *qiru* (often written as *qero* or *kero*) made of wood, ceramic, or metal, were fashioned around the form of a head or skull. In addition, some of the Middle Horizon small bowls and *qiru* have faces painted on them, similar to those of the earlier Nasca region, also expressly seen in the Tiwanaku and Wari tumblers.

Later Spanish historical accounts tell us how the Inka presented gold and silver *qiru* to conquered leaders as emblems for gaining their allegiance, while they themselves drank out of wooden *qiru*. But the Spanish also noted that the Inka occasionally drank directly out of human crania, usually of enemies, in highly charged settings. In this case, the upper half of the cranium was cut and the brains removed, or perhaps literally sucked out (in Aymara this is *lixwi juchhanti*). These historical accounts confirm how victors in battle, especially the Inka leaders, used the trophy heads of their defeated enemy leader as receptacles for drinking maize beer.[1] For example, the Inka Pachakuti was known to have drunk out of the skulls of conquered Chanka leaders.[2] These accounts also note how the Inka covered enemy crania in gold, often putting a silver straw through the clenched teeth to be able to drink (or rather suck) the liquid from inside the head. Chalcochima, Atahualpa's general, is said to have done this with the head of Atoc, Atahualpa's brother.[3] While Atahualpa was in prison under the Spanish, he launched his allies to capture and kill Atoc, who had sided with his other half-brother Huascar, with whom he was fighting for control of the Inka Empire when the Spanish arrived. The cranium was smoothed, the skin dried, the hair curled, and beaten gold attached. Maize beer was then drunk through the inserted tube. Many drawings in the *Nueva corónica y buen gobierno*, attributed to the colonial mestizo chronicler Guaman Poma de Ayala, illustrate these kinds of examples, as do some of his verses. For example, his version of *Tinyacusun* begins "Let us drink from the enemy skull" (*ca.* 1615:f.314).

This evidence suggests that this drinking practice is older than the Inkas' use of it; most likely it continued on from the first Early Intermediate Period or Middle Horizon states through to the Inkas' imperial reformation of the Andean political scene. There is also evidence that the practice was more widespread and a component part of much smaller polities. For example, archaeologist Cathy Costin (1986) describes the use of heads on ceramic vessels in the Upper Mantaro Valley (of what is now Peru) during the Late Intermediate Period, and in this case the local Wanka and Sausa groups were clearly not state formations.

Up to the present day, community-made beer, called *chicha* in Quechua or *k'usa* in Aymara, is consumed from wooden *qiru* in the drinking rituals of the region of Qaqachaka and its neighboring ayllus.[4] These *qiru* are usually undecorated or take the form of wooden or silver cups. In Qaqachaka, sometimes a conch shell is used for making libations in particularly important family rituals.

These modern drinking practices shed light on the way that the origins of drinking maize beer from a skull-like *qiru* might have derived from the bellicose act of sucking the brains directly out of a cranium. This is still done in fierce battles in the region of Qaqachaka, such as the 2000 "war of the ayllus." On these occasions, as we have seen, the warriors seek out the head of a great enemy leader. As an explanation for this practice, the Qaqachakas themselves say that it is to have a "good head," or to "get more intelligence." They also brag how "he who eats lots of brains is the one who can go on firing rifles end-lessly, who sweats a lot and never gets drunk" (see also Arnold, In press; Arnold and Yapita 1996:353).

This act of sucking out the brains might be related to certain uses of the term *jucha*. Although the religious and administrative functions of this term have been widely examined in the historical and ethnographical literature,[5] its bellicose dimensions have not. This is possibly because, in the Colonial Period, the original uses of the term *jucha* became transposed into the more Christian meaning of "sin" and "a sense of guilt," but its alternative uses today clarify its possible historical roots in hostile acts. For example, the verb "to suck out" in Aymara is *juchhantaña* or *juchhjaña*, and the specific act of "sucking out the brains" of an enemy leader is thought to elevate the person doing the sucking toward a higher rank in the community so as to be able to carry out the sponsorship of a feast. In this case, you refer to the person with a driving need to host a feast as *jach'a jucha* ("he with a great burden") or *jach'a p'iqi* ("he with a great head") (Arnold and Yapita 2006:80).

The better known Spanish term for sponsoring a feast in this way is "*cargo*," which means literally "a burden." The burden in question for the feast sponsor, according to contemporary Qaqachaka usage, is that "he carries a head" (*jucha p'iqi*). In *The Metamorphosis of Heads* (2006), Arnold and Yapita propose that this perhaps refers to the time when feast sponsors really did carry an enemy head and when the possession of a head, and its subsequent practices of curation, was what triggered the obligation to host a feast in the first place. In this sense, Andean feasting practices were not simply concerned with a redistribution of ayllu wealth (as others would have it); what was at stake was the victorious celebration of war and the domination over and empowerment of the lands, food crops, and other produce of an adversary. This would account for the more macabre aspects of ayllu feasting—for example, the almost forced feeding and drinking practices that feast sponsors foist on to their guests, who must accept this largesse in food and drink to honor their host.

Many anthropologists' accounts mention taking part in such feasts. For example, Thomas Abercrombie (1993:139–40) in neighboring K'ulta stresses how one's immediate destiny is to become satiated with food and powerlessly drunk in the feast sponsor's presence, leading one to perform publicly this lower but temporary status. This aggressive form of "fighting with food" occurs in different guises the world over, as Young's work in the Massim society of Papua New Guinea shows (1971).

Some of the practices that take place during the famous *tinkus* of another of Qaqachaka's neighbors, the Macha in northern Potosí, clarify the nature of the relations between warfare and sucking out maize beer from *qiru*, as seeds that will sprout in the earth. For example, Tristan Platt (1986) has described how the history of the ritual battles that take place during the feast of the Holy Cross on May 3, at harvest time, derives from struggles for domination between the moieties of "above" and "below." The Macha warriors arrive at the scene of battle dressed in fine and densely woven cloth, wear leather helmets, and bear traditional arms (slings, metal balls, leather gloves, densely woven belts wound around their hands, leather hides around their waists, etc.) to fight man to man.

One characteristic of the Macha *tinku* is that the ayllu men come drinking maize beer and dancing to the sound of panpipes (*jula jula*). Before going out to fight, the combatants take to drinking with the right or left hand (which signifies life or death), while the beer gives them courage and spirit to fight the enemy. In this case, drinking the maize beer out of *qirus* (like sucking the brains out of a cranium) is a means of fortifying these warriors, so that they have valor and overcome fear of their adversaries. The couple responsible for the feast serves rounds of drinks to the warriors beforehand, but the drinking must be moderated; an internal social control of the level of drinking in each group ensures that the violence is relatively controlled and disciplined.

The Patterns of Drinking Pathways

Another aspect of these belligerent drinking bouts merits comment. Several studies show how drinking in the Andes is a means of engaging both mind and body with social memory.[6] In the region of Qaqachaka, like the drinking practices described by Abercrombie in neighboring K'ulta, social memory is called on, above all in the long rounds of making toasts. During these libations, the participants must trace out the historical origins of each and every thematic element they recall in the ritual language of "drinking pathways": whether of the animals, food produced, the ayllu's saints, people's genealogical descent, building construction materials, and so on and its subsequent journey to its current location in the ayllu territory. Abercrombie focused on the cultural dimensions of these drinking pathways, but their equally important political dimensions have been ignored.

It seems to us that this political dimension is traced out spatially in the distinctive patterns of the drinking pathways, on different occasions. For example, this tracing out of origin pathways has *two* distinct facets or patterns with political ramifications: a *centrifugal* one (outward directed) and a *centripetal* one (inward directed), as Fausto (2001) described for the political dynamics of lowland groups. The first pattern traces the expansive intergroup sociopolitical relations of a particular polity from the center outward, while the second traces the concentric and centralizing tendencies of newly absorbed elements, whose origin comes in from the outside. This kind of patterning also seems to be at the heart of the regular designs called *tocapu* that often decorate the *qiru*.

In its political ramifications, the first tendency is more concerned with an expanding model, of, say, an ayllu as part of a wider political system, or as part of a system of political and warfaring alliances, or perhaps of a family as part of a wider system of matrimonial alliances with affines (marriage partners) moving between groups. By contrast, the second inward-directed facet is concerned politically with an accumulating center, where the current living members are reinforced by genealogical or other ties, rejuvenated from the outside. An example of this second pattern might be the libations that record human ancestral ties made at the Feast of the Dead at the beginning of November each year. On this occasion, a family remembers first its recent dead, then the ancestors whose names can be remembered, and finally the long-gone ancestors, converted to dust, fortifying the family genealogical center first with its sense of locality and then with the many ramifications outward to other people and groups.

This practice is also evidently a means of circulating names within one's own group to promote identity from the very center. Another might be the marking ceremony ritual (called *k'illpha* in Aymara) for the animals, described by Abercrombie (1993:149–59) in K'ulta, and Arnold and Yapita (2001:111–13) in Qaqachaka. In this ceremony, the participants first remember the origins of each animal in the family corrals before going on to remember the corrals that are sited gradually farther from home and finally the distant corrals.

The mental maps that underlie the Feast of the Dead genealogies and the marking ceremony libations both take the form of concentric patterns, called *muyu* in Aymara. At one moment, the pattern is read from the inside outward (literally, from the house window out), while at another, the same pattern absorbs elements from the outside. There is an additional spatial patterning to these practices. The centrifugal tendency generally goes clockwise (or anti-sunwise, in this case), yet the centripetal tendency goes withershins (sunwise in the southern hemisphere) in a ritual logic quite opposed to that of the north, where the sun is perceived to move differently.

There might be an additional magical aspect to these practices whereby the centralizing centripetal tendency is life and kin centered, as compared to the death-centered tendency of the centrifugal system. We also suggest that the death-centered expansive centrifugal tendency is managed more by men, based on the knowledge of trophy-head taking, whereas the life-centered centralizing tendency is managed more by women at the stages of curating the spirit of the enemy head and converting it into kin.

An example of the centralizing centripetal system would be of heads some-how converging on the ayllu plaza, perhaps in tributary payments, or in a specific arable area held in common (*manta*), where ritual practice is directed toward appropriating the energy from buried heads to nourish the fertile center. These differential energy flows have their own specific means of symbolic expression. For example, the ritual practices directed toward appropriating the energy from a head to nourish the fertile center are often expressed with reference to a squared concentric pattern, or alternatively in the form of an Andean stepped cross. Zuidema (1989c:305) expresses this same possibility in another way by associating the circle with the top-down or center-out per-spective, and a square with the view from below. Both are finally united in what he calls "the squaring of the circle," which gave the local group and its organ-ization "a kind of dynamic tension and a dialectical quality that it could not have achieved in any other way."

With reference to *qiru* designs, an example of the expanding outward pat-tern would be the zigzag lines, illustrated by the historian Tom Cummins on some colonial examples, which might enclose elements in its inner corners (commonly heads or flowers), or in the lozenge shape of doubled-up zigzags (1998:115, Fig. 14) (see Figure 3.1). Interestingly, the weaving expert William Conklin has compared this design, which he calls the "over-and-under motif," to a weaving figure of zigzagging weft threads enclosing warp threads, said by some weavers to be like seeds in the earth (1999:120ff.). These vessels with zigzag designs are used in the field-planting ceremonies. For Zuidema, the example par excellence of the outward-expanding model is the system of lines radiating from a center, called *ceques* (*siqi* in Aymara and Quechua), that the Inka at the height of their power imposed on local organizations to realign their ritual and political allegiances (1989c:305).

Toward an Iconography of Drinking, Social Memory, and Warfare

Some of the striking designs on *qiru* drinking cups seem to confirm these hy-potheses, although, as a number of other studies have already pointed out, there is a danger of reaching any solid conclusion from sparse data that are not well contextualized.[7] So let us try to contextualize some *qiru* designs, as part of the trophy-head complex and an associated Andean theory of memory practice.

First a question: Why has there been so much attention to the designs on *qiru* drinking vessels, both by the social actors who made and used them as well as by scholars trying to understand them? Peruvian scholar Jorge Flores Ochoa provides some clues. In his 1998 article, Flores Ochoa holds that one of the functions of these vessels in ritual practice was that of "transforming orality into vision and action." For Flores Ochoa, the vessels accomplished

Figure 3.1: Colonial *qiru* Designs Showing Centrifugal and Centripetal Tendencies
One of a pair of *qeros* from Ollantaytambo. The original is in the Museo Arqueológico, Cuzco. After Cummins (1998:Fig. 22, pp. 124), "Let me see! Reading is for them: colonial Andean images and objects 'como es costumbre tener los caciques Señores.'" In *Native Traditions in the Postconquest World*, pp. 91–148. Eds. Elizabeth Hill Boone and Tom Cummins (Washington, DC: Dumbarton Oaks Research Library and Collection, 1998).
Image © Dumbarton Oaks Research Library and Collection, Washington, DC.

this function by transmitting complex messages preserved in the decorative figures, for example those concerning Inka history, through images and visual metaphors (1998:164). Their iconography, by means of drawings, painted images, engravings, and even form, illustrated scenes in which various personages appeared surrounded by their attributes. Flores Ochoa's analysis reveals different levels of meaning, according to a pre-established Andean logic.

According to Flores Ochoa, Inka *qiru* iconography is concerned above all with the Andean religion of the sun god centered in Cusco, a world that he suggests was imbued with the golden color of maize and maize beer that enveloped the participants in their drinking bouts. In these *qiru*, the design narrative deals with these golden sites whose sacred dimension was measured in relation to the center of the sun religion in Cusco. In addition, some of the flowers illustrated on the *qiru*, used as hallucinogens, might have facilitated these kinds of golden-colored visions, in the same way that botanist Richard Schültes has suggested for the chemical concoctions of lowland groups.[8] For example, it is still common in the altiplano around Lake Titicaca for some kinds of angel trumpet related to datura (Sp. *floripondio*, lat. *Daturacandida [Pers.] Soffird*) to be soaked in maize beer, to make it more potent, when it serves to stimulate visions as a part of certain curing ceremonies (Arnold 1994:194). Beer recipes using *Schinus molle* or quinua, instead of the more usual maize, are thought to have been created well before the Inkas' maize beer festivals.

Inka *qiru* designs seem to have expressed this Cusco-centered sun religion partly through the use of certain geometrical designs. In the case of earlier Inka *qiru*, these are decorated with engraved figures, the greater part with incised straight lines in geometrical forms. One common form is that of concentric boxes. This concentric spatial layout can be found in a variety of other cultural practices, for example in the so-called *ceque* lines radiating outward from Cusco, as described by Zuidema (1990:69–78), that we already mentioned. A similar spatial layout characterizes the organization of the important Inka ceremony of *qapaqjucha*, described by Pierre Duviols (1976) and others, in which the domination of Cusco as the religious and political center over the many peripheral groups under its dominion was celebrated in rituals of sacrifice. During this ceremony, local chiefs summoned to Cusco came bearing offerings along their normal routes, but returned along special straight routes called *ceque* (sometimes called *cachaui*) that ignored the normal roads and went directly, ignoring even the contours of the local topography (cf. Abercrombie 1993:159). This same concentric pattern is reiterated in the drinking pathways that characterize ritual practice in parts of Oruro and Potosí (Bolivia) today. Arnold and Yapita (2001:111–13) have described how these libations begin by naming a local site and then proceed by naming more and more distant sites, in the concentric rings (*muyu)* of *kipu*-like mental maps, whose knots trigger off the social memory. In some sequences, these concentric or linear circuits extend until Cusco itself is named.[9]

One methodology used for analyzing this kind of *qiru* iconography has been through semiotics. Following this approach, Catherine Allen (2002) identifies what she calls a "cluster of iconographic elements" and their interrelations, as parts to parts, and as parts to the whole. As examples of these elements and groupings, she gives Inkas felines with rainbows emerging from their mouths, tropical forest plants and animals, and places of encounter, again indicated by zigzags or rhomboids. She suspects that this complex of elements, taken as a whole, is an image of the "liberation of internal force, a dangerous but necessary liberation with the potential of realigning cosmic, moral and political relationships" (Allen 2002:182). We argue in the following section that this liberated internal force was derived originally from having taken a trophy head and that therefore the figures engraved or painted on pre-Columbian and even colonial *qirus*, as stand-ins for heads, are visual representations of this force.

Visual Representations on Colonial *Qirus* of the Potent Energy of Trophy Heads

What is the nature of the visual representation of this force? Again, we should first remind ourselves of the many limitations to free speculation concerning *qiru* imagery. Apart from the general lack of an adequate contextualization on *qiru* findings, we know that *qiru* in general were produced in different sizes and shapes, and usually in pairs for the ritual sharing, libation, and consumption of beer; the problem here is that modern collections often lack the vital pair. There is also a great variety in *qiru* form and decoration in their long history, which goes back to the Late Formative at Pukara to the north of Lake Titicaca, and at Kala Uyuni (Qala Uyuni) on the Taraco Peninsula, followed by Tiwanaku and then Wari examples.[10] As a result, many *qiru* studies, for example those by Allen (2002:182) and Cummins (1998), make a point of differentiating the well-known Inka wooden *qiru* with their more somber appearance and geometric engraved decorations, in stark contrast to the postconquest figurative *qiru* that have brightly colored incised designs often with a resin base inlay. We have already noted how simple undecorated wooden *qiru* are still in use today in the region of Qaqachaka.

Having acknowledged these difficulties and differences in *qiru* studies, what common themes also emerge in *qiru* designs? In her study of postconquest highland *qiru*, Allen considers an associated drinking vessel called a *paccha* (*pajcha* or *phajcha*), where the *qiru* cup, sometimes in the form of a head, is attached to a long wooden stem with a spout, usually decorated with zigzag and snake designs. One of the clues to the meanings of *qiru* imagery is suggested by these *pajcha*. Allen proposes that the iconography of the *pajcha* has to do with their uses in rituals centered around the theme of water, where the mountains are particularly acknowledged as the sources of water for the irrigation canals needed to make the earth fertile (2002:183–84).

In her more detailed iconographic analysis, Allen proposes that in their overall layout, postconquest *qiru* are usually divided into two or three registers or horizontal bands. While Allen focused on these three registers, other authors, such as Mulvany (2004:410), have compared these horizontal bands to those of *unku* tunics, as if a common semiotics underlay the homologies between them. For his part, Cummins proposes that the central band of *tocapu* designs on colonial *qiru* was in an equivalent position to those on colonial *unku* (1993:128). Gisbert and colleagues (1996) make an even wider claim when they draw similarities between the *tocapu*-like designs on *qiru* drinking vessels, *unku* tunics, and the decorative painting on certain styles of tombs called *chullpa* dating from the Inka period, situated on the actual Chile-Bolivian border along the Lauca River. In this last case, the equivalent of the *qiru* head seems to be reconnected to the human body, now clothed in a tunic, and this time with *tocapu* designs around the waist.

For Allen, the uppermost register generally depicts a scene that includes figures of humans, plants and animals, drinking rituals and battle scenes. For her, this upper level is what gives *qiru* their narrative quality. Importantly, the upper level is composed with bilateral symmetry, having to do with the way the *qirus* were paired for drinking toasts.

The narrower middle register Allen calls the vessel's "belt" (Aym. *wak'a*; Qu. *chumpi*), what others call its "waist" (Cummins 1998:118). This is minimally expressed as a simple pair of stripes, but often elaborated as a band of flowers or the repeating geometrical designs called *tocapu*. In some *qiru*, part of the upper register is also composed of these abstract geometrical designs (Flores Ochoa et al. 1999:72).

As Allen points out, the lower register usually includes a repetitive decoration of plants and/or animals. This part was often hidden from view, because *qiru* were designed to be held so that the entire bottom half is obscured by the hand whereas the top half is more visible to the users (Cummins 1998:27).

Allen, Cummins, and others make note of the repeating iconographic themes on the *qiru*'s upper register. These include jungle scenes with palm trees, monkeys, parrots, jaguars, pumas, and large snakes, populated by the Indians of Antisuyo called *ch'unchu*, perhaps as a memory of the lost Inka city of Paititi. Allen describes this kind of social memory among the inhabitants of the region around Cusco today. There is inevitably an Inka presence in this register, and Flores Ochoa (1990) goes as far as perceiving in colonial *qiru* designs part of an Inka art of resistance.[11] In her study, Allen (2002:180) identifies as the "feline-rainbow motif" the common design image of a rainbow emerging from the mouths of one or more felines, which continues as a border along the entire upper register (cf. Gisbert 1999). We propose that this feline-rainbow motif gives us other clues to the visual representation of the power of trophy heads, which may also relate highland warring practices to lowland ones.

Allen does not explore the feline image much, although she does provide some illustrations where the *qiru* itself takes the form of a feline head (Allen 2002:195, Fig. 12). The way that warriors draw on the power of felines before a hunt has been well documented for the lowland region (Fausto 2001:376ff.), although there are fewer studies on this for the modern period in the highlands.[12] Historically, Guaman Poma (Fausto 2001:f.155–56) illustrates what looks like a lowland Indian hunting a jaguar, but which actually is

Otorongo Achachi, the son of Inka Roca, who, it was believed, turned into a jaguar to conquer the Indians of Antisuyu, northeast of Cusco. Throughout the continent, the jaguar is widely thought to be the cannibalistic predator of predators. In the Andes generally, and in the region around Qaqachaka in particular, large felines in their guise as the "Master of the Animals" are also thought to watch over the herds from the mountain peaks, and in this sense are frequently associated with the guardian mountains and the ritual sites of the *wak'a*. In the archaeological record, figures of the *chachapuma* or "man-puma" typically show an anthropomorphic feline holding a human head, and these have been associated mainly with human sacrifice, for example at Tiwanaku in the Lake Titicaca Basin (see below and Figure 6.5). Finally, the feline is a widespread and age-old symbol of the shaman, and the shamanic power of transcendence and transformation,[13] for example in the magical flights concerned with head taking. Taken as a cluster of shifting iconographic elements, it is at least plausible that the *qiru* with a feline form might be interchangeable semiotically with the skull of a trophy head.

Like Flores Ochoa, Allen associates the rainbow on this upper register with the sun. She describes a colonial *qiru* from the National Museum of the American Indian in the Smithsonian Institution in which the rainbow emerges from the mouths of an array of jaguars to form wide rainbow arches under which a royal Inka couple stands in different poses. The man is an Inka warrior with shield and halberd, and wears on his head the *maska paycha*, emblem of kingship. His tunic carries a horizontal band of *tocapu* designs at the waist. This same male royal fringe design is repeated in the space over the jaguar's head, and another image of it appears under another red-colored arch that emerges from more animal heads in profile (Allen 2002:180). The woman on the *qiru* wears Inka dress, and holds a branch of red *qantu* flowers (*Cantua buxifolia* Juss. Ex. Lam), above which floats a red rhomboid.

Various scholars interpret the man and woman as an Inka royal couple (Cummins 1998:130; Allen 2002:180). We suggest that they might represent more specifically the warrior-weaver pair as the ideal married couple, and that their positioning under the rainbow arches, and the attributes they hold, indicate their ongoing role in specific phases of the cycling of a trophy head. This also ties in with the discussions around the male and female imagery on Early Intermediate Period Pukara ceramics by Sergio Chávez, and the cycles this might imply, mentioned earlier and shown in Figure 1.4. In this cycle, first the trophy head is captured by the warrior as an important foundational act for marriage, complemented by female sexuality (represented by the female red rhomboid), that leads to the setting up of a new household, and subsequently a new genealogical line of descent (Arnold and Yapita 2006:126–30). The rhomboid form is associated in Qaqachaka today with the female parts

(Arnold 1988:367–68). Incidentally, many colonial *qiru* designs portray the female Coya figure as carrying a trophy head, if not actually taking the head (Flores Ochoa 1990:Figs. 10, 15, 16). This might be why the focus in the *qiru* designs is on the youthful couple and their combined power to appropriate the spirit of the trophy head and so generate the production of flowers, trees, and other vegetative elements as well as animals across Inka territory.

The range of flowers illustrated on the *qiru* is probably polisemic, perhaps standing in for the trophy head itself, and the fallen in battle, in addition to the new plant life generated from these acts. This is evident on the *akilla* silver colonial *qiru* illustrated by Cummins (1998:115, Fig. 14). As illustrated in Figure 3.2, on one of a pair of these *akilla* a doubled-up zigzagging form encloses heads and flowers in the rhomboids so formed.

Another way of analyzing the flower designs on these colonial *qiru* is as a more general seasonal image, related to initiation rituals and the impending status of warrior for a young man. It is surely not a coincidence that the majority of flowers used in these designs have a red coloring. For example, Mulvany (2004:413) associates the *qantu* flower designs on colonial *qiru* with

Figure 3.2: Silver Colonial *qiru* (Qu. *akilla*) with Bodiless Heads and Flowers Enclosed by Zigzagging Lines

Pair of colonial *aquillas, ca.* 1600. The original is the Museo de Arqueología, Quito. After Cummins (1998:Fig. 14, p. 115), "Let me see! Reading is for them: colonial Andean images and objects 'como es costumbre tener los caciques Señores.'" In *Native Traditions in the Postconquest World*, pp. 91–148. Eds. Elizabeth Hill Boone and Tom Cummins (Washington, DC: Dumbarton Oaks Research Library and Collection, 1998).

Image © Dumbarton Oaks Research Library and Collection, Washington, DC.

the red and yellow or cyclamen pink cantuta (*Cantua buxifolia* Juss. Ex. Lam) or, as the flower of the Inka, the red-purple decanto (*C. tormentosa* Cav., *Perighragmos C. dependens*). Mulvany suggests that these flowers were worn as garland headdresses by the young Inka nobles of royal blood for certain ceremonies, mainly in the rainy season in November and December, called the "time of flowers" (*pawqar waray*), which celebrated their coming of age (2004:416).

During the ritual of Qapaq Raymi that took place in Cusco to celebrate the mature summer sun, various chroniclers narrate how these young nobles were initiated as men, given the royal breeches (*wara*) to wear, which initiated them into warfare, and had their ears pierced, possibly as a kind of male menarche.[14] These kinds of rituals have certain similarities to the lowland initiation rituals described earlier, where young men were introduced to warfare in the very center of the entire political system. In his account, Cieza de León (1945 [1551]: Chap. 142) relates this history of Inka ear piercing to the Caviña groups living up the Vilcanota River. The complex symbolism of flowers here, as both markers of sexual maturity and of initiation into warfare, is also much like the flower and song language of the Aztecs (Duverger 1979). As a broad generalization then, we might say that these rituals are centripetal centralizing ones of initiation, while at the same time they reinforce the warrior activities throughout the Inka Empire, but especially on the periphery.

The Space above the Feline Head

Semiotically, if the feline head has a direct relation with the warrior power at play in the taking of a trophy head, then the use of the space immediately above the feline head in *qiru* designs might also provide clues to the visual representation of the potential gained from taking an enemy head. In the series of colonial *qiru* examined by Allen, although the space above the feline head is occupied by a series of distinct images, these might form part of common semantic domains. On some of these *qiru*, this space includes a series of more male images: Inka headdresses in general flanked by flowers (Allen 2002:190), bodiless or trophy heads as such, as well the Inka's *mascay paycha* fringe, whose pendant threads were said to denote the number of enemy heads he had taken in battle (Allen 2002:180).[15] In other *qiru*, they include a series of female images: women holding native Andean flowers and surrounded by red rhomboids (Allen 2002:188). And on yet others they include more general images of plants, for example a chile pepper plant (Allen 2002:189), which has uses associated with transformation and sacrifice, as we shall see.

We further suggest that the two kinds of arches—the rainbow arch under which the royal couple stand, and the smaller red arches, both of which emerge from feline mouths—express vital aspects of the recycling of the trophy head motif. We propose here that a decomposing trophy head, like the offerings in the mountain chest described earlier, would become part of the chrysalis-mist-rain cycle of metamorphosis. This seems to be confirmed by the illustration of rainfall and rain clouds under the rainbow arches in many upper registers of colonial *qiru* (Allen 2002:180, 189). Perhaps the red arch alludes to a more general haemodynamic cycle of blood sacrifice, and its potent consequences. In other *qiru*, instead of rain, this same haemodynamic cycle, or perhaps its winter equivalent, is expressed in terms of snowfall (Flores Ochoa 1990:47ff.).

In this sense, *qiru* iconography, with its bilateral symmetry, seems to express the two poles of the metamorphosis of a trophy head. First, there is the phase of capture of a trophy head, in the hands of a male warrior, personified by the Inka himself. Second, there is the phase of enemy head curation and transformation into kin, in the hands of a female weaver, represented on the *qiru* by the Coya herself. Whereas the first masculine phase is expressed in the images of fierce felines, the second phase, with its regenerative aspect, is expressed in a series of images of flowers, animals and other objects, perhaps to illustrate the proliferation of babies or *wawa* mentioned earlier.

If the feline were to be expressed as a part of this second phase, then it seems to mark the transitional phase from male-oriented warfare to female-managed regeneration. Importantly, for Allen, the open feline mouth also marks the "doors" to the lost Inka city of Paititi, and so to "the country of the dead" (2002: 181, 198). For Flores Ochoa, this second use of felines might also support a key use of the art of *qirus* in the ongoing resistance of Andean populations to Spanish rule.

According to our interpretation, the spatial dimension of these processes is a vital part of *qiru* iconography. For example, the expansive warrior phase has an outward centrifugal tendency, when the incised or painted concentric squares would be read from the center outward. Similarly, the female curation phases have an expansive quality of increasing yield radiating out from the center. Only during the initiation phase into these bellicose acts and their aftermath, centered in youthful initiation rites, is there a much more centripetal and centralized tendency. The female phase might be specially marked in the *qiru* designs by the zigzagging form, associated by William Conklin (1999) with a woven weft image, enclosing head and flower-like seed images in their interstices, as images of the male warp (see again Figure 3.2). In the *qiru* designs studied by Allen, the role of the female as weaver is implicit. However, in other colonial *qiru*, examined by Flores Ochoa, the female figure is much more explicitly a weaver, and she carries as attributes a spindle or else bundles of textiles as offerings (1990:52). Further afield, perhaps the images on Pukara ceramics of a woman tethering a llama while holding a flower derive from a similar complex of ideas.

Finally, we believe that the *tocapu* abstract designs illustrated in the central register of many colonial *qiru* might express certain aspects of this same logic. If we take the two *tocapu* images illustrated in Allen's article (2002), these seem to express the two poles of the trophy-head cycle we refer to above. In this case, the tongue and throne motif, in a highly abstract form, could express the increased power of the male warrior head taker to command obedience in a defined territory. The rainbow imagery emerging from the mouths of jaguars might be a part of this same semantic domain, of male vocal power. The *tocapu* of an Andean stepped cross, on the other hand, with its red lozenge center, might represent male insemination of the female, and the potency of this seed image, which originally derived from the taking of an enemy trophy head, to regenerate life in the domain under his command, as illustrated in Figure 3.3.

Figure 3.3: *Tocapu* Designs in the Frieze of a Colonial *qiru*

A wooden *qiro* with inlaid decoration, on which rainbow arches are depicted emerging from a jaguar's head. In the central "belt" register a zigzag cuts across *tocapu* designs. After Allen (2002:Fig. 8), "The Incas have gone inside. Pattern and persistence in Andean iconography." *Res: Anthropology and Aesthetics* (2002:180–204). The original is in the José A. Gayoso Collection, Cusco, Peru. Photo by NMAI Photo Services Staff. Courtesy, National Museum of the American Indian, Smithsonian Institution (Catalogue #178956.000).

In both cases, the demand for obedience through increased male vocal power, or the insemination of the female with the energies unleashed from the taken trophy head, would be accomplished in part through the consumption of the seed-like maize beer out of the skull-like *qirus*, in the ritual practices of drinking the power of the dead.

The Nested Power of
Modern Andean Hierarchies

To UNDERSTAND how political power was created, consolidated, and maintained by Andean leadership, in the past as well as the present, we now turn to the role of the head as a key symbol for the appropriation of territorial power. First, we trace the different levels of territorial power that are expressed by heads, from the personal and familial levels up to ayllu levels and beyond, as well as the ways in which political power always included the ancestors. The gamut of forms of leadership is of interest here, too, given that there are many alternatives to community organization, group maintenance, and political power within communities throughout the Andean region over time. These organizational possibilities include dispersed families, stratified rulership, nested hierarchies and/or rotating positions, balanced dualism, or simply having a dispersed power base in multiple domains in a more heterarchic system. Although the identification of the predominant model of Andean political form at any one time is widely debated, mounting evidence demonstrates how political structures are legitimized by territorial, ancestral, and social solidarity.

The segmentary systems of nested hierarchies, widely described by anthropologists in the region north of Potosí from the 1970s onward, were strongly influenced by the Africanist models of the day.[1] Their language of nested "minor" and "major" ayllus applies to closed systems that are also strongly patriarchal in their focus, centering primarily on the hierarchy of male political structures, from the *cabildos* upward. Some archaeologists have even argued that nested hierarchies of this kind have held sway since at least pre-Tiwanaku (Formative) times.[2] However, in practice these nested hierarchies of ayllus, at least in Qaqachaka, are overlapped by a series of other cross-cutting forms of organization (for example, complex gender relations, kinship groupings where brothers and sisters, as well as husbands and wives, play a primary role, the wider *castas* that have both male and female criteria of membership and affiliation, regional marriage patterns, and parallel systems of inheritance). These nested hierarchies also combine centrifugal and centripetal tendencies in relevant ways, implying that they are not just closed systems but also part of wider political formations (Arnold 1988, 1998).

More pertinently, in the modern political nested hierarchy, of which the household and ayllu form just a part, contemporary ethnographic evidence reveals a layering of authority centering on heads that denotes different levels of status. To investigate this embeddedness of the head as a unifying symbol in Andean political life, let us first consider the role of practices based on heads at both personal and household levels, where the handling of heads denotes authority and its contextualization as a part of this nested hierarchy, as well as of wider political formations. Then we shall consider heads as symbols of leadership and authority at an ayllu level. Finally, we shall consider the role of heads in the ritual hierarchy at the wider *marka* and regional levels, as expressed in some contemporary rituals and cultural practices. These have an important bearing on how homologous sets of hierarchical relationships might have been organized in the past. Throughout this chapter, we shall refer to the case study of ayllu Qaqachaka, which Arnold knows best, pointing to comparative material where necessary.

Personal Heads

The construction of the political person in the Andes generally, although related to the construction of personhood in general, is particularly associated with the way that spiritual power, particularly of males, is centered on the head. This implies a series of gendered differences in the construction of political and spiritual status throughout a person's lifetime. The head, then, is the key site of human spirituality and sensibility.

Arnold has described how, in Qaqachaka, conceptions about the quickening of life at birth and its destruction at death draw on ideas about the head as the key location for the entry and exit of spiritual power. In a metaphysical sense, the head (Qu. *uma*; Aym. *p'iqi*), particularly the soft fontanel between the bones of a baby's skull, is considered the point of entry and exit for the human self, whether of a male or a female. Around birth, there are accounts of shamans who can observe the passage of spirit into the body of the mother-to-be, which first enters her fontanel, then passes gradually down the vertebral column to the sacrum during the weeks of pregnancy, and hence into the fontanel of the fetus to announce its quickening (Arnold 1988:391–93; Arnold, Yapita, and Tito 1999:180). Similarly, during serious illnesses, shamans (*yatiri*) might hold onto the fontanel of the patient to stop the spirit leaving the body, and so permit that person to overcome their illness. Finally, at death for both sexes, the spirit is thought to escape from the body by the same fontanel, leaving just the human body behind "as if we were throwing away a pile of old clothes" (Arnold 1988:371).

At the same time, a differential attention to the head from childhood onward helps define the construction of gendered distinctions. For example, in early childhood in the region of Qaqachaka, as well as across the southern altiplano more generally, there is considerable dietary attention paid to the construction of gender difference in children, whereby boys are fed on more solid kinds of meat (kidneys, liver, etc.), as well as meat on bones or parts of the head, whereas girls are fed on the softer portions of fleshy meat (generally muscles). People say that this is because boys must become hard and strong, like the bone casing of the skull, whereas girls are less strong physically and their energies are centered more on the heart. For example, the Bolivian press is full of articles on the favorite food of the current Bolivian president, Evo Morales, said to be heads (in this case of llamas or sheep), which are presumed to have given him the personal power to achieve presidential status. We shall examine this particular difference between head-centered males and heart-centered females later.

Initiation Rites

In adolescence and youth, these psychosexual differences become more exaggerated. In the modern context of the region of Qaqachaka, compulsory military service is still considered a prerequisite for a young rural man before embarking into marriage. When he finally leaves the barracks, there is an initiation-like ritual, called in Aymara *uruyaña* (meaning, literally, "making his day"), prepared by his family. During the feast that accompanies this ritual, the young man has to eat the brains of a ram, taking it out of a hole made in the skull, where the fontanel would be, with a rib bone, while the participants in the ritual look on. This is said to give him strength to take up his future role in the household and ayllu of which he is a part (Arnold, In press).[3]

In this case, the eating of the cranial contents transfers an enabling power to the individual young male in question, demonstrating again that the seat of a man's power is specifically related to the brain matter. This enabling power is expressed as an element of "luck" (*surti*) that the young man obtains on drawing out the brain matter and consuming it (see Figure 4.1).

Figure 4.1: Photo of the Modern Ritual of *uruyaña*, where a Young Man after Military Service, Eats the Brains of a Sheep
Courtesy of the archives of ILCA.

Household Heads

Marriage is a vital stage in the life of anyone in Qaqachaka; from then onward, each member of an Andean couple finally becomes a real "person," in the sense of someone now juridically recognized as such in the community. This juridical sense of personhood is called *runa* in Quechua or *jaqi* in Aymara.

In *The Metamorphosis of Heads*, Arnold and Yapita (2006) argue that the newly married couple is now able to start a new household and expand (or radiate) this potential of accumulated luck, acquired previously by the husband, outward through the series of transactions and responsibilities that they accomplish in their immediate ayllu and beyond. Importantly, in Qaqachaka today the ideal couple is considered to be composed of a warrior and a weaver (Arnold and Yapita 2006:126–30). This has certain resonances with Inka times. For example, Caroline Dean (2001:157–59), in a detailed reading of the 17th-century drawings of Guaman Poma de Ayala concerning the age groups of Inka society, proposes that the point of reference there, too, was the married couple of warrior and weaver (*ca.* 1615:f.194, f.215).

From a contractual point of view, once married, a new couple is increasingly incorporated into a wider set of obligations, both ritual and quotidian, within their families as well as within the minor and major ayllus of which they form a part. In the region of Qaqachaka, this set of obligations seems to draw additionally on those that a couple (as warrior and weaver) would have had formerly before to the Inka state or earlier confederation, as if that particular state provided a template for all other relations to the state that followed. Arnold and Yapita have shown how these obligations are expressed, for example, in the verses of the wedding songs (2004:470–71).

For instance, a part of the bride service obligations for a new husband (which in the recent past lasted some two weeks), and the obligations on the part of a new bride to the household of her husband, to this day in Qaqachaka have to do with male and female abilities in warfare and weaving, respectively. Nowadays, the value of a son-in-law lies not only in his strength and bravery but also in his manual labor, so he must be able to build walls, till land, carry firewood, and so on. He must also be able to sacrifice and butcher animals to the satisfaction of his new relations, showing the rapidity with which he can cut off an animal's head (*p'iq q'achjayaña*). In the recent past, however, a young warrior son-in-law (Aym. *tullqa*) would have been required to capture and bring back a human head in warfare, for the future growth of his family (Arnold and Yapita 2006:128).

In his book *Las voces de los wak'as*, Astvaldsson describes a similar set of responsibilities of a newly married man in the region of Jesús de Machaqa (in Ingavi Province of La Paz Department), who was obliged to carry out an annual period of office as an ayllu "head," although he fails to make the connection with head taking (2000:213–29). There, this service was called *chhiphiña*, a polisemic Aymara term having to do with the relationship between the socialization of male violence and the appropriation of land for agriculture and house building. For instance, according to Astvaldsson, the meanings of *chhiphiña* include: serving the shrine of a local *wak'a*, breaking open the land, breaking stones, clearing fields, thatching a new roof, fighting (particularly punching) an enemy, and being contented, presumably because things are in order and the household is now expanding. These associated meanings seem to derive precisely from the theory we put forward for the trophy-head complex and its subsequent stages of regeneration and production but focus specifically on the male side of these obligations.

On the other hand, a woman as daughter-in-law in Qaqachaka was required to be a good cook and an excellent weaver whose weavings were so tight that they would be useful in warfare, when she would help her husband by using them to carry stones (Arnold and Yapita 2000:233). In the past, in Qaqachaka, a married woman would also have cared for the trophy heads her husband brought back from warfare. The potential agency that results from having first captured a head motivates a series of subsequent actions. In this sense, the warrior husband's earlier actions in head capture impinge on his wife's tasks of weaving and help define the specific terms of gender relations in this cultural setting. In this way, her setting up a loom is still compared to tending the hair of a dead enemy over a kind of rack (Arnold and Yapita 2000:198). Many comments suggest that, in weaving, the warp is compared to the solid head stretched over the loom poles, whereas the movement of the weft expresses the more female activity of recreating new life and radiating it outward throughout the ayllu in any subsequent exchanges of cloth (Arnold and Yapita 2001:66–68). There are also indications that the skull-like solidity of the warp expresses the male sense of vertical genealogical longevity in a place where the residence rule is predominantly patrilocal, whereas the weft expresses the female power of genealogical expansion horizontally across the ayllu because a women moves at marriage to the house of her husband, taking her dowry of household chattels, weavings, and animals with her (Arnold and Yapita 2001:67).

Marital advice from elder relations at a traditional Qaqachaka wedding ceremony must drum in the nature of these changes. In these formal advice-giving speeches, the woman is referred to as a weft thread and the man a warp, and commentators insist that at marriage the ayllu textile repertory is finally completed when the warp is combined with the weft. This happens not only in weaving but also figuratively in all dimensions of social life.

Other comments about female actions in weaving affirm their relation with completing the domination of an enemy head, begun in the husband's initial head taking. For example, the technical manner of tying of the warp threads back to the loom is compared to making a hard skull-like foundational base to the textile before the fleshy substance of female woven cloth is created from it. The many historical examples in other parts of the world of loom weights being formed as miniature stone human heads to hold the warp threads down reinforce the idea that the warp in and of itself represents male solidity and longevity in a place focused on the head,[4] which in this instance is expressed in stone as a permanent element, in comparison with the more flexible and expansive nature of female ties. In this sense, the widespread association in weaving, not only in the Andes, of the warp with maleness, with war and trophy heads, and the weft with femaleness, might have arisen from a common underlying pattern of head taking and its wider socialization in gender relations. We shall see later how the close association between heads and loom poles also seem to mediate the way that the *wara* staff of male office is perceived.

The transition of two young single persons to "become people" (*jaqichasiña*) at marriage also entails a "spiritual" birth, when they become "like babies" (*wawjamaw*), leaving the flesh and bone of their corporal parents to accept the authority and "other life" (*mä wira*) of their spiritual godparents. Arnold and Yapita argue that this spiritual transition is another consequence of the metamorphosis of the trophy head (which the son-in-law had captured to prove his bravery and strength as a warrior) into a series of generic "babies" (*wawa*), whose pathway the couple are obliged to follow (2006:129).

By internalizing the spiritual energies (*ispiritu*) embodied in the trophy head, the new couple capitalizes on its expanding yield to leave their condition as single "natural persons" of flesh and blood, to become "social persons" and more spiritual beings. Through this process of "unraveling" themselves as persons in later years of married life, the couple gradually externalizes the energies of the head-baby under their charge. This process accompanies their initiation into the new social "pathway" of married life that entails their communal obligation to enter the offices of authority, expressed in Aymara as "carrying heads" (*p'iq q'ipiña*), or simply as having a "burden" (the Spanish word "*cargo*"). During this period of office, the spiritual power gained from having captured initially a trophy head generates for the couple a fertile period that stimulates the unraveling in all directions of their potential throughout the ayllu territory and beyond as married persons together with their household contingent of new babies (human, animal, and vegetable), and, in the modern world, their plethora of material objects.

The initial taking of a trophy head to found a new household, and its subsequent transformations in the hands of the newly married couple, also seem to structure the way that the house itself is perceived. In Qaqachaka and elsewhere, ethnographers have noted how the general symbolism of a new house in the Andes concerns its nature both as an offering and burial place as well as the site of an extended wake.[5] This death-centered symbolism centers on a three-year cycle, which is reiterated in various moments of the household's new life. Three years is generally the length of time before a couple constructs their first house and when dowry giving is completed. It is also the length of time for the final departure of a dead spirit from the household in which the deceased had lived. Perhaps originally this three-year cycle was the period for the initial decomposition of the head and the gradual appropriation of its powers. We argue that these homologous time periods would at least seem to confirm the presence of enemy bones (as well as ancestral ones) at the heart of the symbolism of a house and the focal point of the cultural and spiritual practices of a new couple.

Apart from the ever-present memory of trophy heads and other offerings among the foundation stones of a new house, other kinds of heads figure in domestic life. For example a skull, particularly that of an aborted baby (*janq'u qallu*), is kept in the house stores to guard the agricultural products kept there. Catherine Allen (1988:59) reports how in the Cusco region ancestral skulls, too, protect stored goods. A married woman, then, deals with skull management as part of her everyday house chores. In addition, since the Colonial Period, many houses have a family saint or "devotion" kept in a niche in the wall (*t'uxu*), which would seem to replace the ancestral heads kept in household niches in the past (Arnold 1991:10).[6] In this case, even if the original heads are no longer present, their potentially radiating power is drawn on in household rituals and everyday life.

Gendered Heads and the Parallelism of Warriors and Weavers

We described how in the recent past of Andean highland regions such as Qaqachaka, men as warriors were required to capture trophy heads to appropriate the alien force incarnate therein and convert its potential powers into expanding energies now put to the use of his own household and ayllu. Like seeds that sprout over time, the alien forces of trophy heads are thus gradually domesticated and transformed into the babies (the generic *wawa*) of the household under the care of women. In this way, the community depends on masculine physical strength and the male forces of production to attain a new harvest of human children in the home, vegetable offspring in the fields, and animal offspring in the flocks, and then to sustain and nourish them through physical work.

In this wider regenerative cycle, male access to the potentiality of the seed-like trophy heads helps generate the fecundity of women, and, in turn, other reproductive and productive cycles. Male physical force is indispensable in obtaining the basic seeds (trophy heads) and then opening the furrows in the fields, perceived as the warp of the earth, in the ensuing farming cycles. In their accompanying activities, men call the rains with their musical instruments and stimulate production through their sweat (*jump'i*), energies (*ch'ama*), and spiritual strength (*ispiritu*).

In the past, these transformations of the head taker into a powerful and fertile figure may have contributed to the conformation of certain leaders or "big-men," whose prestige was measured by the number of trophy heads he had collected. This is the case in many lowland groups, where trophy heads are displayed in the households of such men.[7] It is also the case in the historical record, in the descriptions of the houses of Andean caciques who had accumulated heads in their porches, or in special rooms set aside for this purpose.[8] And it is probably the case in archaeological settings, for example in some Late Nasca sites (see Figure 4.2).[9]

Figure 4.2: Severed Heads on Poles Painted on a Nasca Ceramic Vessel
In Proulx (1999:325, Plate 165), "Nasca headhunting and the ritual use of trophy heads." Originally published in German in *Nasca, Geheimnisvolle Zeichen im Alten Peru,* pp. 79–87. Ed. Judith Rickenbach (Zurich: Museum Rietberg Zürich, 1999). Courtesy of the Museo de América, Madrid (#8154).

In modern life, the wider demand for male labor in the market outside ayllu localities expands this immediate cycle based on head taking and the former attention to local production. Now men are impelled to "raid" the market place, sometimes going to neighboring countries or farther afield to bring back an array of modern consumer goods for consumption at home, instead of heads. Evidence for the roots of these modern transformations in former economic and political cycles based on warfare can be found in the stressful interrelations between communities with differential access to the marketplace. For example, key economic actors in certain regions of the Andes, generally with greater access to the marketplace and hence power over communities with lesser access to markets, are often accused of being "grease-suckers" (the *kharisiri* or *ñaqaq* of urban folklore) by their less successful neighbors.

This is the case, for example, with the regional market town and municipal capital of Challapata, which has substantial economic and political power over the rural districts or ayllus, including Qaqachaka, under its territorial jurisdiction. These differences in economic and political interests between

Challapata and its districts erupt at times into open conflict. Correspondingly, it is most common for the Qaqachakas to accuse residents of Challapata of being "grease suckers."

This emerging complex of economic and political tensions might also derive from modern reinterpretations of the ways that both individuals and groups gained power in the past by accumulating enemy trophy heads and appropriating their powers. Nowadays, though, the economically privileged groups appropriate the forces of weaker players in a wider economic domain of power, and the trophy heads become metamorphosed into consumer goods. There prevails what Deborah Root (1996) has called "a commodification of difference" based on a modern cannibal culture. This occurs when some communities have greater access to say, tractors, in the wider marketplace, whereas others still use the more rustic *chakit'aqlla* digging stick, or oxen and plow (Sp. *yunta*). But this economic difference is experienced as an appropriation of energies, a taking advantage of the existing potential of others, and this resentment frequently builds up into rampant envy (Sp. *envidia*) that must be avenged.

Feminine authority, on the other hand, is based on household and ayllu production and the upbringing of *wawas* (human, animal, and vegetable). A woman has the productive task of raising human babies at home. There, the initial care of the *wawas*, as transformed enemy heads, includes taming the foreign and uncontrollable forces found at any boundary (of, say, the ayllu ancestors or enemies beyond the ayllu bounds) and domesticating these forces within human society. Only later does a mother release her *wawas* to the more masculine domain, say, of the school. Another productive female task is sowing the baby-seeds in the fields and then tending them in the weft-like to-and-fro routine of agricultural work under the tutelary spirit of the Virgin Earth (the *Tira Wirjina*, more commonly called *Pachamama*). In tending the fields, women embody the maternity of the Virgin Earth; here, the plants are not inert things but have their own spirits or essences: the "virgins" of each house plot. Thus, agricultural production also depends on the ability of women (in their maternal and fecund aspects) and the fertilizing spirits of the place. To this end, in a gendered division of ritual labor, the women sing *wayñu* songs directed at the plants in the rainy season, to the accompaniment of men playing their *pinkillu* flutes (cf. Stobart 1996).

During this productive cycle, the Virgin Earth seems to embody the female forces of production that transform the power of heads, through a period of curation, into household produce. As tutelary spirit of the orchards and house plots, the Virgin Earth herself becomes transformed into the creative mother of the cultivated plants that are her babies. However, as in childbirth, the alien nature of the powers at play can be dangerous; so during the cultivation cycle, both people and their crops are always under the threat of her curse. According to Elvira Espejo from Qaqachaka, the Virgin Earth in general, and the other virgins under her charge in more local house plots, have the power to produce not only the cultivated plants but also the flesh of animals and the making of weavings; in this sense, she is considered to have bestowed upon women the domestic arts of horticulture, cooking and weaving in a wider productive cycle, generated by an original trophy head.

These ideas about the importance of women and female deities in the production of *wawas* in the fields are found in the ethnographies of many parts of the world. For example, this particular configuration of ideas has resonances with the "vegetable garden magic" under the charge of the spirit Nunkui, among the lowland Achuar of Ecuador, as described by Descola (1989), as well as further afield, say in the coral garden magic described in Malinowski's classic study of 1935 on the Trobriand Islands. Although the Achuar and the Trobriand islanders did not actually take heads, they were both a part of a wider regional economy that did. In each case, we argue that the key relation between female gardening "magic" and the power derived from male headhunting should be examined.

Ayllu Heads

We have seen how masculine strength is commonly associated with the head and with the spirit residing therein, nowadays called *ispiritu* in the Aymara of Qaqachaka. The greater male capacity to manage this spiritual power, especially in the context of head taking, is thought to engender both the cycles of agricultural, pastoral, and family production and the domain of political power, through male ability in speech and political oratory.

Although this spiritual power is transferable to women at a certain point in these productive cycles, nevertheless the initial male control over this spiritual power would seem to explain the importance of male political power in the domination of political subjects. A generalized awareness that heads were the motivating force behind wider political relations would also seem to explain the ubiquitous nature of heads in relation to the political symbols of ayllu office.

Heads as Holders of Power; Holders of Power as Heads

In Qaqachaka, the political office of "ayllu head" (called in Aymara *p'iqi*) is reserved for the ayllu leaders called *jilanqu*. In this case, their power of authority as "heads" is held to come from the patron saint of Qaqachaka, Tata Quri ("Father Gold"), considered their common ancestor, their most powerful miracle shrine, and importantly their capricious war leader. Each Thursday and Saturday, other ayllu authorities (in this case, the church guardians, or *mayordomos*) still feed, dress, and offer libations to Tata Quri, just as if he were a mummified ancestor, recording his journey and resting places before he came to the colonial church in the central plaza (Arnold 2007).

The *jilanqu* ayllu leaders still receive from all the ayllus under their charge a tribute of first fruits at Carnival each year. On this occasion, the men and women contributors bring these offerings wrapped like babies (or perhaps heads in the more distant past), in weavings on their backs. The *jilanqu* authorities are also responsible for levying and documenting the head-tax based on the former system of tribute called *tasa*, in September each year, and taking it to the central office in Oruro. Some of the rituals of office executed by these authorities in Qaqachaka would thus seem to illustrate direct ties between the political and ritual power of the *jilanqu* office and an association with heads.

However, such ties between political office and heads are even more developed in the rural community of Jesús de Machaqa, some 25 km from the ruins of Tiwanaku, and 10 km from another important ritual site: Khonko Wankane (Qunqu Wankani).[10] In his studies of this region, Astvaldur Astvaldsson (1994, 1996, 1998, 2000:122, 156ff.) explores the significance of male political power and its association with heads. The evidence from his studies affirms these direct ties between head curation and political power in the Andean region.

In his book *Las voces de los wak'as*, Astvaldsson (2000:122) examines in detail the initiation ritual of new ayllu authorities in Jesús de Machaqa, who are called "heads" (Aym. *p'iqi*), as they are also commonly called elsewhere. In this community, though, the power of authority is held to come from the *wak'a achachila* or "stone grandfathers," who are considered to be powerful masculine deities that possess and control power and strength with their unmistakably masculine qualities (Astvaldsson 2000:128, 136). Astvaldsson associates these masculine qualities with *two* particular domains of power: first the power to speak and the associated command of civil obedience through language, and second the power over the natural forces that fertilize or effect in some way the female earth, the plants, and so on (see also Astvaldsson 1998:250, 254–55).

Astvaldsson emphasizes how the authorities called "heads" derive their power from certain deities associated with "heads." In fact, four of the five deities named in the initiation ritual for the ayllu authorities have, or are heads; the most powerful of them takes the form of a stone head, finely worked. The initiation ritual, practiced until a generation ago, lasted for two days. At its culmination, those who assisted the new authorities in their process of taking power, aptly called "soldiers," went off to the site of the most powerful *wak'a* in the territory, taking with them white cloths. They wrapped these white cloths around the *wak'a* to capture its "spirit" called in Aymara *ajayu, animu* or *kuraji*, "courage" (some of the same terms associated with the powers in a trophy head). Then, on returning to the group of new authorities, the soldiers "attacked them," putting the same white cloths around the necks of the new authorities "to give them the power of public speech" (Astvaldsson 2000:137).[11]

Astvaldsson underlines the warlike aspects of this ritual. He also emphasizes that the power of this regional *wak'a* finally speaks through the voices of the participants, who are said to "growl," perhaps like felines. In this case, the power of the *wak'a achachila* is referred to by two particular terms in Aymara: *ch'amani* (to have strength) and *munañani* (to want or desire, in a capricious sense) (Astvaldsson 2000:138). We suggest that both terms refer to the male "desire" for political power and authority originally derived from having taken a trophy head, now directed toward the stone heads of the ritual.[12]

Other aspects of this ritual described by Astvaldsson illustrate the masculine practices of establishing political power. Although there are many descriptions in the Andean region of woven cloths having been draped over ancestral stones, particularly the *wak'a*, nevertheless Astvaldsson describes the ways in which a particularly male use of cloth is directed toward the embodiment of vocal power (2000:137–38). After the regional *wak'a* have transferred a part of their powers to the incoming leaders, they are constantly reminded of the source of this power through the presence of stone heads laid out on the ceremonial altars of office. Other contemporary ethnographic evidence confirms how these regional *wak'a* are held to engender the ritual speech of male leaders, especially the forms of ritual dialogue between pairs of male specialists.[13]

Emerging regional patterns of increased political savvy associated with the accumulating powers of speech held to derive from having sacrificed ample heads to such mountain shrines, as regional *wak'a*, might account for the rising powers of well-known oracular sites in the Andes. For example, Early Horizon Chavín de Huántar in the central Andes, and Late Intermediate Period Pachaqamaq, near Lima, emerged to serve as cults with universal powers.[14] The same pattern of accumulating claims to power seems to have been centered on platform mounds, at sites such as Caral, Áspero, Cahuachi, Pukara, or Tiwanaku as they became regional pilgrimage centers. La Lone (2000:78) and later Rodriguez Kembel and Rick (2004) relate this development to the fact that many Chavín artifacts are portable, allowing for the movement of high value-low bulk items such as marine conch and spondylus shells over long distances to key pilgrimage sites. Portable items such as conch shells are particularly important in the dissemination of these emerging patterns of political power because they can also "speak" in favor of determined configurations of political relations, when blown in certain locations and in the presence of key authorities. Such concentrations of exotic high-valued goods reinforced claims to status and power, perhaps triggered by the pilgrims themselves who claimed high status from having heard the oracle speak.

The key argument here is that if single heads (whether human or of stone), as holders of the powers of speech, can bestow male authority to ayllu leaders, then a concentration of heads should both constitute and express regional accumulations of power. In the ongoing political relations that draw on this power during the many ritual sessions that the ayllu authorities oversee at Jesús de Machaqa, stone heads thought to date from the Middle Horizon or the Late Intermediate Period, usually wrapped in woven textiles, are brought out and placed on the ritual altars in the sites where these male political gatherings take place, as an expression of regional power accumulation (Astvaldsson 1994, 1998:240). At the same time, the power of authority of local leaders, perhaps derived originally from having taken heads, is integrated into wider centripetal political relations, where ayllu obligations are enacted for higher state authorities, through the system of tribute and "cargos," already mentioned. Within the last centuries, these were obligations that ayllu members had to fulfill to the colonial and republican states, although social memory still relates these obligations to those of former Andean states, above all the Inka.[15]

In the expansive Inka state, conquered ayllus were obliged to work state land, tend the state flocks, and complete state construction projects as recompense for their incorporation into this larger political domain, while keeping some territory for their own subsistence production. In the following centuries, the colonial system of tax tribute to the king of Spain replicated this former system. As Platt points out in his pioneering study of Aymara political thought, the colonial regime recognized the rights of possession of ethnic groups to their lands as an "ancient socialization of the enemy," through their political incorporation into the new state apparatus under the charge of the victorious ethnic lord or *mallku* (1987a:114).

For the colonial state apparatus (as formerly for the Inka state), tribute was the "duty" called in Aymara or Quechua *jucha*, toward the functioning of the wider system, on a par with the communal obligations of sponsoring feasts, standing their turn as authorities, or fulfilling an act of vengeance in war.[16] As we saw, in the present-day language of the region of Qaqachaka these obligations are still experienced as "bearing a sin" (*jucha q'ipiña*) or "assuming a debt" (*juch yanaña*). So a *comunario* might complain: "I've been hauled into this duty" (*jucharuw wayuntxituxa*), because he must forcibly fulfill his obligation and "any demand whatever might befall him." The clear relation, already examined in Chapter 3, between *jucha* and head taking, implies that tributary relations at different times were viewed in terms of a centripetal flow of heads, accompanied by obligatory patterns of labor, from these ayllu peripheries toward the centers of power.

Although these kinds of duties were burdensome in the Colonial Period, the *comunarios* sense that these duties were performed more "willingly" under former Andean states. This was because in the immediate household, the duty holders (husband and wife) were considered to represent the victorious Inka and his Coya exercising sovereignty over their subjects in a common realm, according to a system of laws and symbols of authority constituted differently from today. As Platt emphasizes (1987a), this passing of turns has to do with inter-Andean struggles in which the killing of an enemy gave the victorious *mallku* (or Inka) the right to appropriate the lands of the defeated. This regional logic also relates victory in war with the burden of sponsoring a feast, as a celebration centered on lands and their produce.

In the past, feast sponsors in the Qaqachaka region actually held in their possession a head (as seed that would germinate), although today they carry a decorated woven coca bag (*wallqipu*) hung with tassels instead. It is customary to carry this small coca bag slung from the shoulder, and it is compared to the trophy heads of former times. In ritual language, the expression *jucha p'iqi* ("head carrier") is used for this duty, or *cargo*, of organizing a feast. Moreover, these "head-bags" are considered to command authority, and to have the power to direct the duty holders that carry them. According to Don Domingo Jiménez, a former ayllu mayor of the northern Potosí region, these head-bags "usually talk" to their owners on Epiphany (*Día de Reyes*, on January 6), the very day when the obligation of duty holder is transmitted in the ayllu system to an incoming office holder (see also Arnold and Yapita 2006:80, 157).

At the ayllu level, the equivalent of a head for a female duty holder is her woven coca cloth (*istalla*), which is considered to have the same kind of power to "make everything speak," but this time through its textile mouth. Don Domingo explained how the close relation between these weavings and the enemies killed in battle bestows on them their power of speech, and how, therefore, they have the power of instructing the entering ayllu authorities each year on the duties that will guarantee their continuing rights to land. Instead of appealing to written authority and documentation as the precedence for justifying ongoing and customary duties, this function is attributed to weaving. In this case, material objects express the memory of this long-lived relationship between political authority, heads, and speaking.

The *Vara* Staff of Office

Another key material object that expresses the memory of these long-lived relationships between political authority and heads is the *vara* staff of office.

Interestingly, the use and symbolism of the *vara* seems to articulate both the male and female consequences of head taking. From our point of view, the *vara* (Aym. *wara*), as a key symbol of contemporary male power in the Andes for ayllu leaders, derives its strength from its associations with a trophy head. At the same time, the *vara* is a symbol of the regeneration of this head into new life via the weaving activities of women, although in practice women are not allowed to touch the *vara* directly. More specifically, it would seem that the *vara* staff symbolizes the growing stem that sprouts from a trophy head, having absorbed its physical, political, and social powers (seen also in the many staffs held in Middle Horizon imagery). In the region of Qaqachaka, the *vara* is carried mainly by men of the political rank of authority called *jilanqu* or "head" (*p'iqi*), who are the leaders of the minor ayllus and by the *alcalde mayor* of the major ayllu; these are the Aymara equivalents to the *varayuq* or "*vara* bearers" in Quechua-speaking areas.

Nowadays, as in the past, the highland *vara* is usually made of the hard black palm wood called *chonta* in Spanish (*Bactris gasipaes*) brought in from the eastern Amazon, whereas others are made of the dark wood called *yunki*. Evidently, *chonta* wood has been considered to have regenerative powers from at least colonial times.[17] Chonta palm was clearly an early important exchange item as it has been identified from Initial sites on the central Peruvian coast, as well as Middle Horizon sites in the highlands. In an article on colonial Quechua poetry and song, Mannheim (1999:23), for example, cites the colonial hymn *Hanaq pachap kusikuynin* (Bliss of Heaven), by the Franciscan priest Pérez Bocanegra, whose line 73 translates as "Palm tree that bears tender fruit." This line might be more ambiguous than it seems, because *chonta* wood was also used by ethnic groups in the sierra region around Cali (Columbia) to make the sharp and pointed *makana* lances used in warfare and then staked outside the house with a trophy-head impaled on top.[18] See Figure 4.2 for a comparable image of use from Nasca.

It is possible that the *huarango* staffs made from carob or acacia wood (*Prosopis chilensis*), found among the regalia in the elaborate burials of high-status specialists in Paracas, Topará, and Nasca sites on the coast (200 BC–AD 400), might draw on the same kind of symbolism.[19] Pre-Hispanic iconographic evidence shows how such staffs were grasped by the "flying shaman" figures on Paracas textiles and in the later Nasca burial site and ceremonial center of Cahuachi.[20]

This archaeological evidence suggests that these staffs of office are much older than the Colonial Period and that the colonial staffs of authority brought from Spain we now know were simply appropriated within the symbolic sphere of their Andean forebears. For example, some staffs of office from Middle Horizon Wari seem to have carried a large and personalized ceramic effigy of a human head, with molded facial features and painted highlights, inserted onto the top of the pole.

There are certain contemporary contexts in Qaqachaka and its neighboring ayllus when the *vara* staff of office is directly associated with a head. For example, in their design, many *varas* are decorated at one end with a condor's head, molded in silver, while others are decorated with heads of the ayllu ancestors, especially skulls of the ayllu dead.[21]

In other ritual contexts, for example, during a phase of warfare or one of difficult problems in the ayllu, the *vara* is actually knocked against the head of someone "to give the staff more strength," in an action called *jawq'aña*, "to hit." Ayllu members explain that the *vara* is beaten against someone's head in this way "so that no misfortune comes to pass," and so that the staff is "clean," in the sense of free from wrongdoings. The traditional ayllu authorities present at this event comment on how the *vara* has the power to punish and decide in such moments, and how this sense of authority derives from "the times of the grandfathers who rule over us."

Comparative material from lowland contexts provides more insights into the nature of the *vara*'s power. According to Descola (1993a, 1993b), the authorities of the lowland Shuar carry similar staffs of office made from black *chonta* palm wood, which they relate to both lightning and the trophy heads of warfare. Other comparative material from more distant parts of the world, such as Samoa, mention how their own wooden staffs of office, carried by religious experts, not only had a carved head decoration at one end, but how these "god-sticks" were similar in form to loom poles, and so related to the female activity that paralleled warfare for men. Moreover, these wooden staffs had the special power to call on the help of the gods, but only when a flax thread was tied around the carved head, and tugged on. Speaking of the Maori, Weiner describes how

> religious experts carried wooden staffs with carved heads which they used for calling upon the help of gods; these "god-sticks" were similar in form to weaving poles. But only when the staff was placed in the ground and a piece of flax was tied around the neck of the figure could the god be induced. As the expert tugged on the flax while chanting a spell, the god was attracted to the thread. Without the precious thread tied around it, the figure had no power at all. (Weiner 1992:54)[22]

Similar ideas occur in an Andean context. When the *vara* is staked into the ground, the shaman Don Domingo Jiménez considers it to be bad luck for the Pachamama, done to hurt her and insult her riches. At the same time, the Pachamama herself signals the way that the *vara* should be staked in the earth, "as all things come from her, including the wood of the *vara*, and it's [*sic*] coating of gold and silver." Don Domingo considers that the *vara* "has everything and knows everything"[23]; his comment could be interpreted as an allusion to the fact that the *vara* is an Andean symbol for the riches and knowledge that would have been generated from possessing an original trophy head. In this wide sense, the *vara* also has to do with certain classes of carnivorous birds (mountain caracara, condors, eagles, and falcons), and for this reason, the *vara* is often decorated with the head of a condor. Stories tell of how the *vara*, as a stand-in for the Inka himself, also has the power to move stones, making them sound as they move about.

Like trophy heads, the *vara* staff of office is used in rituals to bring rain, as well as those to send the rain away. In the second case, the *vara* is used to point to *kuysawan mallku*, the Aymara name for a basket for potatoes that people take outside to send away the rain. Inside the basket is a black cloth called *lutu k'uchillu*, similar to the fabric used both in childbirth and to wrap trophy heads. The *vara* is used to point to the cloth, and then release a quantity of ash deposited inside it that is hurled in all directions with the wind to send away the rain. Only when the sky clears are the potatoes finally harvested.

These powerful characteristics of the contemporary *vara* staff of office might perhaps derive originally from the use of wooden lances for attacking enemies and taking heads, rather than other forms of weapon, and then impaling the trophies taken outside the house, whence the women of the household might have begun to braid the deceased's hair into experimental weavings.

The Geopolitical Place of Heads in the Major Ayllu Formation and Beyond

Heads played a symbolic part in the political life not only of couples in local households, or of leaders of minor ayllus, but also in the wider geopolitical configuration of major ayllus, and their relationships to the state apparatus. As already mentioned, in Qaqachaka and many other ayllus throughout the southern-central Andes, the formal political organization of the mayor and minor ayllus of which they are composed is often described according to the segmentary or nested model first described by Platt in 1978, although in practice there is no Quechua or Aymara equivalent for this terminology and it seems to be a stark simplification of a much more complex reality.

Looking toward this more complex reality, many scholars have applied this political model to historical and archaeological settings, and examined its distinctive features. For example, Albarracín-Jordan (1996) applied this model to the political development of the Titicaca Basin, whereas Albó (1977) and Schaedel (1998), among others, have noticed how this structure accommodates the processes of both disintegration and reintegration of political units, and so of the alternative poles of solidarity and factionalism, in different historical moments of a wider political cycle. This leads us to ask: Could these characteristic alternative poles of solidarity and factionalism perhaps be about the precise moments of negotiation and adaptation between centripetal (inward-looking solidarity) and centrifugal (more fragmented and outward looking) tendencies?

In the political organization of Qaqachaka, like its neighbors Laymi, Jukumani, and Macha, there is a "major ayllu" (sometimes called *marka*) that includes a series of smaller or "minor" ayllus within its territorial and political limits. Historically, the major ayllu is usually the territory that once surrounded a Toledan reduction town or one of its historical annexes, whereas the minor ayllus are the smaller political units of colonial *cabildos*. In practice, these minor ayllus are constantly changing their makeup, splitting off from the larger units as a result of disputes between minor ayllus or simply demographic pressure; a total of twelve minor ayllus seems to be the maximum before splitting occurs. A major ayllu may also split into two because of similar reasons. Therefore, what are now known as "ethnic groups" (Qaqachaka, Laymi, Jukumani, and so on), are really the historical break offs from much larger territorial and political units, the so-called nations or *Señoríos* of the past (for example, Charkas, Qhara Qhara, or Killakas-Asanaqi), in the colonial and republican processes of disintegration. This dynamic continues to operate today.

At the same time, this centrifugal tendency to split apart is counterbalanced by other more centripetal tendencies toward ayllu unity that assure that the minor ayllus maintain their allegiance toward the major ayllu. We have already mentioned gendered duality as one of these centripetal tendencies. It is also well documented in the ethnographic and historical records that the overall structure and organic unity of political authority within a major ayllu community is commonly symbolized as a human (or animal) body, with a head, arms, stomach, and feet; in the cases of Cusco and Jesús de Machaqa, these are said to take the form of felines, although this, too, has been much disputed.[24]

In the case of Qaqachaka, as with many other ayllus in the southern-central Andean region, the minor ayllus are thought to represent the different body parts, and these rotate authority among themselves, according to the customary system of annual turns (Arnold 1988:145–48). In practice, while the body-appendage ayllus on the periphery of the major ayllu rotate among themselves, the position of "head" in the sense of overall leadership, symbolized as the central belly ayllu (the *taypi* in Aymara), remains unchanging.

Another striking factor in the contemporary region of Qaqachaka is how ayllu territory, and hence ayllu power, is constituted, in part, through the deliberate placing of heads (formerly human heads and nowadays sheep skulls) in key territorial locations. Thus, the typical ayllu center, in this case the plaza of the Toledan reduction town, or one of its annexes, is marked out by these heads. Similarly, the ayllu borders are defined by a series of heads in key boundary markers or *mujuna* (Sp. *mojón*). A series of ritual practices at different levels (household, minor ayllu, major ayllu, and inter-ayllu), directed toward the well being of each of these units, also reaffirms these configurations of heads during the course of the year.

We propose that this dynamic sense of territorial organization, replicated in numerous cultural practices (dance, weaving, language, ritual, rotation of office) that highlight the changing relations between the ayllu center and the smaller political and social segments on its periphery should be examined with the archaeological data in mind, so that new questions can be asked on the overall siting of objects within emerging political patterns. For example, such fissioning of related small-scale groups is well illustrated in Matthew Bandy's (2001, 2004) recent survey of the Taraco Peninsula in the southern Titicaca Basin, where he charted the clear budding off and merging of small groups throughout the Formative times.

The Ayllu Political Center

Let us examine first the way that the siting of the ayllu center is conceptualized and practiced in the ethnographic present, through this deliberate layout of heads. As in many other instances already mentioned, we shall see how this emerging geopolitical sense draws on the power of captured heads to appeal both to the male warrior nature of head taking and its complementary female counterpart in appropriation, curation, and transformation through weaving.

In Qaqachaka, one of the rituals where this is most evident is the communal *wayñu* song and dance that takes place during the rainy season, in Carnival, and again at the feast of the Immaculate Conception of Our Lady the Virgin, in December. In practice, these *wayñus* are first "stolen" (in the sense of imitated) by stealth by young Qaqachakas from the neighboring ayllus that are their traditional enemies. Then the songs are brought to the central plaza where they are performed first in small groups and later on in the immense *wayñu* dance that gradually develops toward the end of the feast.

Arnold and Yapita explain in their book *River of Fleece, River of Song* (2001: Chap. 2) how this cultural appropriation of the *wayñu* songs from the traditional enemies on the ayllu periphery, and its subsequent remaking as a part of an identity-confirming strategy in the central ayllu plaza, seem to confirm that ayllu identity is constantly enriched from the outside. Here, we can go further and suggest that this strategy of cultural appropriation might have derived originally from the head taking of enemies (though nowadays simply of their cultural patrimony) and the reworking through cultural practice (now as a kind of curation, one step removed) of the power so obtained, in this case to enrich the patrimonial sense of self. This appropriation from the periphery is precisely what should also occur to keep potato seed stock vibrant.

Inevitably, this more *male* reading of the process of appropriating the power of the enemy and converting it into creative performance is aided by the complementary *female* activity of curation through weaving, but now integrated at a symbolic level into the *wayñu* performance. Referring to this creative female aspect of head curation, the weaver Elvira Espejo relates how in the *wayñu* dance performed annually at Carnival in the central plaza of Qaqachaka *marka*, the spatial layout of the plaza dance floor is reinterpreted as a horizontal weaving loom, based on a notional altar situated in each corner of the plaza. (In practice, the colonial church belfry and tower act as two of these altars.) On such feast days, each altar, in turn, is laid out with its own *vara* staff of office and has its own ayllu-head authority in charge. In this way, the altar *varas* in each of the four corners of the plaza act like the four poles of the horizontal loom, each with their ayllu-head guardians. In a homologous layout, a head (nowadays a ram's head) is buried in each of the four streets that join with the four corners of the plaza, in the ritual sites called *iskina*. Once the *wayñu* dance gets under way, the symbolism of the plaza layout takes on the further dimension of a textile in the process of being woven (or else unthreaded) on this giant loom (Arnold 1992:55–58).

As if to emphasize the sense of plenty that is now radiating out from this central ayllu space dominated by heads, and whose power the *wayñu* performance now expresses, the plaza center doubles as a belly. It is filled for the feast with twelve sacks of cooked food (meat, boiled beans and maize, toasted maize, etc.), prepared as collective festive food by the helpers or "guardian angels" of the feast sponsor. In this sense, the plaza takes on the quality of a performative space wherein the power generated from captured heads is transformed, on the one hand, into the aesthetic performance of dance and song, and, on the other, its accompaniment by the sensual quality of rampant feasting and later repleteness from having eaten your fill of produce equally generated from the radiating powers of the originally taken head. This is another confirmation that feasting is a direct consequence of head taking and its enriching aftermath.

The female comparison between the form of the plaza and a giant loom gives rise, in turn, to another: that the overall plaza layout replicates the four corners of an immense mantle (*awayu*) or coca cloth (*inkuña*). During the *wayñu* dance, this immense cloth is thought to become unwound from the corners inward and the colors and designs to be released in this process, inspiring the songs and dances in motion. In this case, two of the plaza sides are like the borders at the ends of the warp (called *pulu*), and the other two like the borders at the ends of the weft (called *k'illpha*).

According to this territorial logic, the performance of the *wayñu* dance in the central plaza during the great festival of the Conception of Our Lady the Virgin (in December) expresses the dynamics of this weaving process as a transformative act that enables the energy or power released in this way to be transferred to the potential production from the land. As Elvira Espejo says, "only an element woven in this way can be grasped by the earth" (personal communication). During the *wayñu* performance, all the different cultural elements—dance, verse, rhythm, and tunes—contribute homologously to this process. Thus, the choreographic movements replicate textile designs in such a way that the heads buried in pots in each corner of the plaza are considered to be like the flower decorations in the corners of the woven mantle that a woman weaves for the feast.

In the very center of the plaza another head is buried in a pot; it is considered to be "flowering" there at the very "heart" of the place. In this way, the territory of the whole ayllu is replicated in miniature in the central plaza, now perceived as an emerging being with its heart and head, and from which other elements are growing. In this solidarity-generating ceremony, then, the four heads in the plaza corners seem to express the geometrical pattern of generative power radiating outward from the key head in the plaza center. The conscious channeling of this power through human creation occurs in what we might call a major geo-ontological enactment of head taking, the conversion of its powers into one's own, and the final irradiating outward of a renewed sense of one's own political power, now superior to that of the enemy (see Figures 4.3 and 4.4).

After victory in warfare, this notion of competitive political relations is expressed by referring to the "domination of one territory over another," but in a language whereby the very earth of the dominating territory is felt to "slide" toward that of the vanquished. This sliding movement, expressed by the verb *jithintayaña* in Aymara, is accompanied by an overpowering of the cultural practices of the enemy Other, when even the victor's aesthetics of weaving invade those of the defeated.

This phenomenon of radiating centrifugal power relations, in its sheer scale, has the capacity to absorb and transform cultural and ritual practice. Finally, cultural and ritual practices themselves become organized by the underlying play between deconstruction and regeneration.

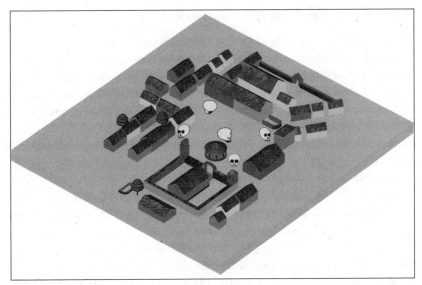

Figure 4.3: Diagram of the Central Plaza of *Qaqachak marka*, with Its Five Buried Skulls

Figure by ILCA with permission to use.

Figure 4.4: Diagram of the Main Plaza of Qaqachaka as an Immense Loom, with the *jira mayku* Spirits Dancing in the Corners

Figure by ILCA with permission to use.

The Ritual of Expanding Power Outward: *Willja*

This strategic placing of heads in the Qaqachaka plaza layout to increase the potential of ayllu political and territorial power is echoed in the agricultural ritual called *willja* that takes place, this time in the huge communally managed fields called *manta*, named like a woman's woven mantle. The aim of this ritual is to encourage greater agricultural yield, not only in the immediate *manta* area but also across the whole ayllu. This is accomplished by "spilling" or radiating outward the ritual power generated in the *manta* ritual, whence its name *willja* (from the verb *willjaña*, meaning "to spread out"). The verb refers specifically to the action of spreading small elements, such as food grains, outward, say on a drying floor (for more details, see Arnold and Espejo 2004). The elements in play in this ritual help us understand how the power of taken heads is thought to contribute to the subsequent radiating yield of agricultural production.

In this ritual, the field layout replicates that of the central plaza and that of the whole ayllu territory. Again, this layout articulates the dynamics of the centripetal and centrifugal forces at play. The social actors involved in the ritual practices that take place there are not passive receptors of predetermined outcomes but vital players in determining future outcomes. The ritual takes place in the aftermath of warfare and has to be agreed on first by all the community in a general assembly; it usually takes place in a field near to an enemy boundary. First, the participants make libations with maize beer. Then a ceramic pot is buried at each corner of this field and a ram's head (*turu p'iqiñay*) placed in each one; the participants in the ritual have already eaten the brains out of these heads. In the center of the field is another pot with a head placed inside. Each pot with its contents is then covered with an upside-down plate. More libations are made "for the growth of abundant potatoes," "so that the *willja* spreads outward," and so on. As in the case of the main plaza, in the past these five heads would have been captured human heads, but nowadays ram heads are used.

Inside each skull is a mixture of ground maize (called *llumpaxa*) and other ritual ingredients (the herb *sanu sanu*, water, flowers, and cinnamon), and each skull is said to be "flowering" there. The meaning of "flowering" here expands beyond the propagation of plants, to apply to the generative and radiating capacity of the heads in their pots. At issue seems to be the idea that the power of these heads is the key motivator of all subsequent plant (and animal) growth in the ayllu territory. The heads have to be kept upright; if they were to be tipped over, "then there would be frosts" and no agricultural yield. The ayllu enemies often take advantage of this idea to tip over the pots and heads from the ritual and so thwart their rival's annual production.

The objective of this ritual is to cure the diminishing "health" of the community," especially after an episode of warfare, with a more robust and expansive sense of "health" in the coming period of agricultural production. In this context, "health" or *salura* (borrowed into Aymara from the Spanish) is a specifically regional reworking of the Spanish term in the context of war and its aftermath. The key idea of *willja* is that the potentiality of new agricultural growth derives from the potent energy inherent in the brains of trophy heads captured in war. The power of the *willja* ritual then expands outward in a predetermined pattern, from the central skull to the four corners of the field, and thence to all the cultivated fields throughout the ayllu. Attention, then, is focused on the potential radiating yield, accompanied by a renewed sense of "health" derived from having conquered heads and absorbed their contents, rather like the additional interest to be gained after first "banking" the heads collectively in the earth (see Figure 4.5).

This agricultural ritual of *willja* replicates at a wider ayllu level another more modest ritual for "taking out health" (*salur waysuña*), again centered on a sacrificed ram's head, which takes place at the household level. But whereas in the household ritual most attention is on accumulating health by consuming the immediate head and brains of an animal sacrificed in a family setting and the interest of the immediate family in benefiting from its associated radiating yield, here in the wider ayllu *willja* the more generalized sense of

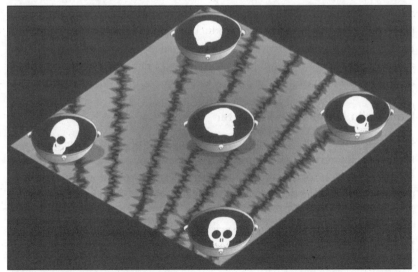

Figure 4.5: Diagram of the Ritual of *willja*. The Communal Field, or *manta*, with Its Five Skulls and Their Containers

Figure by ILCA with permission to use.

communal health is said to be taken "out of the earth itself" (*uraqita*) (Arnold, In press). In this context, the agricultural ritual of *willja* replicates a whole series of other homologous configurations: a similar household level health ritual at a family altar, the general layout of a woman's mantle, and the whole layout of the ayllu territory in which case the four key boundaries would be those of Qaqachaka's neighbors: Laymi, Jukumani, Macha, and Pukuwata, who are occasionally its enemies.

The function of the heads in all of these rituals large and small is to concentrate and then radiate outward the power derived originally from the captured enemy trophy, whether to the ayllu crops or the more immediate well-being of a family. One can see the sense of escalatory economics in these outward radiations of power.

The Ayllu Boundaries

Following this same logical pattern, each of the four main ayllu boundaries of Qaqachaka is in turn reinforced with heads. At the time of the juridical conformation of the various ayllus in the region during the early 17th century (1646, under the Composition of Lands by José de la Vega Alvarado), heads looking outward toward the neighboring territories were placed at key boundary markers, such as Kimsa Mujuna (The Three Boundary Stones). As if to materialize the radiating potential of these ancestral heads, the hair that flowed down behind these heads was thought to become interwoven with the plant roots of the ayllu agricultural production, and so augment their yield. Still today, new animal heads, together with the ritual ingredients of witchcraft for ayllu defense, are carried and buried on the ayllu boundaries during periods of warfare, always facing outward.

From Ayllu Limits to Ayllu Center

In practice, many of these same conceptualizations about the geopolitical layout of ayllu territory are replicated in other cultural practices. It should not surprise us that one of the key practices that reiterates the conformation of ayllu territory concerns the dynamic of weaving techniques, especially in hatbands (that is, items worn on the head).

We already mentioned the observation of the Canadian weaver Mary Frame (1991) that headbands (*wincha*) in ancient Andean cultures, such as Paracas, provided the structural templates that were replicated in all other garments. The continued practice of this kind of phenomenon in modern contexts seems to confirm the presence of a similar pattern of ideas—the common element among them perhaps deriving from the way that the taking of heads from enemies on the periphery was thought to trigger off a set of causal relations in the central aspects of social and political life. In making these former textiles, the weaving technique for these ancient figures begins on the outside of the headband and works inward toward its central axis. Illustrations of this technique can be found in the concentric and uncentered rhomboid in the details of the headbands from Paracas (and Nasca), in which the visual effect corresponds to the compound patterns of interlaced threads, patterned as if they took a tubular form. Figure 4.6 shows how the border threads are tied into an interlaced pattern (if we use Frame's terminology, 1991:132, 133, Fig. 4.18).

In modern practice, according to Elvira Espejo, this image replicates a territorial dimension with geopolitical connotations. It is as if the weaver is "thinking of the ayllu boundaries" and then "moving toward the ayllu center," the central part of the main village plaza, where the new seed is produced each year. Her remark expresses a parallel female concern with appropriating alien energies from the outside and then remaking them in the geopolitical center, where their transformation is perceived as the new seed for agricultural production. In this case, not only the female practices of curation are in play but rather a whole female sequence of appropriation-transformation through weaving.

The Postwar Remaking of Regional Relations between Ayllus

This geopolitical aspect of the dynamic play between ayllu boundaries and ayllu centers, and so of articulating centripetal and centrifugal tendencies, organizes other cultural practices concerned with remaking the relations between the ayllus within the region, after an episode of warfare. Despite the seriousness of their objective, many of these practices are light hearted. For example, this process of political reconsolidation is generated through the enactment of dance choreography performed by young people on the borders between ayllus, with the aim of bringing an end to the boundary disputes over land between ayllus. Here again, the transformations of warring practices into peaceful ones is accomplished through creative cultural practices that rechannel the alien powers formerly appropriated in the head taking of warfare into new and wider geopolitical relations between ayllus (Arnold and Espejo 2004).

This reinterlacing of formerly enemy ayllus is performed in the dances called *achak k'illpha* ("mouse marking") and *sawu tila* ("weaving loom") at the end of the feast of San Juan in June. Adolescents of neighboring ayllus that were previously in conflict go to a strategically sited hill (one lies between Qaqachaka and its neighbor Condo; another is sited between Qaqachaka and its more

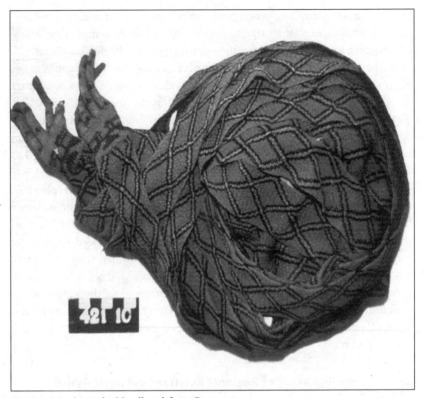

Figure 4.6: A *wincha* Headband from Paracas

Complete headband, top view, with an image of three interlaced strands from the Museo Nacional de Antropología, Arqueología e Historia de Perú, Lima. The headband is still wound in the turbanlike form in which it was worn.

After Frame (1991:Fig. 4.10). "Structure, image, and abstraction: Paracas Necrópolis headbands as system templates." Reprinted from *Paracas art and architecture.Object and context in South Coastal Peru*, Ed. Anne Paul (Iowa City: University of Iowa Press, 1991). Published originally in Paul (1983:Fig. 3). Photograph courtesy of the University of Iowa Press.

formidable enemy Jukumani), taking dung with them as fuel for bonfires to keep themselves warm. There, on top of the hill, they form two lines of dancers, one of girls and the other of boys, like the loom poles of a textile in the process of being woven. In the dance, the adolescents make complex interlacing movements similar to the structure of macramé. The line of girls interweaves with that of the boys, with the aim of interlacing the boundaries of the neighboring ayllus in conflict, represented by the boys (Arnold and Espejo 2004:354). The girls say that their aim is to "sow seeds on these boundaries so that they sprout by the next Carnival time." Again, the female preoccupation here is to reintegrate the boundaries ruptured in warfare by weaving a larger territorial configuration through the complex dance movements. Their attention is focused on transforming the seed-heads captured in battle on the ayllu peripheries into the emerging centers of wider and more peaceful political alliances.

In this complex choreography, the female objective is not only to interweave the boundaries of neighboring ayllus, and so bring to an end any current inter-ayllu conflicts, but also to experiment collectively with creating new textile designs conceived in dance that will come into being the next Carnival. By creating these new textile figures, together with their complex weaving structures, the young women are able to interweave the ayllu boundaries at a regional level, and incorporate therein many more nested, segmented communities. In this sequence of aesthetic transformations through dance, there are *two* key figures related to warfare and its aftermath upon which other variations are made. One is that of interlaced threads, triggered by the two opposed lines of dancers, which serves as the principal image of the ayllu borders. The other is that of a trophy head, created in the depths of cloth configured imaginatively by the complex dance steps, which later serves as a seed-image that will sprout in the period of regenerating production in the war's aftermath, beginning with the rituals of sowing that take place in the central plaza of Qaqachaka territory.

Again, these geoanatomical concepts of territory seem to derive from a wider regional territorial logic in which the generation of new productive forces stems from the remains of the enemy dead, and in which the trophy head serves as a primordial seminal element. Another aspect of all this is that ritual practices seems to be directed specifically at the reunification of the dispersed elements of a common body, in which the various actions of dance, offering, libation making, or weaving interlace the parts of a whole that has been sundered in warfare (see Figure 4.7). The overall dynamic of these movements seems to focus on the interlacing of boundaries with their respective heads, whether in times of battle or the dances of pacification, to appropriate the forces (called *ch'ama*) of the enemy Other and then return with this additional energy to the ayllu center to recreate new definitions of identity and being in the postwar period.

A final question at the level of the major ayllu is how the driving force behind the dynamics of geopolitical expansion is conceived. Evidently, at this regional territorial level, this driving force, just as in the more general expansion of cloth, is conceived as the movement of the tiny warrior beings called *jira*

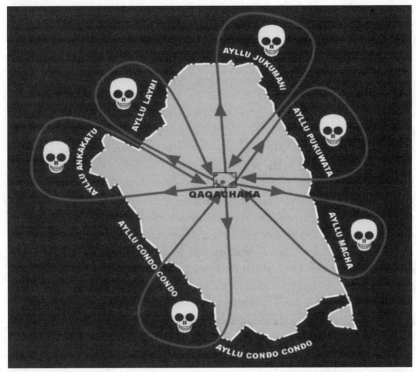

Figure 4.7: Diagram of the Major Ayllu of Qaqachaka. Going to the Boundaries and Returning with Trophy Heads

Figure by ILCA with permission to use.

mayku. We described earlier how weavers deliberately channel the forces of these beings, once they are trapped in the mesh of weaving looms or agriculture fields, toward the productive period of the year during the rainy season until it is over. At the wider territorial level, too, the energies of the *jira mayku* are appropriated during the rainy season until their creative tasks are spent. For example, their dance motion is thought to weave together the plant roots to generate more agricultural yield, inspire weavers to combine threads in cloth, and so contribute to the vegetative covering of the ayllu as well as inspire men in warfare to carry out the dangerous deeds of head taking. Once these tasks are over each year, the *jira mayku* are dispatched from the ayllu, precisely from the piles of stones called *taqawa* where the trophy heads were customarily laid out for display. They are simultaneously dispatched from the whole earth to return to the dark lakes of the Milky Way (sometimes called the "war path of women"), until their return with the rains, a year later (Arnold and Yapita 2001:160, 2006:152, 249).

In these dances and ritual events, we can see how cultural practices focused on heads gather and radiate a fecund power throughout relatively acephalous groups. These practices control and channel both constructive and destructive forces, at times generating their expansion and at others their contraction as the different groups interact at distinct levels of the regional social system.

The Major Ayllu within a Wider Andean State

Now let us turn to the ways that the major ayllu unit might have functioned within a still wider political unit, that of a state or regional system of political power (for example, when the various ayllus of the region of Qaqachaka were integrated briefly into the Inka state). We shall see that this level of integration, too, draws on the power of heads in various ways, not only according to the ritual evidence, but also to the heresay of oral tradition.

One of the ways in which this integration was accomplished was through ritual. We already mentioned how the Inka state's determination to control rain-making in an uncertain environment throughout the whole empire sought to guarantee the production of different crops at distinct ecological levels. This determination motivated a keen interest in the regional rainmaking rituals directed at the guardian mountain shrines. Many studies have shown how, in the past, the sacrificial offerings found on high mountain peaks, including human and especially child sacrifice (for example, at Cerro el Plomo, near Santiago in Chile), seem to have been part of this interest in promoting rain.[25] Alan Kolata (1996) has shown how even today, the rituals of sacrifice at the shrines of the regional *wak'a* and other guardian mountains around the site of Tiwanaku acknowledge the social memory of this wider regional political presence. We mentioned earlier, too, how the widest rounds of libations in Qaqachaka often record Cusco as a historical source of political and ritual power.

Another way in which the shifted alliances of regional polities were strengthened was through a nested hierarchy of dual male and female functions. Let us give four examples of this gendered duality.

In the first, the moiety system that still survives today is nominally gendered. The upper moiety or *patxasaya* is male, whereas the lower moiety or *manqhasaya* is female. Historically, these moiety divisions denoted different functions in warfare: the upper moiety consisted of the warriors, whereas the lower moiety carried their weapons and food, as women do.[26] Still, in the rituals centered on the main plaza and its four corners, these key *saya* divisions refer primarily to these warring functions, since the warriors from each *saya* enter the plaza by a specific corner, oriented toward the direction of their own minor ayllu.

A second example of this duality is the traditional exogamous division of wife givers (female) and wife takers (male), and the reciprocal husband givers (male) and husband takers (female), in the wider patterns of matrimonial exchange. This is overlaid on the ayllu system, which also has important components concerning warfare between groups that hark back to the Inka occupation (Arnold and Yapita 2004:470–71).

A third example is the gendered division of ritual practice, assumed by man and wife authorities, whereby the man is charged with representing the mountains, and the woman, the earth. Similarly, male authorities are charged with rainmaking rituals and female authorities with rituals associated with the land.

A fourth example, particularly pertinent here, is how language maintains this dual system of political power. For example, both song and the ritual speech of authorities are characterized by a parallelism of semantic couplets that reaffirm this gendered identity (Arnold and Yapita 2001:118).

Our argument is that this male-female complementary dualism characterized the dynamic relations between the political center and its constituent peripheral subterritories. Again, this gendered duality was expressed in a number of different ways that draw on the power of heads. It is expressed at times in the terminology of a nested hierarchy of political units conceived as male wrappings (ayllu, *marka*) within female wrappings (*kuntur maman tapa*, *wirjin cabildo*, *tayka comuna*). Historically, the outer male domains might perhaps have fed the conceptually female center through the delivery of harvest tribute, and the heads they had taken. In any case, each subdomain of the wider unity was conceptually ordered in terms of conceptual female and male categories. The constitutive model of the indigenous polity therefore embodied a dynamic symbolic system in which key contrasts of center/periphery, civilized/wild, and female/male provided the basis for the reproduction of a wider political formation.

Territorially, regional ayllus such as Qaqachaka were also brought under the dominion of Cusco by being integrated into the common communication system of Inka highways and way stations, called *tambo*, based on an older system, probably developed by Tiwanaku in the south-central Andes and Wari in the central Andes. The *tambo* way stations, which also controlled food and supply deposits, are said to have been sites where the heads of conquered groups were buried. Again, the potential radiating yield achieved by incorporating conquered groups into a wider political domain, derives from the power of accumulating heads, banked in strategic places. Meanwhile, the storage deposits above ground (*qullqa*, Hispanicized as *colca*) served as visible evidence of this banking power of the Inka Empire.

A third way in which the consolidation of political power would have drawn on heads and their powers is through the accounting mechanisms such as the knotted *kipu* (Aym. *chinu*) used to document the flow of information, labor, and goods within the control of a more centralized polity, such as Tiwanaku or the Inka state. Let us turn finally in this first section of the book to examine how the textual forms of state bureaucracy replicated head management as a vital part of this information flow.

Early State Bureaucracies and the Management of Heads

Weaving and *Kipu* Practices at the Service of the State

It is our contention that these early accounting mechanisms would have been in the hands of the precursors to a bureaucratic class, initially the managers, stewards, or curators of accumulating heads. For example, Topic (2003) writes about this transition from stewards to bureaucrats in Chan Chan (in the Moche River Valley), where architecture, too, was at the service of this information flow. Both in Wari and the Inka Empire, this position seemed to pass to the hands of the *kipukamayuq* or *kipu* holders, who served as the official accountants, and then to Western forms of writing and documentation (Arnold and Yapita 2000:73–75).

In these bureaucratic developments, the later practice of *kipu* keeping would have drawn on the earlier practices of accounting, while systematizing them at increasingly complex levels. In this bureaucratic context, Arnold (2000, 2005) has put forward the argument that the origins not only of weaving but also of the knotted threads called *kipu* derive from trophy heads and their hair. In this context, bureaucratic procedures seem to derive from the subsequent elaboration of the cultural (and curation) practices concerning their elements (the counting, weaving, braiding, whipping, and knotting of the pendant hair) as accounting mechanisms.

The use of numerical *kipu* as mechanisms of state documentation during the Inka period is well attested. According to the evidence, this documentation drew on both the numerical possibilities of the *kipu* (now based on a decimal system) as well as other forms of codification (by color, knot placement, forms of twisting, etc.) that permitted the denotation of populations as well as the amounts of produce, animals, and so on stored in key locations (see, for example, Urton 1994, 2003). Importantly, the *kipus* registered the annual yields of production, allowing a documentation of improvements or setbacks to production in certain territories under Inka command. There were also narrative *kipus* whose coding permitted the documentation of genealogies, the great deeds of Inka political leaders, the narrations and songs considered sacred by a priestly caste, and so on.[27] Although *kipu* keeping reached its apotheosis under the Inka state, a similar use of knotted threads has been documented for earlier cultures, especially the Wari and Tiwanaku states (Conklin 1990:26, 37).

Although the way that weavings might have documented similar cultural and material resources is still not fully understood, evidently common systems of codification were in play. In her book *El tejido andino. Un libro de sabiduría* (1994), Gail Silverman documents the case of the modern woven bags called *taleǧa* in Spanish and *wayaqu* in Quechua (equivalent to the *wallqipu* of Qaqachaka) in the Cusco region of Qeros (Peru), where the width and color of the stripes denotes the quantity and kind of agricultural goods produced there, much in the same way that *kipu* threads were color coded and grouped (Silverman 1994:102–11). This supports the idea of continuities between modern community accounting through textiles and earlier ways of managing such documentation procedures.

We go a step further to propose that the earliest forms of managing such documentation procedures might have arisen from the direct use of heads as the main *kipu* cord, or the foundational edge of a weaving called *pulu*, whereas their pendant hair was used to codify and measure quantity and quality. Hence, the subsequent storage practices and periodic use of the earliest "documents" of this kind, whether as knotted or whipped threads, or different kinds of cloth, would all have entailed at some original stage the direct use of heads (hung from poles or strung across looms) to serve the interests of a particular political class.

Supporting clues for this possibility can be found in the ways in which *kipu* were stored. In a 1990 article, Conklin suggests that both the Middle and Late Horizon *kipus* (later than AD 1400), in their rolled up form, resembled "conical fistfuls wrapped up in a helicoid form," and describes how these had to be unwrapped in order to be read (Conklin 1990:22, Fig. 2). However, a closer analogy to the form of the rolled-up *kipu* might be that of a trophy head, as shown in the following illustrations by Guaman Poma de Ayala (see Figures 4.8 and 4.9).

Today in the region of Qaqachaka, as we have seen, the cultural practices directed toward the communal or household chests of wood or hide that within living memory contained knotted *kipu* seem to replicate former practices directed toward the curation of heads. For example, in the vocalizations offered during the libations for "good luck" when the communal *kipus* were stored in these boxes, the relationship between heads and *kipus* is alluded to. In its rolled-up form, a *kipu* is called "a head" (Aym. *p'iqi*). Before putting the *kipu* in the box, the owner has to pass smoking bittermint over it, and lubricate it with llama fat; if he does not, then it is in vain, and nothing will be produced, neither food crops nor animals. There, out of sight, the *kipu*, as a kind of head, is considered to have the power to regenerate things, but only if it is curated

Figure 4.8: Guaman Poma's Drawing of a Provincial Administrator Holding a Wrapped *kipu* and Another *kipu* Unwrapped

In Guaman Poma de Ayala, *Nueva corónica y buen gobierno* (*ca.* 1615:f.348).
Courtesy of Fondo de Cultura Económica, Lima, Peru, p. 263, (from GKS 2232 4to).

properly first to set these transformations into motion. According to the shaman Don Domingo, the very box itself (rather like a mountain chest) would act as the "foundation" (*simintchixay*) of all the elements produced there, of which the *kipu*-head is the regenerative trigger. But first there must be a final toast

Figure 4.9: Guaman Poma's Drawing of an Inka Warrior Holding a Trophy Head as if It Were a *kipu*
In Guaman Poma de Ayala, *Nueva corónica y buen gobierno* (*ca.* 1615:f.194).
Courtesy of Fondo de Cultura Económica, Lima, Peru, p. 144, (from GKS 2232 4to).

before introducing them inside the box, beseeching the threads to produce offspring of various kinds (Arnold and Yapita 2006:242–43).

Through this ritual process of making libations and generating luck (by focusing on the knots), the *kipu* becomes retransformed into a procreative "head" with the capacity to "give heads" to all the baby products (the *wawas*) of the following agricultural year. In this case, the ritual actions and words that the *kipu* inspires have the capacity of "turning the clock back," to reconvert (or remetamorphose) the *kipu* into a generic head—from which *kipus* seem to have derived historically—as well as constituting its capacity to cause other heads to proliferate. "Having a head" in this context describes the growing condition of the ripening food crops, just before the full production of the harvest. Don Domingo explained how having a head is "lucky": it produces ideas in words, and generates another cycle of production. Note the similarity between this complex of ideas concerning food plants being transformed into heads and vice versa and Proulx's key metaphor concerning trophy heads among the Nasca (Proulx 1999:7).

The power of guarded *kipu* knots, then, does not just denote productive yield in a coded arithmetics in which the knots express quantity. Rather, this power is part of a kind of banking potential, whose accumulated curation procedures (libations, anointments, etc.) contribute to the level of a sort of accumulating interest rate. This, in turn, can be channeled either to agricultural or pastoral production or to the very curation power of its owner to increase his ability to generate the words that accompany this process.

It is our contention that this kind of activity of channeling the power derived from trophy heads was at the heart of many of the rituals of early states centered in accounting practices, especially those included in public ceremonies. This would have been the case for the Inka *kipukamayuq*, as well as for *kipu* keepers of Wari and Tiwanaku, and perhaps even of Chavín and Nasca, to name a few concrete examples.

Conclusions

In this first section, drawing on the contemporary ethnography of a specific region in the highland southern-central Andes, ayllu Qaqachaka, we have illustrated the case of a predominantly centrifugal and expansive political system. We know relatively little about the distant origins of the region, although some archaeologists propose that skirmishes with lowland groups might have been a feature of the region since the Late Intermediate Period. Nevertheless, historical evidence describes how the insertion of the region into the Inka Empire seems to be characterized by the Inka state having used a local warrior culture to serve as its belligerent vanguard against other ethnic groups on the periphery of their expanding empire. We argue that head taking on the external frontiers of the Inka Empire, managed by this regional warrior culture, has characterized the region to this day. We showed how the complex warfaring and ritual practices surrounding head taking and head curation ensures that their powers are appropriated and put to the use of the local ayllu in a new round of productive activities.

Regarding the wider research questions of possible differences between the treatment of ancestral and enemy heads, and how we might identify them, we note that if there is a continuum between these practices, then this might happen only after the conversion of "enemy heads" into "own heads" through ritual activity, curating of one kind and another, and, importantly, the accompanying activities of weaving, predominantly in the hands of women. These transformative practices are consciously enacted at different levels as part of the wider cultural practices of forming and affirming identity, whether in the domestic sphere when a warrior and weaver set up their household, in the premeditated geopolitical conformation of the layout of the central ayllu plaza and its relation to its peripheries, and, as was shown in Arnold and Yapita's book *The Metamorphosis of Heads* (2006), even in the modern-day rituals of schooling.

In each case, these gendered transformative practices also form a part of the dynamic interface between wider centrifugal (outward-looking) and centripetal (inward-looking) tendencies, where the shifting alliances of regional polities are articulated through the nested hierarchies of dual male and female functions. Until now there has been more research and general clarity on the male functions in Andean political life. The new model we put forward helps clarify the female functions as well as the feminine symbolism at play in this larger political setting. It is not just that women weave or cook at home as complementary female activities to those of men. We should now take into account the nested hierarchy of dual male and female functions in moiety organization, in the geopolitical practices of locating heads strategically and ensuring their efficacy in cloth (that is, in managing the relations between centers and peripheries, in rainmaking rituals, and those directed toward the local *wak'a*), in the relations between warfare and wider matrimonial alliances, in the division of gendered labor in ritual and political practice in general, and in the use of language to reaffirm these gendered identities.

We showed how the enormously ritualized elaboration of this warrior-weaver culture over the centuries has meant that the symbolism of heads has become transposed into many other domains of ritual, economic, social, and political life, especially into the powerful symbols of office of the ayllu authorities, such as the *vara* staff of office, or the small woven bags that hang like heads from the waist or shoulder. This means that the gendered parallelism that exists today may even be a result of the long-lived, ongoing, and intimate relationship between head taking and other cultural activities, such as weaving.

Similarly, the parallelism between the qualitative and quantitative aspects of warfare and its aftermath has shaped Andean counting practices and a wider set of gaming practices in general: in the *yupana* counting boards and *taptana* gaming boards, in *kipu* or *chinu* threads, and in the host of games of chance played with dice of one kind and another. In each case, what we have called the "spirit of calculation," with its modern counterpart of a highly ritualized focus on "luck" and "increase," seems to derive from the practices of dividing booty and the practices of judging the value equivalence of commodities in warfare, where previously head taking played a vital role.

Let us now move on to consider the historical roots of these cultural practices, from an archaeological perspective.

Part II

The Archaeology of Andean Head Taking and Power

In Part II, we examine the ways that practices centered on heads might have contributed to the formation of early Andean polities. In our study of how certain power structures might have constructed social identity and social life over the long term, we look at specific archaeological examples that point to the importance of practices concerning heads as consolidating factors in the political domain. There are hints that attention to human heads and bodies, and the meanings associated with them, was not only at the very center of early community life, but also of early political formations. The archaeological evidence suggests that this is manifested in several locations by 2000 BC.

The archaeological examples we present, although illustrating a diversity of activities, nevertheless imply the strong continuity of a constellation of beliefs concerning the head as an instrument of power, punctuatedly through time. Crania are not always uncovered in excavations. Nevertheless, the long-term focus on the body and the many images of the head suggests to us the use of those concepts of corporeal power concentration discussed in the first section. Our aim here, then, is to track the potential importance of heads in past political settings. Our examples include the material use of crania, heads still with bodies, heads now without bodies, and the more general iconographic settings of images or carvings of heads. We are aware that in these different examples the heads could have been curated from multiple sources: they could be the crania of actual ancestors, but they could also have been taken from war captives or simply from unknown burials and curated because of their inherent power, as is common today.[1]

Although it is not always possible to identify direct associations of meaning in archaeological settings, some situations allow for more clarity, and it is these that we shall focus on here. So we shall widen the discussion to include the uses of both ancestral heads as well as those captured from enemies in warfare, identifying the differences when possible.

We concentrate on *three* regions with their distinct histories: the south-central region, which we have already discussed at length in an ethnographic context, the central Andes, and the north-central coast. The historical trajectory of each of these regions, although revealing unique political developments, draws on the imagery of heads in each case. This allows us to trace how some of the same themes presented in Part I might have been present in each area, although they were enacted in a distinct configuration of cultural practices.

Heads and the Consolidation of Andean Political Power

First we present some general theoretical points that should be taken into account when we address an archaeological perspective on heads. We have insisted until now that the recurring patterns of territorial conformation, the power relations at play, and their associated imagery are organized around personal, familial, and corporeal aspects, especially the place of human bodies and above all heads. This is the case with both the principal authority figures of emerging polities as well as with the units of families and groups that made up these polities, whether in a segmentary and nested dispersed political structure or a more centralized hierarchical system.

Historian Susan Ramirez (1996) comments that as late as the Inka Empire, the center of the Inka universe was not a place but a *person* who was itinerant; traveling to the different ceremonial centers recreating the empire through his movements, ritual, and presence. The Inka himself also had many doubles, in carved images and textiles, even sending out a representative to the provinces decked out in his regalia—implying that he could be in more than one place at once to be recognized, honored, and fed—through which he, in turn, fed his people, keeping the cycle of regeneration going throughout the realm. This iconic personage regenerated the world by personifying transference and exchange between the spirits of the earth and the living. He did so especially through feeding and being fed from the largesse of the ancestral dead in different territories.

In this sense, the leadership of the Inka was embedded in, and based on, memories of past rituals, propagated through repetition and long-term resonances that were tailored to the different conquered ethnic groups. But the real evidence of an Inka presence was expressed through his body, particularly his head, as these became the focus of imperial power. It is no surprise that a head was placed on the top of the Inka mummy bundles when they were transported, to remind all of the power of the Inka's entity, focused in the head, as illustrated in one of Guaman Poma de Ayala's drawings (see Figure 5.1, from Guaman Poma de Ayala, *ca.* 1615). At the heart of many Inka rituals that constructed their political power were human dramas of death and regeneration, transposed into other levels of meaning and cultural practice, just as we have argued for the cultural practices of today. Many of these rituals of conquest, whether of planting or calling the rains, required the presence of the Inka's body. The very power of these rituals expressed this cycling of hierarchical largesse, creating a sense of almost forced feeding of the population under Inka dominion, thus providing the power of regeneration.

The Dual Political Forces that Patterned Past Community Formation

The archaeological record has its own particular perspective on political formations. In terms of political structures, the Andean past, like the present, displays evidence in different moments for both steady small-scale, long-lived, and dispersed centrifugal polities that tend to reject any centralizing tendencies as well as more overtly centralizing, aggressive, and centripetal tendencies. The first kind of polity is characterized by more dispersed segmentary or nested models of political organization, whereas the second can lead to larger, more centralized and hierarchical polities. In a classic article of 1988, Schaedel discusses these two political trajectories. More recently Chase-Dunn and colleagues (1997, 2001), drawing on world systems theory, have taken up the theme again. In each case, these studies make a case for both trends being present throughout Andean history. This seems to be the case for the powerful, and long-lived polities such as the Moche-Chimu and Sican as well as for the Wari and Tiwanaku.

The less centralizing segmentary political forms can be found in many regions across the Andes, where long-lived small polities with stylistic continuities show little evidence of hierarchical power concentrations. Within each distinct history, ebbs and flows of power concentrations suggest evidence of both segmentary as well as expansive forces at work. For example, the tendency for expansive political power is documented in historical accounts of the strong forms of organization underlying Inka imperial conquest and examples of Inka direct rule. There are also regions where the Inka maintained what is called indirect rule, using less overt reorganization (D'Altroy 1992).

Figure 5.1: Guaman Poma's Drawing of a Dead Inka Being Carried on a Litter
In Guaman Poma de Ayala, *Nueva corónica y buen gobierno* (*ca.* 1615:f.256).
Courtesy of Fondo de Cultura Económica, Lima, Peru, p. 190, (from GKS 2232 4to).

There are simultaneous accounts of constant rebellions in certain regions throughout the empire during the Inka's reign, evidence of an active desire to resist political centralization. The Wanka/Sausa were a case in point. D'Altroy (1992) mentions how, after a brutal conquest, regular visits by Inka armies, as well as the siting of relocated mitimae communities in the region (state representatives living among the conquered populace) near the large Inka settlement of Xauxatambo, seem to have dampened the centrifugal break away tendencies while strengthening the centralizing imperial ones. Documented litigation proceedings also illustrate how many local lords went to Spanish courts to claim back their group's territories, once the Inka fell.[1]

We have already suggested that these opposing forces are often part of a wider cycle of predatory and reconciliatory practices concerning territorial expansion and consolidation through wider alliances. Now we turn to the archaeological data to chart the evidence of these trends. Our task is to understand how social and cultural practices involving heads might have dovetailed with these political power developments. One goal of our inquiry is to consider the power shifts and meaning structures that wove people together, both in the past and the present, whether in large polities or in community- or ayllu-level social configurations.

Certain assumptions are already evident in the literature. For example, there is much to support the idea that underlying these long-lived polities was the strength of kinship, group, or ethnic identity, usually played out in two or more social units in any one past group (that is, in regional forms of duality, often manifested in periodic gatherings to honor the dead). These activities reflect the centripetal, inward tendencies of communion and sharing through kinship memorialization that Connerton has drawn our attention to in his book *How Societies Remember* (1989). However, it is still necessary to consider whether this duality is primarily "structural" (in the sense of having dual moieties of "above" and "below" that are respectively "male" and "female" as part of a balanced duality) or whether this dual pattern is really the result of previous aggressive patterns, whereby one of the two groups is now subordinated to the other. Remember how, in *Structural Anthropology*, Lévi-Strauss was forced to consider this aspect in relation to the dual patterning of Bororo settlements in the Brazilian lowlands (1967:Chap. 8).

We have shown how the head, in its material and symbolic dimensions, epitomizes in some contemporary Andean groups the essence of regeneration in the cycle of life and death, particularly through periodic cycles of warfare followed by episodes of peace. We now show how these regenerative powers of the head might also have been central to community identity and polity maintenance in the past as well as to the expansion of certain polities. Our purpose is to trace how these concepts, represented in crania, were made manifest through time.

Heads of State

From an early date, the various sociopolitical developments evident in the archaeological record reveal how the head became a symbol not only of the leadership of a family or larger grouping, and therefore of authority and power, but also of the first and founding ancestor of a group. In this sense, power relations are closely dependent on and articulated with social relations. The possession of heads here expresses the power of life through rejuvenation and increased fertility, as well as the identity of the family or descent group—or perhaps groups, in a more bilateral pattern. In this social context, the early practice of grouping together ancestral heads would have brought people together to celebrate regional or descent group activities at a more corporate level.

In this section, then, we examine the role of heads as emblems of consolidating ancestral power in the political situations we find archaeologically, not just of appropriating alien forces. A recurring theme that we turn to, as a way of understanding this difference between practices focused on heads taken in warfare and those focused on ancestral heads, is the distinction drawn by Fausto between centripetal political systems and centrifugal ones (2001:533–37). This difference concerns how groups gained or maintained political power. Also defined by Fausto, this kind of political activity was generated either within the community or without.

Modern Qaqachaka provides an example of the adquisition of power from without. We saw in that context how an expansive centrifugal system demands the regular, renewed adquistion of forces from outside the group to replenish first the ayllu center and then gradually the sphere of one's own group identity. This was done though capturing heads in warfare, thus renewing the growing cycle of both people and potatoes. However, it is possible that historically, there were more centripetal systems that demanded instead the vertical perpetuation of identities, whether through matrilineal or patrilineal descent lines. In this genealogical context, the focus is on a closed cycle of transmission between the dead and the living of the same group, instead of the dead and living of different groups. Here, then, the transmission of names and spiritual renovation, whether matrilineal, patrilineal, or both, is passed down within the same group, bounding and renewing local social relationships.

This is the case today in certain centripetal and generally pacific societies that emphasize the importance of initiation rituals, for example, in the lowland Tukano groups of the Alto Río Negro and Vaupés, such as the Barasana, and the Ge initiation cyles of the Xingu region of Amazonia that Fausto describes (2001:466). These initiation cycles seek to develop masculinity and warrior status in young men. They do so through the potency of ancestral remains and the incorporation of ancestral elements into the living, to renew group identity through each new generation. In these rituals, the attention to ancestral remains and the drawing on ancestral powers generate life-giving potency, but instead of focusing on the capture of trophy heads, this potency is transmitted to the hunt, the growth of plants and animals, or the maturity of babies and female fertility (Fausto 2001:466–67). Even so, it is important to note that the dead ancestors are still considered to be partly alien. In addition, they can be considered to have cannibalistic attributes, and they are often represented as jaguars and other predatory animals. .

It seems possible to us that early Andean societies might have practiced this vertical perpetuation of identities in the political centers of a centripetal system of political renewal centered on practices concentrating on ancestral remains, including heads. This would have continued unless there was a shift into a more centrifugal and expansive political system, this time centered in practices concerning the taking of enemy heads. Although both of these sets of practices might have been present at any one time and place, they would have also become polarized in the dynamics of creating and reproducing opposing political formations.

Heads and Ancestral Power

The *Mallki*

The historical record provides some initial clues to the nature of these earlier ancestral practices. For example, historical research on ancestor cults and burial rituals in 17th- and 18th-century central Peru has shown that each family's history derives from a sacred ancestor or *mallki*. These progenitor ancestors are those placed in caves (called *machay*) where people went to ask for their own regeneration.[2] Mary Doyle (1988) makes a case for the burial of many family members together with the one *mallki* in a single cave, toward which the descendants could focus their prayers. These beings would have embodied the mythic creators of a group as the bringers of crops, good yields, and irrigation systems.

These historical *mallki*, like present-day patron saints, would have been remembered as having arrived along territorial markers and key points of origin in a territory (*pacarinas*), often fighting people to gain new land.[3] In contemporary Qaqachaka, the organic term *mallki* actually describes a sapling and seems to form part of the botanical metaphors used to describe ayllu origins, in what has been called a part of the "trunk speeches" of political power elsewhere.[4] These botanical metaphors of growing, rooting, and flowering still form a vital part of Andean languages. They express the idea of dispersal from a mythical origin place, the "rooting in" and marking of a new territory, and the next generation being produced in that place as new "fruit." In Qaqachaka, the wedding songs, too, describe the way a new wife has to set up house with her husband's family, with the added innuendo that, in parallel, a taken head provides the foundation roots for the new household (Arnold and Yapita 2006:129–30). At the time of the Spanish invasion, ayllus were corporate landholding groups that had mutual obligations with the dead ancestors to take care of the territory, resources, and the descent group.[5] These political entities on the ground were the lowest levels of social authority. When Cristóbal de Alborñoz (1989 [*ca.* 1530–1603]) and Father Bernabé Cobo (1988 [1653]) wrote about religious activities in the 16th century, they noted certain types of sacred places, the *huaca or wak'a*, where mummified corpses of former leaders were worshipped and revered. They were talking about a form of worship specific to the ayllu or family group that descended, truly or fictively, from the ancestors. In their descriptions, they note how the descendants curated the bodies with great care between walls, tending them with clothes, adornment, and goblets, and bringing them out to eat, drink, and discuss matters of political interest. This burial type seems to correspond with the ethnohistorical accounts of *machays*, or mummy caves, such as those by Doyle (1988) and Salomon (1995), but also is evident in Late Intermediate Period settlements as found by Hastorf and the Upper Mantaro Archaeological Research team. For example, Salomon notes that, "In the colonial Andes the delimited space of the dead sometimes functioned as a metaphor for the boundedness of the group with its immemorial and ancestral claim to certain geographical resources" (1995:344).

Evidently, these collective practices focusing on group creation myths and their distinct religious ideas served in campaigns to eradicate other local religions in a common territory, examples of which are known from later Inka history. The new origin myths would be accompanied by a material form of worship via the mummy bundles of these ancestors, just as the new saints introduced into a region are accompanied by their ritual paraphernalia, attire, and other attributes.

The communal rituals performed over time around the mummified ancestors, their bones, and the resting place of the bones to record the generative force behind the living kin group would then create sacred places in the new territories. With demographic growth, small family groups, along with their descendants who practiced such rituals, would become nested into larger and larger sociopolitical and territorial units (like the ayllus of today), who each shared a common ancestor. These same nested structures are also expressed at a territorial level, when the higher peaks serve as the main *apus*, or principal authorities, that rule over a large territory that includes multiple groups. The Inka built their empire on this kind of ritual hierarchy, accompanied by a nested hierarchy of ancestral bodies. As part of a centrifugal and expansive political system, these ancestral rituals were just one pole of other Inka practices concerned with head taking and the appropriation of an alien Other.

The archaeological data, as analyzed by Albarracín-Jordan (1996) and Bandy (2001, 2004), suggest that the early stages of the Tiwanaku polity, building on the long Formative Period of interlocking and fluid political developments, were based on a similar nested hierarchy of ancestral bodies.

Remembered Bones

In a regenerative or transformative sense, this power of inanimate things, such as the *mallki* ancestral bodies, can become transposed to living beings through memory, ritual and other cultural practices, in the same economic sense discussed in Part I. In a modern ethnographic setting, Allen (1982, 1988) has shown how ancestral power permeates certain places, activated through the re-membering of the dead. There, the prior corporeality of those now dead continues to play a part in the lives of Andean residents as they live and move through their territory. For Allen, the living members of a community draw on this power to seek well-being from the dead ancestors as well as the continuing productivity of the crops and the animals. Was this, in fact, an old tradition, and what was its influence in political settings?

In practice, the living tend to focus ritually on ancestral bones to seek the continuity of this power. Allen notes that the people of Sonqo (Peru) save the bones of their dead as a focus of power and protection, as well as of identity: "Kept in a niche of a storeroom wall, a skull is said to provide *khuyay* (protection and care) for the room and its contents" (1982:184). These hard rounded skulls are sometimes associated with small, curiously shaped stones called by different names: *illas* (usually little carved animals made out of clay or stone), *qunupa* (or *conopa*, carved stones in the shape of food stuffs), or *inqaychu* (Aym. *jayintilla*, which are bezoar stones from llamas in the shape of heads and potatoes). Allen (1982) suggests that their gloss in English might be "the energy of the living ones." These skulls and stone shapes are periodically honored with presentations and offerings, because they are considered to hold power over the fecundity of the living.[6]

Examples such as these reveal how social identity, as well as the communal capital of the animals and crops, can all be centered in the head of an ancestor or some other representation. But instead of focusing on the power contained initially in the gray matter inside the cranium as in the case of trophy heads, the longevity of ancestral worship shifts attention to the hard bone skulls as the principal seat of power.

The development of these kinds of powers and energies, focused on the worship of heads and other ancestral bones, might well have occurred in

the face of the unpredictable highland climate, with its dangers of bad har-·
vests and erratic rainfall, with intense floods at one extreme and droughts
at the other, many of them caused by the periodic episodes of El Niño (or La
Niña), as well as possible enemy aggression on one's territory. In this context,
heads would have been used to try to keep the world steady and the crops and
animals productive.

Heads and Rains

Indeed, one ubiquitous and dominant theme in Andean patterns of worship
and ritual in general, in both the archaeological and ethnographic record, is
water and water control. We have seen how, in various settings, ritual practices around heads are often related to the control of water. In some settings,
these rituals may have been concerned with keeping the flow constant, as
in the coastal valleys; in others, people were more concerned with controlling
the timing and quantities of rainfall, as in the altiplano. Although we cannot
present all the archaeological evidence for water rituals here, many studies
tend to presume that crania and head images were connected with these pleas
for control over life-promoting water.[7] One problem we face is that in the
ethnographic record the evidence is more ambiguous, so we need to summarize some of its findings in relation to rainmaking rites before moving on to
examine the archaeological data in more detail.

In modern Qaqachaka in Bolivia, ancestral skulls are taken out of the church
by the ayllu authorities and ritual specialists (*yatiri*) at key moments in the year
to call the rains in a drought as well as to calm a particularly torrential period
of rain, when the skulls tend to be exposed much longer. Almost a century
ago, Bandelier found a similar Aymara practice of exposing the skulls from
chullpa tombs to "dissipate the clouds and release the rain" (cited in Llanos
2004:164). In his own community, Don Domingo Jiménez differentiates between the use of *copal* "passed over" skulls to "draw the clouds together" and
bring the rain, perhaps accompanied by libations with local beer, as opposed
to the ritual use of *incense* to diminish the strength of excessive rain, when the
skulls are requested to "rest in peace" (*tiskanst'amaya*).

However, in other parts of the altiplano and along the Titicaca Lake shore,
skulls are *never* used to bring the rain, only in rituals to dispatch the rain after
a period of excessive rainfall. Is there a pattern, then, to these rituals for rain or
for controlling excessive rain and their relation to heads that we can begin to
piece together from the ideas we have presented until now, even at a tentative
level, before going on to detail the archaeological data?

First, there is the overall annual context of seasonal rainfall. In the contemporary Andes at least, there is a marked dual pattern to the year, both climatically

and at a more cosmological level. Broadly, the dry season is considered to be the time of war and destruction, or at least the absence of production, and this season is held to be more masculine. In contrast, the rainy season is the time of revitalization and growth after the time of war and destruction, and this is held to be more feminine. Thus, the major features that we described of a dual cosmological pattern in Part I—of Proulx's two complexes of "death, head-taking, and blood" and "regeneration, rebirth, agricultural fertility" (1999) and Chávez's identification of two distinct rituals, one male and destructive, and the other female and creative (2002)—are perhaps replicated here in the annual cycle. Proulx (1999) even implies that in the early Intermediate Period Nasca there may have been a cosmogonic cultural pattern in which key ritual specialists personified these dual tendencies (seen in the masked figures depicted on their textiles and pottery) of sacrificer and regenerator. It is also possible that in the more uncertain climatic periods influenced by El Niño (or La Niña), these annual cycles got out of step, and longer cycles of time may have taken on these overall identities. But this is just speculation.

Second, what do we know about the current thinking of Andean populations concerning the origins of rain and its relationship to the ancestors, or alternatively to an enemy Other? In one key ethnographic text about ayllu Laymi (Harris 1983), the origins of the rainy season are clearly associated with the ancestors, and their annual coming to the ayllu coincides with the start of the rainy season, currently around the Feast of All Hallows. No bones are taken out or disturbed on this occasion. Participants simply visit the cemetery and make altars to the ancestors and the recent dead in their houses.

The problem is that, again, there is a certain ambiguity here because the devil spirits called *jira mayku*, as spirits of the vegetation associated with the rains, are also held to be present in ayllu Laymi during this time. These spirits are also considered to be both warriors and invading Inkas and are certainly associated with the dead as well as with the premonition of deaths in the coming year. As we have seen, this whole complex of ideas is very similar in neighboring Qaqachaka (Arnold 1992). This would seem to be the essence of the problem: We are dealing with complexes of ideas and the resulting flows of energies addressed in ritual action during the course of the year in which skulls are vehicles of ritual power and creative potential in this flow of events.

Another key Andean ethnography, *Deathly Waters and Hungry Mountains*, by Peter Gose (1994), focused on the Apurímac region of southern Peru, locates ideas about rain in a much wider ritual and conceptual sphere. Here, the *farmers* think that water is circulated through the community's territory, especially through their bodies as they work on the land. They fear the cold mountain waters, associating them with death, while they regard the towering mountains (*apu*) as hungry for sacrificial offerings. In this context, they regard work on the land as a kind of salvation; they sweat human energy, depleting their bodies of moisture, taking them closer to the dry mummified condition of death. Specifically, their sweat returns to the hungry mountains from whence it came, creating an eternal cycle of hydraulic passage continually fed by human ritual intervention.

But again, the overall relations in this hydraulic system are still ambiguous. Clearly, water is associated with an ancestral cycle, but the mountains, as figures of authority, are alternatively considered to be ancestors (and condor spirits) or else as conquering outsiders (the Spanish class of *patrones*). So the enemy here, as Gose perceives it, is the second manifestation of the mountains, the patron class of notables in the wider set of class relations, those who manipulate the commoners' work for their own ends. Thus, water can have two forms of transference—life giving but also death giving.

Gose's ethnography (1994), like many others, does make the connections between the mountains and the dead, and between death and dryness. And this recalls the direct association made in other ethnographies between heads, in general, and dry skulls, in particular, with the mountain peaks. This association also seems to impinge on Arnold's proposition that the origins of *kipus* can be found in the pendant hair of a skull. The terminology for the main *kipu* cord (as an equivalent of a skull) is often related to the word for mountain. Similarly, the pendant cords are often considered to be associated with water and rainfall, and thus with productive potential, from that mountain (see again Arnold and Yapita 2000:344–53). As another variant of this theme, we saw in Chapter 3, with reference to Allen's work on colonial *qirus*, how the spouting *p'axcha* variant of the *qiru* cup is also associated with water flow in general, and with rainfall from the mountains in particular, and how its main bowl is invariably shaped like or decorated as a head.

So, how do the actual rainmaking rituals of today fit into this wider cosmological system and what might they tell us about the past? In the allusions we have already made in Chapter 2 to the rainmaking rituals carried out on the mountainsides of *wak'a* sites in the region of Qaqachaka, generally in February each year, the essence of these rituals seems to draw on the expansive energies derived from reconstituting the carcasses of sacrificed herd animals, and then awaiting their decomposition and metamorphosis into rain clouds. Here, the rain is held to emerge from the decomposed carcasses of the community animals under the charge of the guardian mountains and these, in turn, have important ties to the ancestors. In another set of communal rainmaking rituals that takes place in December in the same region of Qaqachaka as described by Sikkink (1997) and then by Arnold and Yapita (2000:Chap. 7), the essence of these rituals, called *yaku cambio* in Quechua and *uma turkaña* in Aymara, is to collect together water from distinct sources in a specific territory, and, through collective ritual action, promote a more effective circulation of the waters throughout this particular territory to coax the rainfall when desired.

Similar rituals occur throughout the Bolivian altiplano. For example, David Llanos (2004) has described the complex collective, annual rainmaking rituals of the Charazani region, called there *luxchi*, again directed at energizing water circulation; when they are ineffective for any reason, they are further reinforced by a follow-up ritual called *yapachiy*. For his part, Tomás Huanca (1989) has described a similar ritual complex in the region of La Paz, where a local *yatiri* calls on the powers of certain skulls (called *riwutu*) in his possession to communicate first with a round of the regional *wak'a*-like Catholic saints and then to the mountain guardians (or *achachila*) of a vast territory, to bring the rain for the fields.

Similarly, in the water-focused rituals already examined that take place between the rainy and the dry season (and vice versa), or between the periods of office of incoming and outgoing moiety authorities (for example, in those described by Salomon in the town of Pacota, as a part of Huarochirí, in Lima Department, in modern-day Peru), the *comunario* participants concentrate on generating good luck and plentiful production for all, inspired, in turn, by a couple of ancestral skulls that are the "mountain owners of the water." We suggest that these transitional rituals seek to promote luck and plenty for the coming rainy season or the new period of office.

To sum up, in this first group of rainmaking rituals each set seems to play on constituting the expansive and generative nature of the desired water production through concerted ritual action. The idea is to promote and then hold on to a lucky streak. All of this is often directed, in turn, toward the powers held in certain crania. Within this form of a wider dual model, we locate the rituals that focus specifically on the suffering of a contained being within a restricted space. Such dual, dissonant rituals occurred in the mountain chest complex we described in Chapter 2, or even the known instances of human sacrifice, as perhaps ritual reinforcements enacted only in uncertain climatic circumstances (and when all else fails), to achieve the desired efficacy necessary to generate sufficient production for survival.

A second set of rituals is concerned with stopping continuous and excessive rains. It equally centers on the use of bones, in general, and skulls, in particular, but is qualitatively different in kind from the first set of rituals just described. These rituals depend, instead, on a deliberate "ritual inversion" to achieve their efficacy that is quite at odds with the normal process of generative growth. In addition, the association of these rituals in contemporary settings with "black magic" and the layout of "black altars" means that they are *not* carried out by the practitioners of their opposing (or complementary) set of rituals but by other ritual specialists. This second set of rituals also tends to be specific to a difficult moment in any one particular year rather than the annual cycle, although they are also organized by the ayllu authorities and in a collective way. David Llanos (2004) describes two rituals of this kind in the Charazani region, called *chullpa-uma uqhuchiy* or "the exhuming of the *chullpa* skulls," and *chullpapat-plaza chajmay* or "the plowing of the *chullpa* plaza." In both cases, the skulls and bones of local *chullpa* tombs are disturbed and disinterred deliberately in their state of natural decomposition to thwart the excessive rains. This kind of disruptive ritual action is evidently carried out all over the altiplano today, although it has been documented much less in the literature.[8]

In this second case, the skulls are again ambiguous in their identity and origins; they may be considered to be ancestral or alien, depending on the context. They are certainly non-Christian, and in this sense are different from living populations. Our argument in this case is that this second set of rituals is organized more along the lines of war-centered actions, intent on thwarting the normal course of events as a way of forcibly rebalancing ritually the forces already in play. At least in its attention to defensive measures, these rituals also have much in common with attacks of envy by enemies, as we might expect.

To sum up: In the first set of rituals to promote rain, the ritual action is directed toward the bones of the dead who are still intact or toward the ritual reconfiguration of sacrificed bones into a complete carcass again, to achieve the generation of productive desire and good luck. In the second set of rituals, ritual action is directed toward the inversion of this state of completeness, generally through the deliberate disturbing and disorganization of skulls and other bones of the dead to halt rain.

With these brief reflections on the differential relations between heads and rituals concerned with rainmaking, as compared to those for the control of excessive rains, let us now consider the archaeological data to see to what degree material remains might conform with one or the other cranial use.

Ancestral Heads in Archaeological Settings

Archaeology provides abundant evidence that early in Andean history, and surely by the Early Horizon–Middle Formative phase, cultural practices around the head had became a focal point of group activity, whether to call on the powers of the ancestors to help with matters on earth, to call the rains, or simply impel the production of other living things.

Evidence of this kind of activity is found at some of the first edifices in the Initial Period coastal sites (2200–1400 BC), such as Asia. Engel (1963) describes how, under a floor of a special-use room on top of a mound, a cache of eight human heads wrapped in matting was unearthed. This early evidence of curated heads suggests that the residents of Asia perceived their occupation of the land as related in some way to the power that resided in human heads. Whether these are trophy heads or family heads is still unclear. They were clearly meaningful in the construction of this coastal society, as it was increasingly able to mark the terrain with farms and villages in the river valley. This would suggest the presence of a more kinship-based society, where the handling of ancestral remains would have served to perpetuate the genealogical nature of group identity.

This more aggressive symbolic construction of group identity is expressed by the presence of stone heads at other archaeological sites. For example, carved stone heads have been found in altiplano settlements from the Late Formative phase, dating to between 200 BC and AD 300. They are found in special ceremonial buildings at sites such as Chiripa, Kala Uyuni (Qala Uyuni), Santiago de Huata and Titimani,[9] in later Pukara,[10] as well as in the coastal Nasca Valley during the Early Intermediate Period.[11] These carved heads were often associated with images of power, and placed in locations where people congregated. Their placement and existence suggests that they were part of an interest in regeneration. At least around the lake, the stone carvings often were located such that the heads looked out on the lake and the mountains, to promote visual links between the heads and the water giving spirits. Individually crafted tenon heads increasingly occurred in large structures in the Middle Horizon, at Tiwanaku and Wari, placed in walls of semi subterranean enclosures and also in outer walls, respectively. These locations imply a collection of enemy heads to gain power for the residents.

These examples of heads, both inner directed and hidden as well as outer directed and displayed for many to see, as the essences of power and symbolic links to larger nested powers, seem to have played an important role in the politics of the region as well as in the creation and maintenance of society since settled life began.

The significance of heads was probably brought to the fore in social events. However, we propose that the role of such heads, as well as their multiple levels of meaning for the social actors of these former societies, might be interpreted as a part of political practice and not simply as ritual veneration. By reconsidering them in this light, with evidence from the past and from historical and ethnographic accounts, we can begin to reconstruct the ideological and political importance of these practices.

Rituals Centered around Tombs, Body Parts, and Images of the Dead

The ways in which the ancestral dead, rather than the enemy dead, continue to inhabit the lives of the living has an impact not only in social and cultural matters but also in political ones of today. These kinds of impact are evident in ritual and ceremonial examples where certain aspects of the ancestors are present. This is the case especially where the place of bodies is emphasized in rituals and political gatherings, and the presence of the body, especially the head, is vital.

The *Ñatitas* of Contemporary La Paz

A modern example of ancestral body worship can be found today in the context of the city of La Paz in the way that Aymara speakers, especially market women, hold dear a particular skull taken from the general cemetery, to help give them luck and economic success in their businesses. These contemporary rituals shed light on the possible ways that heads were acknowledged in the past.

Martha Sandra Bustillos and colleagues (2005) describe how these skulls, the so-called *ñatitas* or "little turned-up noses," are generally kept at home, wrapped up, or in a small box. On November 8, a week after All Hallows (the eve of which is our Halloween), they are taken to the cemetery in hundreds to be decorated with flowers and addressed with libations and prayers. Sometimes, the skulls are brought out for the household altars earlier, at the Feast of All Hallows (also called All Saints, or All Souls) on November 1 and 2.

However, the main feast of the *ñatita* skulls occurs on November 8, sometimes called the Feast of the *Riwutus* (from the Spanish *devotos*, "devoted ones"), after the human skulls used for worship as well as for general consultation, whether about day-to-day matters or important business enterprises. These heads are also called simply "skulls" (Sp. *calaveras*), "crania" (Sp. *cráneos*) or the Aymara *t'uxlu*. According to Bustillos and colleagues (2005), the skulls in question are usually of people who have died a sudden or violent death and may also include thieves or those involved in contraband, although their precedence may just as well be unknown. This association with violence, theft, and contraband seems to place them in a similar category to trophy heads taken from enemies, rather than from kin. Even so, the relationship with the skulls on a day-to-day basis is familiar and affectionate (as if they have been tamed in some way from their violent origins), and often expands to include complex networks of relations and affines (in-laws) as well as of friendship and acquaintance. Crucially, the main owners of the skulls are women.[12] So, in this modern urban context, we find a similar relationship between heads and their careers as we found in archaeological and ethnographic settings: violent origins, a subsequent transformation into the familiar realm, and then female management.

Bustillos and colleagues (2005) relate how the decoration of these heads on the Day of the Skulls is equally light hearted, some painted in red, some with colorful decorated hats and knitted caps, and many with a cigarette in their mouths (see Figure 5.2). They come in fancy glass boxes, on silver platters, in plastic bags, in shoeboxes, and in baskets. Apart from market women, the skull bearers are often medical students (many of them female), who have become attached to a certain skull during surgical practice. The skulls are also acquired somewhat illegally by the cemetery workers who take advantage of those who default on their cemetery bills by removing the pertinent skull from its niche. The skulls then pass down from generation to generation.

According to Bustillos and others (2005), the sponsors of the Day of the Skulls go with their followers to the main cemetery of La Paz in black mourning dress,

Figure 5.2: *Ñatita* Skull Decorated with Flowers and Smoking a Cigarette
Photograph with permission of Martha Sandra Bustillos, for the student work "Las cabezas de Todos Santos" in the course Duke in the Andes, La Paz, Bolivia, 2005.

carrying their skulls covered with flowers, blossoms, and ribbons, often with an additional garland headdress, in their ornate niche-like boxes, to be blessed by the Catholic priest in the cemetery chapel. The women carry them in bundles, like babies, and the skulls without names are baptized after the mass, the skulls are laid out on tombs, not generally of their own but rather of the other dead (see Figure 5.3). Believers in this rite who do not actually possess a skull stay near the tombs to take part in the celebrations following the mass. The skulls are set out in rows at the base of the tombs, with their names written above them, and a series of libations and prayers is made to them by all those present, with offerings of alcohol (mainly beer and 40% proof), coca leaves, cigarettes, flowers, and crowns. The skulls are also acknowledged by groups of musicians who play music of different rhythms to cheer them: *tarqueadas*, *morenadas*, *kullaguadas*, and so on.

The skulls, meanwhile, are held to listen and respond to the demands people make of them. People who carry out this rite ask the skull owners for the name of the skull and then address themselves to the skull in question, asking for protection, economic security, and for the skulls to help them in legal suits. Another common request is that the skulls help them find robbers and name them through the power of their spirits (or *ajayu*), and so make the

Figure 5.3: *Ñatita* Decorated with Flowers, Laid out on a Tomb after the Mass
Photograph with permission of Martha Sandra Bustillos, for the student work "Las cabezas de Todos Santos" in the course Duke in the Andes, La Paz, Bolivia, 2005.

thieves tremble. The skull owners, in turn, welcome those who come with offerings and tell them stories of the ways the skulls have helped them in family matters. There is always a double edge to these stories, however, since the skulls are extremely demanding on their owners, they are jealous of their time and require constant attention. If the owner should fail to make sufficient offerings, then the skull might turn on its owner and even cause their death. According to Spedding (personal communication), some skulls "fall in love" with their female owners and become tremendously jealous of competing male suitors.

After leaving the cemetery, the sponsors carry the skulls like trophy heads in the streets outside, before returning in procession in funeral cars, equally covered in flowers, with the niche-like boxes placed on the car hood (bonnet). Once they are home, the sponsors and their followers celebrate the skulls, now laid on ornate household altars, replete with bread, food, and drink as offerings, all prepared to honor the Day of the Skulls. The house, too, is covered with black decorations.

Bodily Relations in Architectonic Form

These modern examples also provide clues as to how ritual practices around heads were incorporated into archaeological sites in the Andean region. For example, throughout the prehistoric into the historic period, we find evidence that ritual centers were built around tombs, body parts, and the heads of the dead. The material expression of these bodily relations in architectonic form seems to confirm a preoccupation of the social actors that built them with the powers of the dead and their participation in the politics of the day. Thus, human bodies and heads are common among the things curated in ceremonial-ritual contexts. Here then, bodily relations are homologous with political and even moral relations.

Evidently, the head as a powerful symbol of identity and authority could mobilize not only family or ayllu gatherings but also immense public ceremonies. This is brought home more clearly where the curatorial places include space for large gatherings and rituals, which happens at sites on the coast as well as in the highlands in sunken enclosures. In fact, possibly every mound-plaza we find at archaeological sites could have been charged by power generated from the dead, as there are often caches of heads, stone carvings, or sacrificial bodies in key locations associated with such ceremonial mounds.

Jerry Moore (1996) has shown how a study of these spaces informs us of the size and structure of the group that would have gathered at one time for a ritual or a meeting with the elders. In many cases, the labor force necessary to construct or maintain the larger platform mounds must have been greater that the nearby resident populations, suggesting that folk from a much wider area were called on periodically to pool their labor and construct or refurbish these monuments. The motivation behind this effort could be, as Earle proposes, the ability of such monuments "to be experienced simultaneously by large numbers of individuals" (1997:155). But the political nature of these gatherings could have taken many forms. The Mississippian gatherings in the American Midwest, which Pauketat discusses in his 2001 article, is an example of this undertaking, where a case is made for a community gathering that reconstructs a mound in a communal fashion for those who surely must have also participated in the ceremonies of those spaces.

Such monuments are, then, the materialization of these common experiences directed toward the dead and the powers that they draw on, with all the memories and traditions of the people that constructed them. The material placing of heads in the chambers and niches of these platform mounds implies that these very mounds were thought to draw on their reproductive powers. One such example is Chavín de Huántar, where large transforming human heads were tenoned around the outside of the large cut-stone-faced mound. These heads must have communicated power and shamanistic capacity to the local residents and fear to foreigners.

Another example of a modern monumental acknowledgment of the power of heads is found in Qaqachaka. Arnold (1993:66–67, 75–76) has described how, in its colonial history, the local version of the colonial monumental structures of church, plaza, and *calvario*, around 1562, would seem to have reappropriated these new ceremonial spaces into the meaning system of previous customs, where temple enclosures, plazas, and mounds were the order of the day.

We mentioned earlier how, in the *wayñu* rainy-season songs and dances that take place in the plaza (now reworked as a dance-floor), the participants reinterpret the colonial plaza form as a loom in the process of weaving certain items and then unweaving them, depending on the time of year. We also described how the *wayñu*, as a song and dance form inspired by the dead, is part of a wider identity-creating sequence in which songs are robbed from the ayllu periphery of neighboring ayllus to be later appropriated in a collective reconstruction of identity in the central village plaza. These cultural practices are not only inspired by the dead; the remains of the dead, in particular skulls, were actually buried in key ritual sites in the center and four corners of the plaza to participate in and oversee these activities.

Historically, the *wayñu*, like the *wanka*, was a dance of victory in warfare, where the victors celebrated by literally dancing over the bones of the dead enemy.[13] The plazas associated with the pre-state platform mounds found throughout the central Andes suggest versions of these activities in the shadow of these human constructed mountains. In both modern and past settings, then, the power of the cultural practices in such ceremonial events reconnects the present with important physical places marked by the remains of the dead, jogging the memory while connecting the past to the present for the future. In the next chapter, we turn to a series of examples of this kind of situation, laid out diachronically.

Heads and Andean Political Change from an Archaeological Perspective

Let us turn now to four regional studies, where archaeological evidence of practices centered on heads help us reconstruct the cultural history of political formations.

The South-Central Andes

With reference to the archaeological evidence, we will begin with the southern examples, which are illustrated in Map 6.1.

The South Coast

Paracas

On the Paracas Peninsula on the south coast of what is now Peru, in the Early Horizon Period around 900 BC, concerns with the dead became centered on a series of now famous cemeteries. In these immense necropolises, bodies were interred wrapped with beautifully made woven cloth, many covered with images. This tendency continued into the Early Intermediate Period, from 100 BC through AD 200, when these kinds of textiles were still being buried with elite members of Paracas-Topará society.

This dry southern coastal region was the site of important developments in the Ica and Nasca valleys. The histories of these valleys reveal a sequence of quite small-scale societies, where farming communities were dotted along the rivers, watered from the highland rain-fed rivers. Here, we never

Map 6.1: The South-Central Andes, with Sites Mentioned in the Text
Map courtesy of ILCA, La Paz.

see the development of the large-scale ceremonial centers so prominent in the northern coastal valleys; rather, smaller settlements are the norm. These southern rivers have much less water, and many of the tributaries flow only seasonally. Thus, the inhabitants of this region occasionally had to seek out water, dig wells, and later on build elaborate *qanat*-like irrigation systems.[1] So, not surprisingly, the evidence suggests that both the Ica and Nasca drainages were occupied by people obsessed with water. The populations were never very dense, and, according to Silverman (1993), they were not politically hierarchical. Rather, the populace invested their labor in many beautiful crafts, textiles, ceramics, and geoglyphs, to name the longest lived remains, as well as farming. These people were inward looking, living in segmented, even autonomous communities, coming together perhaps only for the large rituals that focused on protection and water, at Cahuachi or in the pampa between the rivers.

Group cemeteries near the ocean were not new to this region, when we recall the Chinchorro mummies of the Initial Period, located to the south. These group burials go back thousands of years earlier, to river dwellings at the edge of the Atacama Desert. At Paracas, the elaboration of each burial in its distinct wrapping first caught the eye of Peruvian archaeologist Julio C. Tello, inspiring him to launch his systematic investigation. Years later, Mejía Xesspe and Tello (1959, 1979) published details of the now famous structures located in several places along the peninsula, which were filled with individually wrapped mummy bundles (*fardos*). The extremely detailed and beautifully made weavings that enveloped the tightly flexed bodies crammed into buildings that had been residences provide clues to the society of these inland farmers and coastal fisherfolk. Figure 6.1 illustrates the detail and surreal elaboration of costumery that these inhabitants thought important enough to depict for the dead (and see again Figure 1.6). Clearly, the making of these weavings demanded a great deal of time in people's lives, and so were highly important at many levels. These burials, however, were not the only evidence of the dead in this society.

Many bodiless heads have been found in these Paracas and Paracas-Topará cemeteries. Kroeber (1944) describes nine human heads dug up by looters at an Ocucaje cemetery in the Ica Valley in 1942, some of which had carrying ropes projecting from the forehead area of each skull, as in the later Nasca examples.[2] He calls these "trophy heads," after an earlier paper by Tello (1918). Pezzia Assereto (1968:100–02) records a group of thirteen heads buried together in a Paracas cemetery (called Cerro de la Cruz).[3] Five of these heads had carrying cords and most had mask-like preparations with the skin of the faces and hair intact. These heads were then wrapped in layers of cotton before burial.

Figure 6.1: A Paracas Textile with a Figure Holding a Trophy Head

In José Antonio de Lavalle and José Alejandro González García, *The Textile Art of Peru* (1991:79) (Lima: Industria Textil Piura, S.A.). Courtesy of Industria Textil Piura, S.A.

Hundreds of other crania have been found in the Paracas Peninsula cemeteries, especially in the Cavernas burial precinct, although the conditions of their finding, in the back-dirt left by tomb robbers, makes it difficult to say if these heads were buried without their bodies. Many of these crania were missing the lower jaw, like some trophy heads in different parts of the world.

Anne Paul (2000c:73–76) recently questioned the previous tendency to call many of these heads "trophies" and to see the images on the Paracas Necrópolis textiles as "warriors" holding these heads. Paul's painstaking work on over 300 images of bodiless human heads embroidered on the Paracas Necropolis textiles leads her to challenge interpretations of Paracas as a warlike society. According to Paul, there is little representation of fighting on the textiles; instead, these are people dressed as supernatural beings, or perhaps as shamans. Added to this, the number of representations of heads on the textiles is much greater than the number of heads actually found in reality, so the textile representations of heads do not seem to reflect real practices. She divides the images of heads embroidered on the textiles into two types: those with carrying ropes (some 25%) and those carried just by the hair (the remaining 75%). Traditionally, putting a hole through the forehead and attaching a carrying rope has been attributed to captured "trophy" heads. Such captured heads were then carried, hung, or worn as icons of captured power, as discussed in the previous sections. Even so, Paul insists that the evidence is too weak to support any conjecture about whether some of these are trophies while others are ancestral heads (2000c:77).

However, Paul does point out a difference in the incidence of these distinct forms of head preparation over time. In the 300 images of heads in forty-six bundles of study, with proportionally different percentages of textiles present from each time period, she found the following data concerning the overall depictions of the heads. In the Early Horizon epoch 10, 43% of heads had carrying ropes (as the presumed trophy heads) and only 18% of the heads are without ropes. Later, in the Early Intermediate Period epoch 1, 52% of heads have carrying ropes whereas 48% of the heads are without. Later still, in the Early Intermediate Period epoch 2, there are only 5% of heads with ropes and 30% of heads without. These values imply that there were more heads with ropes (the possible trophy heads) in the earlier period and more without (more probably ancestral heads) in the later period (Paul 2000c:76). In addition, Paul points out that the illustrations of both kinds of head on the textiles are disproportionately large in relation to any bodies that were represented.

Both of these tendencies in the archaeological record lead Paul to propose that the heads on the Paracas textiles are not "literal depictions" of human heads but rather "symbols of the intense concentration of power in heads." Here she supports the earlier argument by Tello (1918) that human heads, as the repositories of the "vital essence of living after death," were fetishes. Because of this, "they were depicted over and over again in ancient Andean art" (Paul 2000c:77), conferring supernatural power on those associated with them, who were probably the powerful and/or shamans with whom these textiles were buried. The fact that the illustrations of heads in the textiles do not seem to differentiate between the ones with carrying ropes and those without, and that therefore both types seem to be "symbolically interchangeable," leads Paul to conclude that the overriding central idea in these illustrations is that of the "collective importance of heads" (2000c:77).

Earlier, Paul and Solveig Turpin (1986) interpreted this textile iconography as expressing a key relation between head taking and shamanic activities. The images embroidered on many of the textiles are illustrations of elaborate beings with their hair streaming behind, and their legs flung back. Often these flying personages carry severed heads by their loose hair. Paul and Turpin's thesis is that these are depictions of drug-taking shamans who "fly" to visit ancestral spirits (or appropriate enemy ones), to gain power to deal with vital issues. These beings sometimes carry other items of power, such as the *huarango* staffs found in the later Nasca burial site of Cahuachi, as well as throughout the Ica Valley.[4]

Other beings illustrated on these textiles, in the form of birds, felines, fish, and vegetation, also fly through the air. These images might suggest shamanic reinforcement of ancestral control in the cycle of life and death, or perhaps shamanic reinforcement of warfaring activities. The accompanying illustrations, together with the heads, of bird, feline, fish, and vegetation, might also imply that the Paracas practices concerning human heads included ceremonies with the participation of interpreters of these life-forms, who ensured that the power of these heads was disseminated more widely to the pending fertility of the animals and crops (Paul 2000c:78) (and see again Figure 1.6).

But although Paul and Turpin (1986) interpreted some of the beings illustrated on these Paracas textiles as "flying shamans," Frank Salomon disagrees. Their skull-like faces and exaggerated rib cages have led him to interpret them instead as the ancestral dead revisiting the living. In an ethnohistorical approach, Salomon has examined how the living might have retrieved the powers of the dead through these flights, as an impulse for more generalized powerful and productive forces (1995:323, 336–37 and cited in Paul 2000c:77–78).

Salomon finds certain clues for this interpretation in the Paracas textile imagery. For example, in the figures on Paracas textiles, a third of the heads illustrated are placed near the mouths of whole figures or are attached to the long tongue appendages of front-faced standing figures, as seen in Figure 1.2 (see also Paul 2000c:77). This leads Salomon to propose that the location of the head held near the mouth in these images might express ritual practices entailing verbal descriptions of ancestors (say the *mallki*), whereby a religious specialist would summon the persona of a dead human, whose spirit (*upani*) returns to the living through this ritualized enactment of speech. That is, the dead soul would adhere to the living person during these sessions, thus the speech of the dead ancestor would pass through that person's body (Salomon 1995:323, 336).

According to Salomon, the essence that returns as a "light volatile component" would be the person's productive, fertile personal qualities. In this setting, the priest would reconstitute the ancestor temporarily while speaking to the dead powers within (cf. Paul 2000c:78). It is worth noting that these historical descriptions Salomon describes are quite similar to the ways that specialist *ch'amakanis* in the region of Qaqachaka call up the dead today. They also reflect a commonly held assumption about some prehistoric pilgrimage sites where oracles spoke for larger powers. One of the most famous is Chavín de Huántar, where the large mound has tenon heads depicting people transformed by hallucinogenic plants into jaguars and the dead. Whether the original images on the Paracas textiles actually dealt with magical flight or communication with ancestral souls, many of them have a sense of overwhelming power with a sense of dread, as illustrated in Figure 6.1.

Many of the beings on the Paracas textiles have their tongues sticking out with heads attached (see also Figure 1.6). Mary Weismantel (2005) has made a case for the active power of the tongue in these ancient iconographies. Tongues help people speak, so they are often a sign of power and authority. Tongues also express the relations between generations, while the smaller beings sitting on the tongues could be the voice of the soul of the person depicted. All of these images seem to portray the strong powers of heads; a simultaneous sense of ancestral power is expressed through the children (or ancestors) who some of these characters hold in their hands, as well as on their tongues. A simultaneous sense of ancestral power is expressed through the children (or ancestors) held in the hands or placed on the tongues of some of these characters.

This generalized preocccupation with the power of heads is expressed in Paracas textiles at other levels as well. For example, another feature of Paracas described by Paul (2000a, 2000b) is the way that cloth was enfolded over the body and the more specific way that certain garments emphasize their relation to the head. This draping of garments was part of a visual language managed by the weavers of Paracas, who viewed the body in terms of a play of alternating gyrations around the neck, waist, and knees, according to the design configurations of the different garments. At one level, Paul notes how these alternating gyrations seemed to define a "personal sacred space" (Paul 2000b:165). But at another, she notes how, curiously, the pattern of designs on some garments make a rightward gyration around the head while those on others make a leftward turn, as if to suggest a distinct relationship with the head between the two classes of garment users (Paul 2000a). This leads us to wonder if the garments with one of these directional gyrations around the head were about marking the attire of the ritual sacrificers of heads in Paracas society, while the garments with the opposing gyration were reserved for more common use.

The later Early Intermediate Period evidence from the Nasca Valley has allowed us to better understand the earlier Ica *and* Paracas cultural life. We have learned that these small farming villages were intimately tuned into the cycles of life and death and how their populations spent much of their time depicting their views about the power of the dead over the living, made manifest through the head. Although some of the heads they focused on in their ceremonies might have been trophy heads, as suggested by the carrying rope through some of the curated heads, many heads could just as well have been ancestral heads. We also have to take into account here Paul's disagreement with the generalized archaeological view, initiated by Tello, that all heads with carrying ropes were necessarily "trophy heads." However, the evident presence of at least some trophy heads with carrying ropes does suggest to archaeologists that there must occasionally have been some skirmishes between the local communities, much like those of Qaqachaka of AD 2000.

Even so, such forms of capture and rechanneling of power could also have been for nurturing the plant "babies" as well as human babies, as suggested in the textile images. Plant production in this region was always risky because of the irregular amount of water in the rivers. Thus, although there are hints of centrifugal outward tendencies in the Ica Valley, this was contained within a small-scale, segmented society that showed little evidence for political hierarchy. Many of the dead were buried complete and curated heads that were not trophy heads have been found, both of these supporting the idea that some textile images expressed ancestral ties through speech. This suggests that these people were more concerned with issues of fecundity and survival than political or territorial conquest. In this sense, once these people gained their heads, they seemed to believe these were central in the power to communicate with the deities and to ask for life-giving water, plants, and fish.

Nasca

In the Early Horizon Period (900–100 BC) along the south coast, there is still insufficient evidence to define the extent of warfaring and head taking. In contrast, ample evidence would suggest that both of these activities were prevalent in the next temporal phase: the Early Intermediate Period (100 BC–AD 200). Most research for this later period has been conducted in the Nasca pampas, just to the south of the Ica River Valley. There, cranial images are related not only to concerns over fertility and its expression in the family or descent group centered ceremonies of a centripetal political system in the early phases, but also to the political consolidation through warfare of an expanding centrifugal system after AD 500.[5]

From the 100 years of archaeological research in this network of semipermanent rivers across the Nasca pampa, we have learned that, like their neighbors to the north, these inhabitants were quite acephalous politically. The river tributaries were apparently filled with small farming communities, linked by paths across the dry plain. Silverman (1993) describes how, between AD 100 and 400, these communities clearly worked together to construct and maintain Cahuachi (Qawachi), a large ceremonial center spread out along the river containing forty platform mounds, with many burials and animal offerings. This site was abandoned later in the valley's Early Intermediate Period history and used only for burials after that.

However, the extensive eastern survey conducted by Schreiber and Lancho Rojas (2003) and Vaughn (2004) tells us that there was a Middle Horizon threat from the highlands, of a Wari and/or Tiwanaku incursion around AD 600. This pressure from the east, in addition to a long drought between AD 560 and 600, probably led the people of this area to build larger, more defensive settlements on hillsides. Most valley settlements along the water courses remained small, though they, too, displayed increasing preoccupation with defense.

There are prominent geoglyphs throughout this time period, which still survive in this valley network. These have had many interpretations, but the general consensus is that they were part of more extensive ritual constructions where ceremonies were performed to honor and communicate with the deities, most likely to ask for successful harvests and enough river moisture to complete them. Thus, the history of this region is similar to that of the Ica Valley, but on a slightly larger scale, and implying a segmented and decentralized society with a centripetal trajectory. The main view seemed to be to the earth and sky deities. After years of survey, Silverman (1993) believes that the valley network became a confederation of kin-oriented groups, segmented for the most part, although sharing the same ceremonial ways, sharing Cahuachi for important burials and rituals. In comparison, Zuidema (1972) finds more dualism at Cahuachi, with two groups in a dyadic relationship. In the Nasca region, then, cranial images are increasingly related not only to concerns over fertility, and its expression in the kinship-based ceremonies of a centripetal political system, but also to the political consolidation through warfare of an expanding centrifugal system that continued until around AD 800.

In the Nasca Valley river system, findings of crania are common. Archaeologists are more likely to call them "trophy heads" because of their treatment. For example, Browne, Silverman, and García (1993) have recently uncovered a cache of twenty-two crania at the important center of Palpa and another forty-eight severed heads at Cerro Carapo in the Nasca Valley.[6] These late Nasca crania (AD 500) are again presumed to be trophy heads by the authors because of the hole in the front of their foreheads, suggesting a postmortem treatment that allowed them to be carried and displayed on a rope.[7] Such finds have been reported since Uhle (1918) and Tello (1918) first noted the prevalence of such heads in the region's ceremonial precincts. This kind of treatment, as well as the caching of heads, suggests the heads were considered to hold much power and that this power passed to those who carried them, giving them greater prestige, status, or voice in society. One claim by Browne and colleagues (1993:291) is that the Late Nasca leaders, as head conservators, may have been trying to consolidate the personal gains they achieved through trophy head–taking into effective social power, as manifested in the ceramic portraits of richly attired, trophy head–bearing leaders.

Another series of Nasca heads was excavated by Kroeber in the 1940s. Kroeber reported on this in 1956; more recently, Forgerty and Williams (2001) have restudied these crania, describing all 145 that had been uncovered. Some of them were plastered, like the earlier Chinchorro faces, suggesting that the heads might have incarnated a continuing essence of power after life (much like the *sami*-filled wooden spoons, described by Allen in her book of 1988).

However, Kowta's (1987) finding in the Acari Valley, the next valley south, reported on by Browne et al. (1993:288), of five heads each wrapped in cloth and each found within a cooking vessel, suggests that not all heads were necessarily the result of warfare. Indeed, some of these crania were probably venerated kin. This kind of evidence leads Browne and colleagues (1993) to conclude that in earlier Nasca times (40 BC–AD 160) there were *two* cranial lines, one of enemy trophy heads and the other of ancestral heads. Only later, in Nasca 4–5 times (*ca.* AD 320–430), did trophy heads begin to dominate. This evidence could be attributed to a greater attention to ancestral worship and genealogical reinforcement of kinship identity and nurturance in the earlier centripetal period, with increasing outward aggression and a centrifugal tendency, centered in defense, warfare, and accompanying shamanic activity, in the later periods.

John Verano's (1995) detailed anatomical work on trophy heads demonstrates the elaborate processes of head preparation in the Early Intermediate Periods in settlements along the coast, especially the south coast (40 BC–AD 800). It is important to note that the Nasca area has many more curated heads in caches than all the other regions we consider here,[8] although only a few of the locales studied (four of eleven) contain multiple heads. This distribution would suggest that this period was increasingly one of head taking, elaborate curation measures, and finally a developing interest in the accumulating or banking of these heads in special caches. Such an accumulation of heads must also have expressed political functions, with the greater powers of the head-taking accumulators over the head givers.

This leads us to ask whether such elaborate curation procedures were practiced more in relation to enemy heads or those of kin. This is particularly relevant with respect to the so-called shrunken heads. Historical accounts certainly describe cases where such shrunken heads are ancestral. For example, according to the colonial chronicler Estete (1938 [1535]:208–09), the heads of the dead in Pasao (on the Ecuadorian coast) were mummified with certain balsamic substances and shrunken in a process quite similar to that described for the Jívaro of the eastern Ecuadorian mountain slopes.[9] We also know that the Chinchorro of northern Chile prepared and curated their own dead through similar processes. So, are these Nasca shrunken heads only of enemies, as some have suggested, or of important members of society, curated with care as were the Chinchorro bodies? Not all the heads found in these particular sites have such processing, leading Verano to suggest that such treatment might have been reserved for certain significant crania but not others (1995).

It is worth noting that the use of balsamic substances for embalming has continued into historical and recent times. For example, in the region of Qaqachaka, according to older people, the dead only a few generations ago were placed in a flexed position and then covered with layers of the herb bittermint (Aym. *muña*), to avoid foul odors. They were then wrapped tightly with twining made from local rough grass. As the bittermint dried out, it turned black and the dark liquid seeped into the twining, giving it a bitumen-like appearance.

The fact that the iconography of the southern coastal area of Nasca has survived in textiles, ceramics, and geoglyphs allows us to ask whether heads were a part of the domain of a ritual leader or simply a part of a family's collection of preciously guarded objects used for curing, healing, and maintaining their identity. In any case, the ambiguity surrounding these heads within archaeological debates still stands. The question of whether they were ancestral kin or from enemies captured in warfare also has consequences for the kinds of practices centered on them and the kinds of power issues that were at play in these practices of head management.

Donald Proulx (1971, 1989, 1999, 2001) has written most eloquently about the place of heads in Nasca society, in his work on head imagery on Nasca ceramics. Proulx takes up the issue raised by Verano's analysis: that distinct heads could have been processed differently and therefore have varying significances, especially through time. For example, Proulx notes how, in the Nasca Valley, head imagery on textiles and ceramics had been assumed by previous scholars to be centered in war victims. But, to their credit, both Proulx as well as DeLeonardis (1997, 2000) allow for other interpretations: that the heads could perhaps represent icons of family and ancestral lines, and therefore that the practices of power concentration would have been related to certain deceased people, emanating from the ancestors.

Not only are there naturalistically made ceramic heads, some in the image of the curated trophy heads with twine through a hole on the front of the forehead, there are also many images of highly stylized nonhuman heads painted onto pots, often as if these were an added design element. Most likely these additions were not just decoration, but attention to the value and powers that such heads would provide. More heads perhaps meant more fertility. This would seem to confirm the findings of Browne et al. (1993) that both sources of heads, kin and enemy, were present in the Nasca sequence and that their meaning remained centrally important to the Nasca people.

Overall, we suggest that the common occurrence of heads in late Nasca reflects the preoccupation of these people with water and the associated fertility that it brought. Although the valley land is quite fertile, it requires additional water to produce a viable yield, and this comes out of the mountains on a seasonal basis, depending on the highland rainfall. The Nasca rivers flow underground in several parts of the basin; this means people had to dig for water as well as learn where the aquifers travel near the surface. The quantity of water also varied due to the annual amount of mountain winter rainfall. In this context, the necessity for collective rainmaking rituals might have been a key organizing principle in Nasca society as well as a key organizer of the symbols of office and more general iconographic trappings of ritual specialists.

Another interpretation of the prevalence of heads in Nasca concerns gender identification and gendered practices, as well as key ambiguities in the expression of gender relations. For example, in the site at Cahuachi, Silverman (1993) has identified early Nasca 3 androgynous people holding heads painted on ceramics, suggesting that heads were important in ritual contexts. It should be noted that the Nasca ceramics are some of the most sophisticated in the Andean region. Not only are the polychrome pots thin walled and delicately crafted, the painting style is highly refined, with the subtle use of earthy colors. Through time, the images become increasingly stylized as the earlier spaces are filled in. For most of the Nasca sequence, the images are clearly identifiable. Although some of the ceramic shapes and images are realistic portrayals of animals and humans, other images are quite surreal (the horrible bird, the oculate being, etc.). These prominent images are also drawn on the ground in large geoglyphs, including images such as monkeys, birds, and sharks. Yet, it is the surreal images that seem to haunt the Nasca people, as did the stalking masked beings on the Paracas textiles.

Heads are a key part of the repertory of this image palette of the Nasca. They become so common that whole pots are made in the shape of heads, as if they, too, were curated trophy heads. The images on these pots have the same pinned-up mouths as do trophy heads. It is these kinds of "pinned-up" mouths with spines from the local *huarango* tree that led Uhle (1901), and more recently Verano (1995) and Proulx (1999), to compare these Nasca trophy heads with the modern Jívaro (Shuar) shrunken heads whose mouths are similarly pinned.

The Nasca human heads are often associated with a series of important deities, including the horrible bird and the harpy eagle, thought by Anita Cook (2002) to be the patrons of the eastern sky (from where the water comes). Iconographic analysis of these Nasca images suggests that the horrible bird is the sacrificer, the killer and taker, even the eater of heads. This is the image that Cook (2002) thinks becomes the front-faced deity that is a key concept in the Middle Horizon highland states. Her supposition implies that the importance of this sacrificer deity, whether as the horrible bird, or its variant first seen in the *chachapuma* or "man-puma" figure (Aym. *chacha* = man) in the highlands, accompanied the greater accumulation of heads in Middle and Late Nasca times, from *ca.* AD 280–430.[10] In this case, an evolution of this image in the region might relate head-centered activities to increasingly powerful shamans and an accompanying elaboration of the anthropomorphic mythical beings represented in textile iconography, who collect and hold human heads in later Nasca times. Equally likely is that this increased focus on heads and their powers might have been due to the ever-increasing worry about water for crop production.

Lisa DeLeonardis (1997, 2000) discusses an important shift in head imagery in Nasca ceramics after Nasca 4–5 (in the Early Intermediate Period,' AD 320–430). Before Nasca 4, most images were of naturalistic animals and plants, strongly associated with regeneration and fertility, whereas after Nasca 5 there is more emphasis, in pottery for example, on warfare, weaponry, and decapitation. At this stage, there are pots in the shape of human heads and ceramic pots with heads decorating bowl rims. DeLeonardis notes that increasingly through time, both males and females (and increasingly androgynous humans) become associated with heads, especially with the front-faced deity (the sacrificer) who manages such heads. Furthermore, the humans portrayed in this later imagery hold domesticated plants and deceased humans as well as heads, suggesting that the power of these heads, while related to death, also triggers the fecundity of agricultural plants.

Browne et al. (1993:290) also note this radical increase in head collecting in later Nasca times, but they do not give a cultural or political reason for it. Insofar as they offer an explanation, they suggest that the heads were sacrificial, playing a part in some kind of elaborate death ritual. They also suggest that an ancestor cult might have been escalating at that time.

We do not agree with this interpretation. Rather, we support both Cook's (2002) and DeLeonardis's arguments (1997, 2000:381) that the increasing association between accumulating heads and accumulating political power is not based simply on ancestor cults but arises from the reaction to increasing aggression coming from the outside. In these later Nasca phases, DeLeonardis also notes the additional evidence for increasing stratification, as shown by relatively fewer graves having greater quantities of burial goods in relation to the majority of graves that had fewer goods.

The Nasca archaeological data would, therefore, suggest that practices centered on heads were central to the spiritual and political lives of their populations; they would cache power at ceremonial centers, drink out of pots in the shape of heads, and so on. Such practices must have played a pivotol role in the consolidation of political power during the Nasca sequence, especially with the increasing pressure from the east.

Regarding clues to political formation, the iconography of this small-scale confederation of communities was clearly centripetal in the early times, focusing on the settlement of Cahuachi, perhaps characterized by local processional rituals across the pampas, led by shamans, to request water, fertility, and life in general. But with increasing political pressure from the outside, not only from the east but also possibly along the coast, warfare directed outward in a more centrifugal political model grew in importance. This is evident in the history of Nasca interactions with heads. In later times, the populace seems to be reaching out to the deities through shamans and their practices around heads, to gain more power through head capture. Here, the more heads you accumulated, the greater your political power over those who had surrendered their head. Such a shift in Nasca is not surprising as it is accompanied by similar changes in Wari and Tiwanaku polities that also became outwardly oriented at the start of the Middle Horizon Period.

For the Nasca, the balance seemed to shift between these two tendencies. At the frontiers, there was an expanding centrifugal system based on warfare and head taking. In contrast, the very center of the Nasca mindset was still interested in the power of certain communities and their productivity through practices of head management concerned more with ancestor worship.

The Lake Titicaca Region

The Formative Phases

Let us turn now to the huge Titicaca Basin, east of this coastal region, with its larger lake to the north (Lake Titicaca proper, sometimes called Lago Chucuito) and smaller lake (*Wiñay marka*) to the south. All around Lake Titicaca, there is evidence for an early but different material focus on heads. We know that the coastal Nasca region was in fairly regular contact with the people of the altiplano basin, through many shared traits. So, although the styles and cultural histories of these two regions differ, we can identify and follow certain resonances throughout the prehistoric sequence.

From the start, the Titicaca Basin dwellers focused on human heads in their ceremonies. Archaeological evidence shows that as the ceremonial centers were built and proliferated, the place of the head remained important. In this region, the inhabitants of the Titicaca Basin seemed to draw on both the powerful ties to ancestral heads to help with crop and animal fecundity and the additional powers gained from captured enemy heads. The archaeological sequence shows evidence for both of these uses of heads and the mounting evidence through time confirms that the Tiwanakota actively used both ancestor and enemy heads to consolidate their political success.

Another use of heads seems to be concerned with the early marking out of ceremonial territories in the region. Along the southwestern side of the large lake in the Titicaca Basin in modern Peru, inland up the Llave River, Mark Aldenderfer's team has excavated several stone piles that contained a series of crania.[11] These are rather like the modern *taqawa* in Qaqachaka that we mentioned earlier, used to display trophy heads. Although the date is not firm, Aldenderfer believes that the stone piles were constructed sometime around 2500 BC. These small mounds seem to be from the Early Formative (Archaic) phase, and so would be attributed to forager-hunter-herders, before the construction of permanent settlements in the basin. We do not know if these were ancestral or enemy heads, but this shrine clearly implies the central importance of heads in this region at the beginning of the ceremonial marking of territories. This evidence suggests that these early forager-herders sensed the meaningfulness and power inherent in the human head.

The first settled communities increase in frequency around the lakeshore in what some call the Middle Formative phase, dating between 1500 and 100 BC. This phase shows the first evidence for ceramics and other symbolic cultural representations crafted by the inhabitants as they settled in the region. Stanish's regional survey (2003) shows how the early small settlements were located primarily along the lakeshore, where the climate was more moderate.

Although a series of sites have been noted around the whole lake, the most detailed excavations from this period have been carried out at the site of Chiripa on the Taraco Peninsula in the southwestern area of the smaller Titicaca lake (*Wiñay marka*), a site first occupied around 1500 BC.[12] Hastorf and her team's excavated material inform us that these first settlers were farmers and herders as well as fisherfolk and birders (1999). In the small settlements of these early times, no more than 0.5 ha in size, families lived in ephemeral houses around ceremonial courts and sunken enclosures. The fact that the earliest permanent architectural evidence is public in nature and not residential informs us of the priority that the inhabitants gave to ceremony. Early associated material includes ceramics, bone tools, and carved stone images.

Synthesizing previous work completed at the site, and in the Titicaca southern basin Formative Period, Ponce Sanginés (1957), Cordero Miranda (1977), and Browman (1978) have reported on a series of stone heads and other stone carvings first uncovered at Chiripa and dating from what we call the Late Chiripa phase, from approximately 800–100 BC. Middle Formative stone carvings, begin with surreal animal images concerned with life in moist areas, fecundity, and animals that live in such environments: frogs, snakes, lizards, and fish.

Through time, the individual images become more surreal and yet increasingly human-like, with a repeated focus on heads with toad-like prominent eyes (see Figure 6.2). These heads are androgynous, with a stylistically prominent "T" for the nose and eyebrows, and appendages emanating from the four corners of rather square faces. The specific carvings depicted here suggest a direct relation to productivity. These bud-like appendages, which seem to express the power of these heads to regenerate plant growth in sprouting and rooting forms, are similar to other vegetative images on later Tiwanaku stonework. In fact, many of the stonecarvings toward the end of this phase have this characteristic sprouting nature. In addition, four camelids were placed around the outside of the enclosure into which this emanating energy is pouring.

The surreal stone head carvings develop through time into more elaborate presentations of powerful beings that later appear in the Titicaca Basin in the form of two human-like beings, a male and a female. These have been called the Yayamama or Pa'ajano (Aym. *Pä Ajanu*: "Two face") tradition, dating to around 100 BC-AD 500.[13] As defined by Sergio and Karen Mohr Chávez (1975), the Yayamama religious tradition includes stone sculpture, temple centers, ritual ceremonial paraphernalia including ceramic trumpets, incense burners, and a "surreal" iconography with felines, faces with rayed heads (like the budding appendages described above), divided eyes, and tear bands. There is also a generalized focus on communal feasting (Mohr Chávez 1988:17, 21) (see Figure 6.3). The supernatural iconography of felines makes an early appearance here.

These characteristics are very similar to what Portugal Ortíz (1981) calls the Pa'Ajano *style*, typified by human-like images on both sides of a standing stone that have their hands crossed or are holding things, often heads and ritual bundles. These surreal beings suggest deities (or their attendants) preoccupied

Figure 6.2: A Chiripa Carved Head-stone Plaque
Courtesy of the Museo Nacional de Arqueología, La Paz, Bolivia. Photograph by Christine Hastorf.

with managing heads, although these male and female figures also carry a strong sense of dualism and balance. These elaborate dual images are found on the peninsulas of Santiago de Huata, Copacabana, and Taraco at sites associated with rich agriculture and lacustrine access (Lemuz Aguirre 2001; Hastorf 2003).

This evidence for dualism hints at moiety development in the social and political fabric of settled society in the basin, although again it is necessary to ask if this development is a unifying force politically or simply served in ritual and ceremonial organization. These early populations seem to have been built on ayllu-like kin groups as the basic units, with their respective symbolic figureheads at an authoritative level. The stones and other objects that seem to be associated with fecundity provide a common motif for group identity

Figure 6.3: A Pukara Ceramic Fragment Feline Face with Rays or Tears Coming out from the Eyes
Photograph by Christine Hastorf.

and unity. Again, there is a certain ambiguity around the heads: whether they were predominantly ancestral or accumulated from war captives, where we might expect the feline imagery to be more dominant. The Early and Middle Formative images (1500–100 BC) still do not include felines. Like their coastal neighbors, water, rain, and crop productivity were more central to the security of these early lacustrine settlements.

Regarding the budding appendages on the head at these sites, as Paul (1982, 1986), Arnold (2000), and more recently Mary Weismantel (2004) have suggested, the budding features of substances flowing out of the head could be the vehicles for transferring the vitality of life flowing from one body to another to maintain life. This "flow of life," as Paul calls it (1986: Figs. 3–31) emanates outward in these lake culture images. In other imagery in the lineal style, especially those that characterize Paracas turbans, a similar flow seems to pass between paired figures and the heads of snakes, felines, or trophy heads (Paul 1982: Figs. 4–30). Again, this "flow of life," although seemingly derived from the power of heads, is not just limited to this domain; instead, it spills over into many other elements of the ecological system: flora, fauna, birds, and so on, as we would expect from the expansive dynamics portrayed in stone by the Titicaca folk (cf. Paul 1992:286).

These Yayamama stone images might equally have referred to ancestral or to enemy heads, although there are no aggressive images or ropes associated with the heads. They seem, rather, to express living heads with open eyes. However, there is evidence in this period for the development of political hierarchies. For example, throughout this Formative sequence in the Titicaca Basin, the shift from animals to more human-like images might have accompanied the development of more expansive political structures in the region. As Roe (1982) reminds us elsewhere, this trajectory occurs when humans become the powerful mediators between the deities and those living on earth. In the Titicaca Basin, this trajectory began materially in the Late Archaic phase, around 3000 BC.

The Middle Formative: Chiripa

The Taraco Archaeological Project, under the direction of Christine Hastorf and Matthew Bandy, which combines U.S. and Bolivian archaeological expertise, has made advances in our understanding of this relation between material culture and political development. Recent Formative excavations by the project suggest that the first settled peoples in the Titicaca Basin constructed their society around concepts of their place in the terrain and the ancestors. In this case, the early architectural manifestations at Chiripa, like the Aldenderfer mounds, celebrated family ties on the landscape, with multiple burials in tombs, usually with a woman as the central figure (Steadman and Hastorf 2001; Hastorf 2003). Further evidence for this notion are the progressively more elaborate architectural manifestations built at Chiripa related to the role of the deceased and the kin group. This would imply an early societal focus on the matri-line, in a small-scale, segmented centripetal political system that stresses rituals that affirm and reproduce identity in a genealogical sense. From Leo Benetiz's measurements at the site, we have learned that the ceremonial buildings were aligned with the lunar cycle and the main *apus* (sacred mountains) of the region.

The Taraco Archaeological Project defines the Formative occupation of the Chiripa site in three phases: the Early, Middle, and Late Chiripa phases, 1500–100 BC. These three phases are expressed materially in the site in its three culturally contoured terraces rising up from the lake. Twelve Chiripa-phase burials outside of the later mound have been studied recently by Blom and Bandy (1999) and Hastorf (1999), in addition to the later burials uncovered on the mound. Most of these subterranean burials were intact, but some included bodies without heads.[14] We suggest that these heads were ancestral and probably kept in niches in the ceremonial enclosures of the mound.

To date, the archaeological data imply that the residents of Chiripa began to hold regular and protracted rituals surrounding the burial of dead adults. Furthermore, the pits were occasionally reopened to add other family members to the group of previously interred cloth-wrapped adults. The architecture for these practices also becomes more elaborate. This is evident in the shift in importance of the burial placement at Chiripa from subsurface pits enclosed by an adobe wall, to semi-subterranean enclosures with niches (where important bodies would have been placed), to subsurface lined pits within a platform mound accompanied by large enclosed niches that could have held important, cloth-wrapped ancestors (Hastorf 2003).

In form, the later multiple, above-ground bins, built within a series of elaborate structures, are like dark, small cave-like places, which could have held, among other curated items, wrapped mummy bundles that were taken out periodically for rituals. This resonates with the elaborate descriptions of such mummy bundles in the 17th century that Doyle (1988) has drawn our attention to. Again, these kinds of structures with their antechambers are also similar to the later Inka niches, for example those at Coricancha (Qurikancha) in Cusco, where the Inka mummies were displayed. In Chiripa, this civic core area was evidently expanded and rebuilt many times, in elaborate acts of renewal. As yet, we do not have a full inventory as to what was actually stored in these niches; whatever was guarded there was moved out years ago. We can say that some of the small chambers held special foods and ceremonial ceramics. Indeed, heads could have been one of the things curated in these niches.

The presence of stone face carvings, like that in Figure 6.2 found at the Chiripa mound, added later to the site's assemblage, suggest that such heads were not used by the inhabitants of the site in any one exclusive way; rather, multiple manifestations of the head were important to the Formative people. Nevertheless, ideas centered in the potency of these heads must have contributed to the way settlements such as Chiripa retained local influence, drawing in new residents throughout the Formative Period as well as to the way that local authority structures and power relations in general were perceived and symbolized. Bandy (2004) shows that by 100 BC, Chiripa was one of the largest settlements on the peninsula.

Similar preoccupations of the populations of the time with the siting and symbolism of heads have been noted in many sites around Lake Titicaca that are contemporaneous with Chiripa, dating to the Middle Formative Period between 800 and 100 BC. While the Chiripa tradition on the Taraco Peninsula was characterized by carved stela within enclosures on a platform mound, as well as in sunken enclosures, complete bodies as well as bodies without heads have been found with the same date at Ch'isi and at Titimani.[15] In addition, at Titimani, on the eastern shore of the large lake, Portugal Ortíz (1988) found some carved stone animals that were brought to the enclosure. At Kala Uyuni (Qala Uyuni), also on the Taraco Peninsula some 7 km from Chiripa, a carved stone was found *in situ* at the base of a standing stone in the center of a sunken enclosure (see Figure 6.4).

This might suggest that these stones were perceived by the local populations rather like the mobile stone *qunupa* and the *inqa* or *jayintilla* bezoar stones of modern times, as seed-like reproducers of animal and plant growth. Alternatively, these stones might have served as solid and permanent memories

Figure 6.4: Carved Middle Formative Rock from Kala Uyuni (Qala Uyuni) Enclosure, Taraco Peninsula

Photograph by William T. Whitehead. Courtesy of the Taraco Archaeological Project.

of the power of earlier taken trophy heads, in a similar way to the wrapped, carved stones taken out and used today in altars for ceremonies of the highest Aymara authorities in the region of Jesús de Machaqa, not far from the lake, as described by Astvaldur Astvaldsson (2000:145, Figs. 5.3–5.5).

Overall at Middle Formative Chiripa there is no real evidence for the curation of separated heads as such, but rather for the curation of the whole cloth-wrapped bodies of people, hence what Hastorf perceives as an ancestor focus. There is little trophy head management until perhaps the creation of niches in the upper houses, which date to Middle and on into Late Formative times (600 BC–AD 100). More secure evidence for trophy heads from captured enemies or sacrificial practices only begins with the *chachapumas* in the Early Intermediate Period, at Pukara, continuing on at Tiwanaku.

Late Formative/Early Intermediate Period (Tiwanaku I, III): Pukara

During the Late Formative Period around the same Titicaca Basin, some local ceremonial centers grew and became regionally important. In the northern basin, the large ceremonial complex of Pukara grew to its height between 300 BC and AD 200. This site was built up the side of a hill, with a series of terraces running up to a set of sunken enclosures. At this site, as at Chiripa, a similar importance is given to curated bodies as well as heads.

At Pukara, the practices around head and body curation are housed in specific architectural forms. Excavation evidence by Wheeler and Mujica (1981) at the site revealed a pre-Pukara truncated step pyramid dating to around 300 BC on the lower portion of the terraced hillside. Within this small mound, there was a rectangular room with four niches. Two of these niches were on either side of the east-facing doorway (facing the rising sun) and two were on the western wall (facing the setting sun) (Wheeler and Mujica 1981:29). These two western niches each contained a human-like carved stone head, one attached to a small body. These stone heads were multicolored and embedded in clay within the niches to conceal them.

This location of images of heads and human bodies within the niches of Early Intermediate Period Pukara strongly supports the suggestion made for Chiripa: that these niches held heads and that such cave-like spaces were used to commune with the deities. Several crania were found within one of the sunken ceremonial courtyards (Kidder 1956; Stanish 2001). The presence of these heads, along with a complete body uncovered in a long niche-like bin, further support the widespread practice of ceremonial customs around the entire basin centered on heads and the appropriation of their powers.

Whereas Hastorf (2003) thinks it is more probable that the Chiripa heads channeled the ancestral powers of former kin group leaders, in later Pukara there is strong evidence for the curated heads representing the capture of enemy powers. In Pukara imagery, heads are commonly represented on poly-chrome ceramics. Sergio Chávez (1992) has called these images "trophy heads," alluding to the contemporaneous Nasca head images, although there is no evidence for holes in the foreheads or twine for carrying. For Chávez, these heads are associated with "ferocious" males, or warrior shamans, reminiscent of the fierce Paracas shamans illustrated on the necropolis textiles. So, these heads might represent enemy heads and power gained via their capture, but they might also express the epitomy of life force passed on from kin, or even both at once.[16] However, the fact that these rows of heads on the ceramics are often near a feline personage, similar to the destroyer aspect depicted in the later *chachapuma* statues and similar to the Moche feline warriors that seemed to have control over death and life, suggests that an expanding warrior culture becomes predominant during this time.

This implies that the placing of the famous *chachapuma* stone sculptures in ceremonial contexts throughout the Titicaca Basin at this time develops along the same lines as the placing of the front-faced destroyer images in coastal sites, as seen in Figure 6.5. These Early Intermediate Period figures (in Tiwanaku I and III phases) are realistic, kneeling anthropomorphic felines holding a human head in front of them with both hands. The human head held by them often has open eyes and flowing plaits, as if it were flying. Most probably, the *chachapuma* figures represent ritual specialists with feline masks or in a feline-like state after taking a hallucinogenic plant. Here, the strong

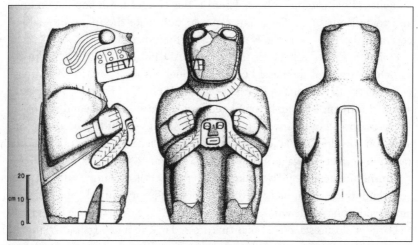

Figure 6.5: *Chachapuma* Stone Figure from Three Sides, Uncovered from the Base of Akapana, Tiwanaku

Alan L. Kolata (2003b:193, Fig. 7.22), "Tiwanaku ceremonial architecture and urban organization." In *Tiwanaku and Its Hinterland*, pp. 175–201. Ed. A. Kolata. (Washington, DC: Smithsonian Institution Press, 2003).
Courtesy of Alan Kolata.

sense of power attributed to the heads that they hold seems related to the notion of feline power over human life and death, whereby the feline not only has the power to kill but also the power to hold (and so contain) the life force embodied in the head.

A number of studies have discussed this theme at length in other settings; see, for example, the classic works by Roe (1982), Lathrap (1977), and Valcárcel (1932, 1935). But here, in these Titicaca Basin sculptures, we emphasize the political nature of these postures. For us, the Titicaca Basin feline-humans display the head as if to express feline power over humans, or, more precisely, the power of those ritual specialists who impersonate such felines. This suggests that in this region, heads are directly related to powers greater than humans, as if to suggest a political escalation from the kinship-based leadership of the earlier Formative Period to a political system where priestly or military leaders, perhaps from certain families, rise in prominence.

Middle Horizon Tiwanaku

The major ceremonial center of Tiwanaku, today situated some 10 km to the south of the southern lake's shore line in Bolivia, also has Formative habitation, beginning around 800 BC. However, during Early Intermediate/Late Formative times (300 BC-AD 300), the settlement grew, as did Pukara, with the building of the immense ceremonial compounds, described by Ponce Sanginés (1990), among others. Then, as the Titicaca Basin population grew and trade flourished, Tiwanaku came to dominate the many other local ceremonial centers, eventually even the northern basin.

Finally, in the Middle Horizon (between AD 450 and 1000), Tiwanaku became the largest of the nested centers throughout the basin, in what archaeologists call the Tiwanaku IV and Tiwanaku V phases.[17] Even so, Tiwanaku's regional influence was ephemeral and sparse, within and beyond the basin. It was built on a vast network of trade routes, but with little settlement construction outside of the Titicaca Basin, implying that Tiwanaku was a centripetal rather than a centrifugal polity at heart (Goldstein 2005).

During the height of Tiwanaku's powers, a set of monumental structures were built in the expanded ceremonial core of the city, with the most elaborate carved stone of the whole Andean tradition. The carved stelae that graced the large enclosures depicted shamans dressed in elaborate regalia carrying the ritual implements of *qirus* and equipment for sniffing hallucinogens (others suggest these are *tumis* instead of pouches) (Figure 6.6). The evidence suggests that these priests led elaborate rituals in the various settings of the ceremonial enclosures, communicating with the deities, much like the shamans

Figure 6.6: A Front-faced Image from Tiwanaku, the Ponce Stele
Photograph by Christine Hastorf.

of Paracas, to bring the rain as well as maintain the well-being of the populace. The front-faced deity is an important image here, highlighting the tensions between the figures of destroyer and regenerator.

The presence of the *chachapuma* figure continues into the later, expansive Tiwanaku IV and V times, as uncovered in the excavations at the Akapana stepped platform mound at Tiwanaku. There, Alan Kolata's team found a *chachapuma* figure at the platform's base, in association with a sacrificed human burial (Kolata 2001; see again Figure 6.5).[18] In the same precinct, many of the offerings of human burials, of men, women, and children, had been disarticulated postmortem and reordered into groups of crania, lower limbs, and so on. Sonia Alconini (1995:209) has suggested that this Andean practice of reordering bones in secondary burials, as at Tiwanaku, may have been a way in which an elite priestly caste reestablished political alliances between the center of Tiwanaku and its various peripheries. Also at the base of the Akapana there was an offering where many drinking vessels (*qiru*) used to consume maize beer were deposited (Alconini 1995).

Again, this implies that such locations became a focus of the enactment of ritual practices concerned with sacrifice and politics, harnessing the powers of the human soul, as illustrated in the consuming of maize beer from the crania of defeated enemies, rather than ancestor worship through more benign propitiations. Some of the central plazas at Tiwanaku are immense, suggesting that congregations of thousands might have participated in ceremonies of awe and honor (Isbell and Vranich 2004).

The architectural expression of heads in the early political expansion from Tiwanaku during the late Early Intermediate Period developed with the use of immobile stone tenon heads that formed friezes of one kind and another. These were crafted in architectonic form around the sides of the semi-subterranean enclosure at Tiwanaku. One interpretation of these is that they were shamanic heads expressing transformative power, like those around the earlier outer face of the Early Horizon Chavín de Huántar platform mound.[19]

A more likely interpretation for the rows of stone heads facing inward in the sunken enclosure at Tiwanaku, according to several researchers (Ponce Sanginés 1990; Hastorf 2003; Couture 2005), is that they represent the regional leaders of ayllus or similar social and political unit "heads," probably brought together symbolically if not corporeally to one ritual locale during a time of increasing political centralization. Again, the accumulation of heads, this time in stone, is associated with the consolidation of political power, where the different features of each individual head would represent the different ethnic or tributary groups under the dominion of the Tiwanaku leaders. An associated view, applying our thesis, would be that these heads represent enemy heads captured in warfare and brought to Tiwanaku, where their regenerative powers could be harnessed by the regional leadership.

Put another way, the individualized nature of the tenon heads placed within this Tiwanaku enclosure illustrates the increasing influence of this ceremonial center and its capacity to support a centralized form of leadership. As with the trophy head imagery seen on Tiwanaku pottery and textiles, there is a sense, in these walls of heads, of concentrating metaphysical power in a classic centripetal manner. This concentrated power is not reciprocal, but depredatory and centralizing (cf. Fausto 2001). The configuration of the heads growing out of the older form of the semi-sunken enclosure also echoes the power of such conquered heads to generate organic development, like potatoes buried in the earth.[20] To us, these material heads seem more like the actual local leaders of certain groups, as compared with the surreal entities of other architectural uses of head imagery, and this is very likely, given the history of stone carving in the basin. Such imagery could have had the aim of symbolically and spiritually (if not forcibly) trying to aggregate a dispersed group of people into one unified group, at least for ceremonial and ritual events.

This imagery builds on the long-term Formative traditions of the Titicaca Basin, where semi-subterranean enclosures provided a venue for communal centripetal gatherings motivated by an effort to consolidate a form of worship of ancestors in common. Following this same form and by siting the enclosure with a lunar orientation like earlier Formative enclosures,[21] this semi-subterranean enclosure would have provided a forum for ancestral worship for the newer residents, with several carved stelae in the center of the court but an additional twist: the ceremonial organizers also had the power of the threat of head taking if tributary payments were not fulfilled.

In either case, this concentration of heads in the semi-subterranean temple would express the political force of the burgeoning Tiwanaku leadership, who now had the power to appropriate the symbolic image of the heads of regional leaders, and perhaps even force them into sending the ancestors of the groups conquered in the region to this ceremonial center, in much the same way as the Inka demanded that conquered *mallki* be brought to Cusco. The semi-subterranean location of this display might also emphasize the power of these heads, "taken politically" rather than in direct warfare, to help regenerate and disseminate the wealth of agricultural products under Tiwanaku's charge, especially the potatoes that sprout from the eyes of tubers underground.

The forming and painting of human heads onto ceramics became common in Tiwanaku's well-crafted pieces, especially in association with the front-faced deity as a highland variant of the coastal destroyer.[22] In this sense, these images of heads at Tiwanaku articulated the appropriating and expanding power of a rising state, building on its ancestral forebears to augment its expansive practices. The Tiwanaku ceremonial sequence, like its precursors in the basin region, used the image of the head to consolidate their political power along both axes. But the Tiwanaku leadership used the image of the head in its more ancestral form as well, focusing not so much on a fecund power of appropriation, but rather on the ancestral power to control death and renew life.

Were ancestral bodies and heads curated at Tiwanaku? The Qalasasaya enclosure implies this was so. In the classic phases, Tiwanaku leadership constructed this much larger walled enclosure that dominated the sunken enclosure. Within this large space, there was a series of small rooms. If these were used like the D-shaped structures of Wari or the small rooms of Chiripa these would have been the likely "mountain boxes" for corporeal storage. Similarly, the sets of neatly made small rooms on top of the great Akapana pyramid were probably ceremonial curational chambers, too, although no evidence of human bones has been uncovered in these places. Even so, these storage spaces seem to be sites of homage to the nurturing regeneration derived from ancestral life participating in Tiwanaku's statecraft. The two mounds at Tiwanaku, Akapana, and Pumapunku both have elaborate cut stone canals that would have ushered water periodically out of central cisterns. This obsession with water control is also noted in the channeling of the Tiwanaku River around the ceremonial core of the site in a moat. These concerns with water at the core of the precinct show us again the close material links of water and heads.

Finally, another source of heads helped constitute this form of political maintenance. Practices centering on enemy trophy heads, with their focus on death and regeneration, were also operating at Tiwanaku. This can be seen not only in the sunken enclosure of heads gathered together but more importantly in the front-faced destroyer deity (see Figure 6.7) that regularly oversaw ceremonial rituals within the enclosures of the most central part of Tiwanaku.

Middle Horizon State Developments: Wari

Let us now examine parallel state developments in Wari (or Huari). The fact that the central role of head imagery on ceramics, in cut stone and sometimes in

Figure 6.7: Gateway of the Sun Image of the Front-faced Destroyer, Tiwanaku Redrawn by Christine Hastorf.

actual heads, is equally prominent in the Middle Horizon images of both Tiwanaku and Wari leads us to suggest that these two great polities were related through similar practices that this common imagery expressed. Although Wari devel-oped after Tiwanaku was influential, there are important differences between these two polities (we could compare them to the contemporaneous Greek and Rome polities). The Tiwanaku expansion of its religious ideologies and trade routes was centered on the dissemination of ancestral values and the shamanic harnessing of their powers, but Wari expansion seems to have been more militaristic in nature, in the sense of its sending out people to build Wari towns, organize populations, and rule away from the main center in multiple subcenters.

The center of Wari developed on an eastern ridge in the Ayacucho Valley overlooking several small rivers, in conjunction with Conchopata on the western side of the valley. The Ayacucho Basin is dry, yet can support rainfed agriculture. Although the Huarpa population had resided throughout this basin during the Early Intermediate Period, these centers, larger than all the other settlements, developed around AD 500.

The drought that affected the dwellers on the Nasca plain also probably had an impact on this process, for this is when the Wari were on the move, seeking out arable areas with water. Glowacki and Malpass (2003) note that the Wari's great concern with water, and hence with productivity and fertility, was a driving force of their polity and a main focus of their rituals. We know that there were vast beautifully cut stone water canals that laced throughout the site. No wells or springs have yet been identified in the settlement and civic center, suggesting that the few water sources the residents had access to were especially important. As we have suggested, water and rain as sources of life are associated ambiguously both with the ancestors and with appropriating the energies of enemy others. In either case, head curation would have been part and parcel of the Wari rituals based around this primary concern over water. The most sacred sector at Wari, Moradchayoc has a wall of niches for such things as bodies and crania.

Wari grew rapidly to its maximum extension around AD 800, when its cultural styles spread throughout much of the central Andes. But by AD 900, it had collapsed to a small community again (Isbell and McEwan 1991). The central precinct of this huge city contained beautifully cut stones, some forming rectangular compounds with small chambers surrounding inner courtyards, used for priestly or elite activities. Some of these precincts highlighted elaborately boxed burial chambers and ritual-sacrificial D-shaped structures. These architectural features share the use of cut stone and the double layering of the walls; each had an inner chamber enclosed within another. Although some of the stone techniques are distinctly Tiwanaku, in style their constructions are their own.

Unlike Tiwanaku, Wari had a large and imposing wall, as if it was on the defensive from the start. Wari then, much more than Tiwanaku, gives the impression of a conquest state, expansive and centrifugal in nature, with the accompanying production of characteristic artifacts in Wari style. The Wari leadership built a series of settlements along a road system, following strict architectural codes, as conquered people were resettled along these roads and ceremonial outposts were built (Schreiber 1992). At the same time, the Wari were constantly looking over their shoulders to the south and the large sister polity of Tiwanaku in the Titicaca Basin. There is much evidence of exchange between these two polities, including deities, technologies, plants, and religious ideas, creating a unique bipolar dynamic in the highlands that has never been recreated.

Their shared cosmology is evident in the dominance of the front-faced deity at both of these state centers. Like the earthly leaders, such deities displayed on the large beer presentation jars of Conchopata and the stone stelae of Tiwanaku had the power to take heads, and use them to promote life through death (see Figure 6.8). A strong case can be put forward here for the increasing role of these kinds of practices centered on heads at a community and supra-community political level, whether in real ceremonial events or merely in the iconography that depicted ideal events. This possibility is supported by images of warriors holding heads throughout the later Early Intermediate Period phases in the Wari valleys as well as of the power emanating from heads becoming associated with all things powerful in a more generalized way.

The earlier Yayamama imagery of sprouting and surreal heads, oriented toward a common regeneration of fertilizing potential, became transformed by the Middle Horizon into a more overtly powerful, menacing, and individualized visual language. At the same time, ceramic and stone carvings begin to portray more realistic human heads (see Figure 6.9). We see examples of this process on the famous large Wari face-neck urns that were probably used for the brewing and presentation of beer (*chicha*)[23] (see again Figure 6.8). Some of these vessels were covered with images of sprouting or growing plants, expressing the power of regeneration, while many of the necks of the vessels were now decorated with heads that carried the insignia of leadership. These vessels served as body effigies from which the participants attending a meeting or celebration would receive drink, as they were reminded of who was really providing the drink at the specific ceremonial context.

Figure 6.8: A Conchopata Face-neck Liquid Storage Jar
Courtesy of William Isbell.

These evocative pieces found in Wari centers seem to express the dominant role of the regional lord as the provider, not just of beer, but also of communion with the deities through transformative drink. This same role must also have accompanied the regional systems of tribute and recompense administered from Wari. In this sense, the expression of largesse of these local lords, illustrated and individualized in the portrait vessels, was not simply that of a two-way system of reciprocity, but rather of power relations over local populations—their territories and produce—controlled through the festive medium of drink.

Portrait vessels are present at both the Wari and the Tiwanaku ceremonial centers. For example, Figure 6.9 shows a Tiwanaku drinking vessel where the head is quite naturalistic and clearly powerful. In such vessels, the largesse of the Tiwanaku or Wari state and its leadership is portrayed precisely in this context of the distribution of drinks at ceremonies.[24] In this sense, the images of power that had first emerged in the Early Intermediate phases of Pukara, Nasca, and Moche became central during the Middle Horizon in the conformation

Figure 6.9: A Tiwanaku Portrait Head Gray-ware Tumbler from Kalasasaya
Photograph by Wolfgang Schüler. Permission courtesy of Alan Kolata.

of these state centers. There, a combination of the spiritual power that generated fertility and raw political power becomes evident in these new media,
where diverse kinds of heads again illustrate the continuity of this dominant image of political power. We learn of the extent of this political power
through the architecture, as we have no direct militaristic evidence from
either polity.

The expression of power relations implied by deliberate cranial placement
within state ceremonial architecture is evident in the presence of niches found
at major Wari sites. These become formalized as a key component of the
generalized D-shaped structures found, for example, in the central temple of
Moraduchayoc in Wari, at the site of Conchopata, at Cerro Baúl, and other
sites.[25] Earlier versions of these D-shaped structures had already emerged
over a wide area: at La Galgada, Kotosh, Huaca de los Reyes, Pacopampa, and
Pampa de las Llamas de Moxeke as well as at Chavín.

Investigations of these D-shaped buildings have led Cook and others to
make a strong case for their ritual importance. Cook (2001a) argues that the
D-shaped enclosures within larger rectangular niched halls probably served
complementary functions in the staging of private and public components of
ceremony. Although the activities conducted in these spaces are unknown,

sacrifice, propitiation, and food consumption seem to have occurred in and near them. Iconographic evidence, also analyzed by Knobloch (2000), suggests that participants consumed psychotropic plants such as *Anadenthera columbrina* (ground vilca seeds) to achieve altered states and adopt the forms of feline supernaturals.

Cook mentions how, in 1997, José Ochotoma and his students excavated a well-preserved D-shaped structure in which were found broken oversized pottery, subfloor llama offerings, pits for the placement of oversized cone-based vessels, and a cache of human trophy (*sic*) heads (cited in Cook 2001a: 147, Fig. 7.6b). This led Cook (2001a) to suggest that these D-shaped enclosures were focuses for rituals, the display of heads, and even human sacrifice. Surrounding these small enclosures are niched halls that did, in fact, contain several children's bodies within the niches. Although these could be respositories of the dead, they could also have held offerings. Regeneration seems to have been central in this architectural feature of the Wari polity throughout its area of influence.

The ubiquitous presence of enclosed small rooms for ceremonies located on the top of mounds had already been a major and long-lived form at many ceremonial sites throughout the Andes. This kind of architecture was built from about 2500 BC onward, for example in Áspero on the coast, and can be found at Chiripa and Pukara, as well as at La Galgada, Cahuachi, Cerro Sechín, Kotosh, and many other sites. It seems rather that, as in the case of Cahuachi, the earlier uses of these rooms seem to be more renewal and ancestor focused, whereas the rise of these later Wari D-shaped structures with their niched halls seem to express a substantive change toward housing the more aggressive centrifugal warfaring activities that include head taking and sacrifice.[26]

Gordon McEwan (1998) has studied the highly formalized organization of the Middle Horizon Wari sites south of the Cusco area. Within this group of very regular and planned structures, one type has rounded corners, like the D-shaped structure, but larger, and with rows of niches at eye level, in so-called niched halls (McEwan 1998:80).[27] In one of these buildings investigated at Pikillacta, a very important Wari site, McEwan (1988) uncovered a cache of human skulls. It is not clear if they were skulls of ancestors or of enemies. However, in this period of active expansion, it seems more likely that they were of enemies rather than of ancestors, as suggested by Cook at Wari (2001b). McEwan, however, defends the ancestor hypothesis, especially when he sees the continuance of such ancestral, corporeal storage at the later, neighboring Middle Horizon–Later Intermediate Period site of Conchapuquio.

This provides us with Middle Horizon evidence for specialized skull curation and care, but also of human skulls stored in what both Topic and

McEwan calls "lineage halls (*sic*)" at the center of an expansive centrifugal system. McEwan thinks these were feasting halls, used for ancestor remembrance and perhaps the incorporation of fictive kin into a family line, under a common ancestor (*mallki*). In this case, these niched halls would be the locus of new social interactions promoting political cohesion as well as providing a place to legitimize new family histories, by materializing the heirlooms of ancestral images (cf. Joyce 2000). If this was so, then this Middle Horizon site, Pikillacta, would provide a direct link between the earlier Formative "lineage houses" of the Titicaca Basin, found on the platform mounds at Chiripa and Pukara, and the much later Inka Coricancha niches in Cusco that housed the bodies of all of the important past *mallki* (in this case, the Inka emperors). Heads were stored in some of these niches, and people surely feasted and called on them to help define and legitimate new political regimes, just as we see them doing in the practices of ayllu consolidation today.

In her studies of a set of small turquoise figurines at Pikillacta, Anita Cook (2001b) claims that the cached curated bodies at this site are ancestral and compares them to the tenon heads at Tiwanaku. Cook studied these figurines in detail, finding sets of pairs, based on clothing style and size. Basing her analysis on the unique outfits, especially the hats worn by the figurines, she claims that these are ancestors of the many groups that came together within the Wari state. In this case, the different hats denote the presence of different personages from distinct groups, communities and/or ethnicities. Her conclusion is based on the application of a long-term symbolic system for the figurines, where she associates the color green with the ancestors. At the end of her article on the figurines, Cook relates these human effigies to the ancestors. Like *illas*, they are protectors of the crystallized essence of life and thus form part of the practices around ancestor veneration.

Patricia Knobloch offers another interpretation of Wari heads. She warns against interpreting all Middle Horizon images of the human head as simply ancestral (1993, 2000),[28] and proposes that Wari iconography of human heads with distinct headdresses and facial markings (what she calls "agents"), such as the turquoise figurines, could have been documenting the traits of particular leaders or perhaps trading partners and tribute participants from the different ethnic groups living under Wari's expanding sphere of influence. That this iconography illustrates such local leaders or trading partners is also a reasonable thesis for the use of the tenon heads at the semi-subterranean temple at Tiwanaku, as argued by Couture (2005). In this case, then, we have suggestions for both foreign (or enemy) as well as ancestral heads and bodies being important to the Wari leadership. In spite of not always being able to clarify which source these heads were from, heads in and of themselves seem to have been important to the Wari because of their tie to sources of earth, water, rain, and therefore fertility.

* * * *

This vital dimension of heads as channels for rituals centered on water and fertility in general, as well as their potent association with leadership, may explain why, at both Tiwanaku and Wari, the central place of heads is celebrated in important buildings, hosting ceremonies with political if not sacred dimensions. Interpretations of their precise use and meanings still remains open, but the evidence suggests that they played an important part in the practices of political consolidation both at the core and at the periphery of state development in the Middle Horizon, and in both centrifugal and centripetal political systems. This allows us to return to the issues that we brought up in Part I concerning radiating yield and the economics of heads. Our argument is that this archaeological evidence for head gathering seen in these Middle Horizon centers once again illustrates the central place of the metamorphosis of the commodity in the retransformation of essences associated with heads. More explicitly, the use value of these heads would have been appropriated many times over within these political domains.

At a more symbolic level, the groupings of small dark rooms on platform mounds, built across the Andes from the Initial on through the Middle Horizon, seem to replicate precisely the idea of the "mountain chests" with their trapped sacrificial offerings that we described in Part I. Although the mountain chests are used today only intermittently for the interment of animal bones, the logic of their power as sites of transformation, seems to derive much more directly from a context of domination of the dead Other and the appropriation of its powers.

There, in the stone-lined "mountain chests," set out like horizontal niches, the decaying remains of sacrifices could have acted like *illa*-seeds, becoming converted gradually into the rain clouds that initiate the production of the land and the flocks. The cultural practices focused on these transformative processes seem to have been housed in the small dark cave-like rooms at Chiripa as well as in the rooms on top of the Akapana at Tiwanaku, and the D-shaped structures and double rooms of Wari. In each case, one of the ritual goals would have been to initiate the rains, perhaps by concentrating ritual power onto the creative potential of ancestral and enemy heads.

It is probable, then, that the Wari, like the other political entities we have been discussing throughout this book, contributed to more generalized regional practices that emphasized fertility and pending production, at least as they expressed themselves ceremonially. More specifically, the leaders of both small and large polities seemed to have been particularly responsible for bringing the rain, as *yatiri* still are today in the altiplano.[29] Glowacki and Malpass (2003) make a case for Wari settlements being located next to lakes, again supporting this water-rain emphasis. Moreover, ever since the Formative period, offerings such as marine shells at such sites imply that rainmaking rituals were practiced there. Similarly, the evidence for burning patches on the floors within Wari structures suggests the burning of ritual altars (*misas*), whereas the presence at Chiripa, Tiwanaku, and Wari sites of incense burners also suggests offerings to the sky and clouds. All of these point emphatically to the underlying importance of rainmaking rituals, with their political dimensions.

Central Andean Political Developments

W E CLOSE this comparative archaeological study of Andean polities with a review of some material from the central Andes. Geographical definitions of the internal divisions of the Andean region are rather fluid, so we are calling the "central Andes" the highland regions north of the Ayacucho Valley, Vilcashuaman, and the Upper Mantaro Valley, on up through the Callejón de Huaylas. This includes what is traditionally considered the region that had patchy, but extant Wari influence, encompassing several intermontane valleys and their slopes, up to the two parallel mountain ranges of the cordillera (see Map 7.1).

Each highland and valley area had its own distinct cultural history and political trajectory. Nevertheless, the central region shared some broader symbolic systems with the south-central regions we have just presented. For example, the evidence suggests that the imagery of heads and their uses played a significant role in the construction of social and political formations. This confirms that we are dealing with a widespread and generalized phenomenon of political development throughout the whole Andean region. The following simply selects some pertinent data that support our hypothesis.

Early Ceremonial Centers of the Central and North-Central Andes

Interestingly, at the early Initial Period ceremonial site of Kotosh, in the Huallaga Valley on the eastern slopes of the north-central Andes, studied by

Map 7.1: The Central Andes, with Sites Mentioned in the Text

Map courtesy of ILCA, La Paz.

Izumi and Terada (1972), we have provocative if indirect evidence for the power of heads within the ritual-political sphere. For example, the twin mounds at this settlement, sited at the meeting of two rivers, are composed of a sequence of single room structures on top of a mound that each include a central hearth and ventilation shaft for dark, small group ceremonies that focused on burnt offerings. This same kind of structure has been uncovered by Grieder and colleagues (1988) at contemporaneous La Galgada, to the north and west, off the Callejón de Huaylas.

These hearths seem to have had a ritual purpose, for C. Earle Smith found chile peppers within them at the site of La Galgada (Grieder et al. 1988:141). This pungent and burning plant might have been used to test initiates, as it is used, for example, among the Barasana of the Columbian Amazon, or they might have been simply sacrificial plants.[1] In the Bolivian altiplano today, burning chile peppers are so pungent that they are used on occasion to suffocate unwanted children as well as being used more deliberately as a form of sacrificial death through suffocation and in malefic witchcraft.[2]

These small rooms at Kotosh are encircled by a series of niches at eye level. Izumi, Terada, and their team (1972) report that nothing was found in these niches. However, one room had two modeled crossed arms directly below niches on either side of a large stepped niche. This strongly suggests that a cranium or a stone replica of a head was placed or stored in these two niches, harkening back to the whole body of which it was once a part in a regenerative way. The use of the crossed-arms position leads us to suggest that this head was from a captured enemy, in which case its power was appropriated by the ritual practitioners resident at the site. If that is so, as Fung (1988) argues, then this architectural entity, called the Mito culture, would seem to use niched heads as the ritual trigger for the double-edged sense of the sacrificer and the regenerator.

This ancestral context of either natural or accelerated death links to the later evidence from the colonial chroniclers who tell us how the Inka sovereign's cadaver was placed in such a flexed position—arms crossed over the chest and with the head positioned over the tightly crossed knees—before it was dressed in the finest cloth and wrapped in great quantities of cotton and the face covered.[3] Today, in areas such as Qaqachaka, important Inka burials are still recognized by this characteristic positioning, as are many *chullpa* burials across the altiplano.[4]

The most prominent central Andean Early Horizon site is undoubtedly Chavín de Huántar, situated in an eastern valley off the Callejón de Huaylas in what is now central Peru.[5] We have already mentioned the use of tenon heads around the largest ceremonial structure, as if to channel the sacred power within these marked confines. As we have seen, some authors, including

Burger (1988, 1992), Cordy-Collins (1977), and Rick (2000), suggest that the Chavín de Huántar carved heads placed around the largest structure represent the power of shamanic transformation, as seen also on the Paracas textiles. Particular details on the tenon head images (for example, the mucus coming out of the nostrils) are associated here with the taking of certain plants to reach this stage of transformation. These images suggest that those who participated within the mound were involved in this shamanistic form of ceremonialism. In fact, one of the galleries was full of marine conch shells, looking very much like heads and is probably associated with rainmaking rituals (Rick personal communication 2005).

Heads appear in other arenas as well. For example, there are multiple head images found on the stone carvings of the Lanzón. This standing stone is a double-sided stela whose engraving illustrates primarily a cayman, with plants and heads sprouting out of its body. Much of this imagery illustrates fertility, like the contemporaneous animal moisture-loving images from the Titicaca Basin.

However, the most important images are found on another stone stela, called the Tello Obelisk (see Figure 1.5). The surface of this thin staff-like stela is filled with engravings expressing the fecundity of the cayman being. An important image repeated in the iconography on this stela are the heads growing out of other living things, perhaps as a celebration of their powers to procreate and generate new life, in what we described in the first part of the book as the female pole of the captured head sequence. This more female semantic complex centered on the regeneration of heads can be contrasted with most heads on other stonework, such as the Raimondi Stela, which illustrate heads with gnarling tooth-filled grins, clearly suggesting the more masculine warrior-like power to devour and kill in the first stage of the sequence. Although in a completely different style, these two images mirror the two main images on the ceramics at Pukara, the aggressive (sacrificer) male with trophy heads and the front-faced life-giving female.

These chthonic sequences, so manifest at Chavín, became commonplace throughout the Andean region in the Middle Horizon Period, manifesting themselves in representations of the powerful forces of nature most clearly seen in images of the pan-Andean staff god, or the dual-sided sky and underground figures, always symbolized by heads. In one and the same ceremonial setting, these representations invariably express the two poles of the sequence, with heads related first to the violence of sudden death, and then to the gradual processes of imminent fertility, reproduction, and transformation. In each case, the heads seem to be both vehicles and concentrators of the power flows of ritual concentration and action, affirming the inalienable power of the metamorphosed head.

North-Central Peruvian Coast

We are aware that the north-central Peruvian coast is far from our main ethno-graphical and archaeological examples, and the vast literature concerning the role of heads in this area would be a study in and of itself. Nonetheless, it warrants mentioning that in this region, too, there is ample evidence for a political dynamics based on the use of heads, whether of the processes of pol-itical expansion at the outer limits of control, or consolidation of power in the political centers. Here, we just mention a few comparative points, rather than going into detail.

For example, the Casma Valley contains many sacred sites that house a range of ever larger politically sacred meeting areas. At the start of the Early Horizon–Formative times, Cerro Sechín was built into the form we now know. Cerro Sechín was really a small ritual building associated with the larger Sechín Alto complex that dominated many hectares of the valley. This side building consists of a small mound with dense square rooms on top with rounded cor-ners. It was built up against a hillside as if it were a part of the hill shrine itself and encased with stone carvings of plumed surreal soldiers and body parts, including heads. Drawn on the surfaces of these stone monoliths are what look like executed heads, stacked with their eyes closed. Along with the body parts, and what seems to be frogspawn, are parading warriors (Wickler and Steibt 1982). There is consensus that this iconography represents the con-quering power over a dead enemy of those who illustrated these images and the subsequent curating and sharing of the taken heads. This is accompanied by the parallel theme of fecundity, via the frogs and sprouting heads (Jennings 1978). In fact, heads are a leitmotif within all these carvings.

The iconography of heads continues to be represented in this region at Pampa de las Llamas-Moxeke and at the Huaca de los Reyes mound, which is adorned with huge feline heads (Pozorski and Pozorski 1986). There is a sense of the political power of control over death associated with the feline warrior at these mounds. But the association of the power of heads with political con-trol is illustrated even more clearly in the Early Intermediate Period along the north coast, in the Moche River area. Moche portrait heads express not only individuals who likely were political leaders, but also a myriad of deities and important figures in the culture, from real potatoes to surreal skeletons (see Figure 7.1).

The famous Moche "portrait" head vessels are not *qunupa* in the sense of carved forms in the shape of something particular, but carrying-vessels used for propitiating the deities and, as elsewhere, subordinating local popula-tions in rituals of serving. Many of these "portrait" head vessels were placed in

Figure 7.1: A Moche Portrait Head
The original is in the UCLA Fowler Museum of Natural History, Los Angeles, CA,
X71-145. Courtesy of Chris Donnan.

important burials. Were these images individual enough to be family ancestors,
family members, or just important political characters that people felt the need
to have nearby? We still do not know. We can only surmise, like Weismantel
in her pertinent article on "Moche Sex Pots" (2004), that these ceramic heads
were imbued with the kind of power linked to warfare, warriors, and ruling
families. Some of the Moche ceramic drinking vessels are formed into perfect
human crania that illustrate the characteristic decapitation scenes, described
by Chris Donnan (1978, 2004).

Depictions of heads are also painted on top of poles (like the Nasca example
illustrated in Figure 4.2), or with a rope through their mouths, illustrating
the same kind of treatment of heads that was practiced by the Inka. These
heads are considered to be Moche trophy heads associated with the sacrifice
of war, as we discussed in Chapter 2 on the spirit of calculation. Interestingly,
Anne Marie Hocquenghem in her book *Iconografía Mochica* (1987:116–17)
makes the case for the close association between warriors and seed imagery
in Moche iconography, which might confirm the presence of practices based
on the death-head-seed-regeneration cycle we already identified in other parts
of the Andes.

Regarding the political formation of Moche, we have learned over the past ten years that even though the Moche polities were decentralized across several valleys without one capital, the leaders were still powerful enough to manage settlement patterns and production across the entire region, while having power over life and death. This is most cogently expressed in the recent and ongoing excavations by Uceda and Bourget on the top of Huaca de la Luna in the Moche River Valley, where young men, probably captured warriors, were tied down and left to die, probably as an offering for the rain gods (Bourget 2001a, 2001b, 2005).[6]

Further excavations in the domestic urban area of this same part of the river valley and time period have uncovered two skulls in niches within a domestic setting near the Huaca de la Luna (Verano et al. 1999:59). The finding of actual heads is rare in Moche, so this treatment seems particularly poignant near the Moche mounds. The modifications of these protected cranial offerings, defleshed after recent death, further suggests that these were collected from the captured warriors as part of the sacrifice to the deities associated with rainmaking rituals. However, these heads were not processed like the Nasca trophy heads, and although they imply the actions of a polity seeking "power over" others, they are not threaded with rope. Rather, they were used as drinking vessels, but probably in the same sense of the largesse-forced-subordination practices of giving while taking.

The Late Intermediate Period

The political setting of the Andean region shifted dramatically around AD 1000. The Late Intermediate Period (AD 1000–1450) displays ruptures in many practices, including those concerned with heads, which we shall mention again only in passing.

With the radical shifts in population settlement across the southern Andes after the demise of the Tiwanaku and Wari polities, new aggregated settlements tended to be situated on higher ground. Although this relocation must have been disruptive in some ways, the advantage was that many residents of these upland sites moved nearer to the caves that held the dead as well as to the new *chullpa* or burial houses built for the dead (Dean 2005). With these new settlements, people also began to place their dead in caves, in small constructions, and especially under the floor of their dwellings.

The construction of these *chullpas* began earlier. However, William Isbell (1997) holds that they became ubiquitous throughout the Andean region in this Late Intermediate Period. During this same time, these houses of the dead were often placed among the houses of the living. Another major shift was that heads were no longer cached or prominently depicted in textiles and on vessels. Rather, as Isbell (1997) shows, the Late Intermediate Period is characterized by the importance of mummy bundles and their curation in separate houses throughout the Andes. The power of the head "went inside."

These broad tendencies parallel the political changes brought about by the demise of large political formations and the breakdown of these political structures into more dispersed and possibly multiethnic settlement patterns, where small family rituals centered on their ancestors would have predominated. This suggests a dramatic change from a more expansive centrifugal political pattern to a more centripetal, inward-looking, and ancestor-focused one.

The many skirmishes within and between neighboring groups are mentioned often in the stories of the time before the coming of the Inka, suggesting that protection, whether real or imagined, loomed large for many. Centripetal political forces seem to have been dominant as much effort went into reforming internal, local communities. Heads were still being removed from bodies, as revealed in the Upper Mantaro Valley data, whereas many dead were wrapped and stored in caves and designated tombs. Evidently, these same people wanted to be closer to their dead, bringing them into their homes and communities.

This is the time when the political configurations we associate with the Inka Empire were being formed and consolidated. Many of the structures and images discussed in Part I were initially developed by various highland groups in the Late Intermediate Period. This implies that the shifting place of the dead within these changing societies is an important project to be studied in the near future.

Late Horizon

The Inka and the Colonial Period

This is not the place to detail the many Inka practices concerning heads, or the memory of these practices as recorded by Andean populations living today. Nor is there space to detail the many colonial accounts of the practices encountered by the chroniclers at the time of the Spanish invasion, or of what violent episodes of head taking followed as a consequence of changing political relations across the region. Here, we simply summarize some important details of the political use of heads under the Inka and in the Spanish colony that take us back to some points made earlier in the book about the role of heads in the conformation of economic systems.

In general, the Inka state was an expansive centrifugal system fed by the constant conquest of new regions and the incorporation of new populations with tributary obligations. Interestingly, the expansive nature of the Inka state, which was certainly characterized in part by the practices of head taking in warfare on the frontiers of the empire, was described by more than one chronicler in terms of religious practices that emphasized growth and sought a continually expanding productive system. Tantalean Arbulu, in his article "El circuito macroeconómico incaico" (1998:240), draws our attention to one of the songs or religious prayers collected by Molina (1943 [1573]:43) that illustrates this Inka preoccuption with economic growth:

> Oh Viracocha, and your son the Inka,
> Whom you gave us as Lord,
> While he reigns, may things multiply and be guarded safely, free from danger,
> May the times be prosperous, and the fields and people and herds all grow in number.[7] (Our translation)

This song might very well have had a European influence, but even so, the prosperity it calls for is markedly economic. This implies, as Tantalean Arbulu points out (1998:242), that the Inka state appears to perceive the utilization of its resources according to what Godelier (1971) calls a specific form of intentional economic rationality, in the sense that it sought the production and reproduction of its own organization. Even though the economic sphere was not separated from other spheres of human activity, evidently the whole set of cultural, religious, political, and kinship relations interacted here as a whole, motivated and driven by an intense desire for growth, fecundity, and prosperity.

Could it be, then, that the prevalent expansive nature of this state, characterized by head taking with the ethnic groups on the periphery, led to this radical reworking of the different spheres of human activity, now in expansive economic terms? If this were the case, then the generating yield obtained from the taking of heads might have been reconceptualized in the initial stage of a differentiated economic domain. Might this even have been an independent development of an incipient form of capital expansion, as we discussed in Part I?

We know that enemy heads were important for the Inka and were used by the leadership on many occasions.[8] Evidently, heads taken in skirmishes on the periphery of the empire were then transferred to its center in Cusco and integrated into ancestral practices. For example, it was considered important to bring the conquered enemy, dead or alive, into the empire and into Inka settlements. This was done at many levels, for example, by bringing into

Cusco the actual bodies of local leaders after death, or simply their crania, or even just their skin. Similarly, the Inka state constructed its centralized polity on the basis of a common ideological formation in Inka religion, statecraft, and sumptuary laws. To this end, local rulers' children were brought into the center of the empire, to attend special schools in Cusco. The ancestral dead were also acknowledged in many ways. For example, important dead from across the empire were curated as wrapped bundles in special death residences in Cusco.

The political use of the head also became important in Inka practices of statecraft. Chroniclers such as Cabello Balboa (1945 [1586]) describe how conquered leaders were often killed in ceremony, flayed, and the heads placed on stakes or carried in victory processions. Other documents and reports offer descriptions of how the Inka cut off the heads of their enemy leaders and carried them into Cusco for display. For example, Murúa reports that the head of a rebellious chief was carried in the hands of the effigy of Huayna Capac on an entrance into Cusco organized by Huascar (1946 [1590]:116, 118).[9]

For his part, Betanzos tells us how, under the Inka, rebel "trophy" heads were kept of many leaders, especially the Colla leaders, as prized possessions (1996:95 [1557]). We also referred earlier to Guaman Poma de Ayala's account of the way that some heads were transformed by the Inka into drinking vessels for maize beer (*ca.*1615:f.164). This transferred the enemy's strength to the Inka leader who drank from the enemy head, gaining not just the transformative maize drink but also some of the leader's essence. This resonates with what we know about Amazonian habits in certain tense times.

Under the Inka, too, miniature heads and bodies were important energy holders. Effigies of the Inka were carried into battle, as if the actual leader's being were there. There are also descriptions of how non-royal folk made masks (*huayos*) of dead enemies in central Peru. These were used to promote harvests by harnessing the energies of the deceased for regenerative purposes.[10] Apart from these characteristics of an expanding centrifugal system, the center of the empire was characterized by practices that sought to acknowledge and reproduce the powers of the great Inka lines, through attention to the Inka mummies, or in the initiation rituals of the young Inka nobles that we have already described.

* * * *

In the Colonial Period, some of these practices continued. At the same time, the tensions and apparatus of conquest and the forging of new alliances promoted a new wave of violent practices. More work needs to be done across the Andes to determine the range of patterns of power and resistance and how practices concerned with head taking or with ancestral heads changed.

More systematic work on head taking has been done in the northern Andes (Ecuador and Columbia),[11] rather than in the southern-central Andes and central Andes that we deal with here. These northern sources, based mainly on the documentation provided by Cieza de León in his *Crónica del Perú* (1553), refer to a region characterized by various frontiers, including the limits of Inka penetration northward, that, as a result of the political and social disintegration provoked by the Spanish conquest, suffered a time of intense warfare, including acts of cannibalism and head taking between local groups. Many other chroniclers (soldiers, travelers, evangelizers, and administrators) confirm this phenomenon, although most of them ignore its ritual dimension (Caillavet 1996:68).

There are certain works, though, on the central and south-central Andes that provide a historical perspective on practices around heads. For example, Mary Doyle (1988) and Frank Salomon's (1995) work on early colonial mummy veneration offers a major insight into the historical past by informing us of how the associated family lines of certain mummies were manipulated to aid in increasing the power of certain leaders in the Arequipa region. This is a strong case for their supra-family line potency in fictive kin groups. While operating within the structures of an ayllu system, political boundaries are manipulated using the ancestor as the focal point in both internal *and* external political affairs.

Reread from the perspective based on heads that we have developed here, these changing indigenous practices in the colonial period might help us ask new questions about colonial power relations in general. Evidently, the newly consolidating Spanish centers of power seemed to play on the symbolism of indigenous Andean warfare to simultaneously reinforce their own emerging forms of centripetal power, while managing an immense effort at centrifugal expansion. In parallel, Andean peoples, struggling with the destructuring forces of colonial expansion at all levels, seemed to resort to strengthening their own centripetal ancestor-based practices simply to survive.

* * * *

Throughout the archaeological sequence we have examined here, although we can see some discrete shifts in the use and place of bodies and crania, there are also some surprisingly resonating themes that continue to resurface, whether in the northern, central, or south-central Andes. We wanted to write this book to document and reflect on the provocative common uses of heads in these diverse settings, while we attempted to highlight similarities and differences in the use of heads in time and place. The use of head-shaped drinking vessels, for example, seems to be a shared aspect of head imagery throughout much of the Andes, whereas the place of the shaman's voice was not so uniformly materialized. We are not saying that all groups used the human head in the same way; in fact, it is quite clear that different cultural groups interacted and saw the place of the human head differently.

Our principal argument has been that these distinct uses of heads, rather than being simply ritual appendages, were always concerned with wider political aspects. Studying the history of crania use within these societies has allowed us to perceive this political past from a different perspective, permitting us to ask new questions, suggest tentative models of analysis, and propose preliminary answers.

Conclusions

THE MAIN thesis of this book is that many of the cultural practices centered on heads in the Andean region, like elsewhere (we mentioned mainly Indonesia, Melanesia, and Amazonia), are not simply ritual practices as they have been described until now. Rather, these practices are intensely political in nature and concerned with the accumulation of power for certain determined groups in a wider regional setting.

Building on this main thesis, we developed a series of political models, with various axes, to account for the similarities in practices as well as the differences, grounding them in specific societies, historical situations, and regions. We tried to avoid treating these practices as timeless, essentialist, or uniquely Andean. However, among the variety of practices presented here we also identify specific trends historically and similar semantic domains that can be compared across regions and time.

This includes our proposal that many common warfaring practices centered on heads were practiced in both the Amazonian and Andean regions because of the complex and long-lived historical contacts between them. We make a case for the possible historical Amazonian links of the Qharaqhara-Charkas confederation, of which Qaqachaka once formed a part in pre-Inka and Inka times, and the way that the social memory of these interrelations was still drawn on in the early Colonial Period, and, indeed, how it erupts occasionally today. However, these historical contacts were not limited to those of the south-central region. Linguistic and iconographic evidence suggest that the cultures of Tiwanaku, had important Amazonian links, perhaps even regular trade.

A gamut of historical studies has also examined these Andean-Amazonian links and their possible warfaring connections further north. Moreover, there are strong suggestions that ongoing interregional trading relations between key Andean regions and their Amazonian hinterlands may at times have erupted into warfare.[1]

Among our specific interests in the study of these practices around heads were two preoccupations. The first was to understand practices around heads as the point of reference in defining primitive forms of accumulation and exchange, or their symbolic precursors, that could possibly be applied to non-stratified and early state societies in the Andean region. The second was to develop a methodology that would allow us to examine ethnographically the practices around heads in some contemporary settings and then compare these practices with archaeological evidence from the past.

We dealt with this second more treacherous enterprise by attempting to express ethnographically a synthesis of some sequences of ideas, through structural and semantic domains, and the logical connections between them that make sense today to the social actors in the region who exercise such practices. Then we asked to what degree we might apply this kind of modeling of cultural and political practice to the archaeological data, which, although much sparser, suggested certain resonances with these contemporary practices. The key element of comparison here was the way that the political practices centered on heads generated and reproduced common political formations. In this study, we came up with nine axes of current and future research. These are the areas we found to be the most compelling for future Andean scholarship.

1. Heads as Symbols of Political Power

Our thesis that practices surrounding heads were a major principle of channeling power in different Andean societies implied that these practices centered on heads were directed toward political reformulation. In this sense, heads were key symbols of power, uniting populations and territories and activating change. Heads became key symbols of political office; headhunting, head taking, and even curating ancestral or enemy heads were all political acts. Similarly, the role of heads in political negotiations often provided the symbolic basis of authority and power in the Andes. Moreover, as a consequence of the immense power believed to emanate from heads, the power of heads and the symbolic configuration of their potentiality became transposed into many other domains.

At the same time, the archaeological examples we illustrate through time and across the Andes demonstrate the different uses of the power derived from heads in the formation of many past societies. Here, we had to weigh carefully the evidence to consider if people were using heads to gain new powers or primarily to maintain a steady life force. In this context, we had to ask if the "pathways created by heads" might have escalated in the past to create and legitimate certain groups or else expand ethnic polities and their power bases.

We also had to consider the differences in practices centered on heads in terms of the sources of these heads: Were they friend (ancestral heads) or foe (enemy heads)? One factor that we took into account here was the possibility that the intense rituality centered in the conversion of an enemy head into an ancestral one may have been the point of reference that defined thereafter a common set of relatively benign heads, minimizing the difference between them. From there on, the treatment and curation practices concerning both types of head would have been roughly comparable. For their part, ancestral heads were already relatively benign, with the immediate possibility of curation and other practices to draw on the more generalized power of the dead to help the living, help the crops grow, and substantiate and symbolize family-line power in ritual contexts. Enemy heads first needed these long ritual and practical procedures to convert them into a head of one's own, before these more generalized properties, political and otherwise, could be drawn on. This conversion procedure, however, had the potential to generate more power.

We are acutely aware that these metamorphoses of heads, in both cases, were much more complex than we have outlined. The evidence suggests that they entailed long cycles of transformations, with symbolic, seasonal, astronomical, cosmological, political, and other dimensions that also shed light on Andean political settings and their temporal transformations. We leave these issues for a later study.

Among the political theories we applied to our thinking concerning the political strategies based on heads was an overtly "power over" model. These are essentially predatory theories concerned with the way that economic practices and warfare are interrelated and how the power strategies of coercion and warfaring are deployed with these interests in mind. We found that this kind of model was more appropriate to certain archaeological settings, especially to the tactics applied to the frontiers of expanding centrifugal systems, whether in the northern and southern Inka activities as well as within former long-term polities such as Nasca, Wari, and Tiwanaku.

Another political theory we considered was "contract theory," where political power is thought to derive from the control of forms of accumulation and dissemination. Here, we perceived the role of head taking and head caching as early banking and conversion practices, perhaps in the control of local or regional elites. Our discussion of Marxist theories of the accumulation of possessions as commodities, and therefore as imminent forms of capital, was also relevant here.

In terms of wider models of alliance, including those of kin and exchange networks, we underlined the greater status of warriors who were head takers, as opposed to men who had not taken heads, and the way that their elevated status as the accumulators of heads has an important role in their subsequent status as wife takers. In a broad sense, the accumulation of "heads" accompanies an accumulation of wives.

We also showed how the political power centered on heads is reinforced by shamanic activities, such as the control of captured heads and specific shamanic practices concerned with the potency of flying heads. And we noted how this role of head converters and curators locates shamanic activity as a part of the more female domain of head taking and curation as a posterior phase to the warrior activity of head taking. Such logic hints at the potential for women's political power in a range of past settings often overlooked in archaeological discussions.

2. Heads and Regeneration

In relation to the regenerative power of heads, the ethnographic details of the case studies we present show how taken heads are considered by the social actors concerned—and not only the anthropologist—to contain a vital force of soul substance, thought to be located above all in the gray matter, and how this soul substance has real causative agency. In this sense, although acknowledging the doubts expressed in the classic article by Rodney Needham on "Skulls and Causality" (1983), we take this indigenous causative theory as our starting point for elaborating a series of logical consequences derived from head taking.

This also allows us to compare our findings in the Andean region with a wider anthropological debate. We compare both Mauss's classical studies on the Maori idea of *hau* as a kind of radiating yield and Hubert and Mauss's studies of the Pan-pacific notion of *mana* as the "idea of difference in potential," that which extends its *aura* to other possessions, with the generative power called *ch'ama* in the Aymara of Qaqachaka, obtained by a warrior from having captured a trophy head.

This generative power derived from the seed-like head of an enemy is thought to disseminate and proliferate productive processes in a series of different levels, from the localized head outward, first to the warrior's wife and immediate family and then into their wider ayllu territory and the domains of animals, plants, and sociality in general. This disseminating sequence, derived from head taking, would account for the way that practices around heads seem to generate, in an almost causative manner, the impulse to accomplish a series of other contemporary social and ritual practices, such as those around house building, the breaking in of fields, the activity of weaving, the initial demands, especially those of bride and groom service to their families in the life of a couple, many early marriage obligations, including having children, the taking of ayllu office, and so on. This same sequence would also seem to structure the polisemic way in which heads are perceived of as a part of a dynamic logic of biological transformations, especially those of flowers and fruiting trees.

Here, we identify *two* distinct stages in the cycle of head taking. The first is the actual warfaring practice of head taking and the immediate practices carried out on the taken head (boiling, burying, shrinking, plastering, displaying), all managed in general by male warriors. These activities are essentially death centered. Then, in a later phase, the warrior passes the head for curation purposes to his wife, which initiates a second sequence in the cycle, this time concerned with the creative and life-giving regeneration of the head in which head wrapping and unwrapping play a vital feminine role. This twofold model of male-controlled death dealing and the subsequent processes of female-controlled regeneration has been noted by other scholars working in the Andes (for example, Sergio Chávez), and it has frequently been illustrated on pots and the drinking vessels called *qiru* as part of a wider cultural and visual repertoire. This is first manifested in the south-central Andes in the Late Formative–Early Intermediate Period.

In these interrelated cycles, the vital force contained originally in the taken head provides the generative seed-like substance that facilitates the radiating yield from head to immediate family to wider kin and alliance groupings, and hence the proliferation of offspring for the head taker's group. Even so, the original source of this generative power is always acknowledged. We suggest that this is why, even today, the birth of babies into a family is fraught with the idea that they may have derived from hostile acts of the past, so babies are thought of as enemies to be tamed.

However, any defined point of generative agency is difficult to determine, given that women, too, in Qaqachaka, say that they goad their menfolk to go on the war path (*wila thakhi* in Aymara) in the first place, "in order to have more babies" (of various kinds), so claiming for themselves this initial agentive act. In this sense, there is only a more generalized and dispersed sense of agency, claimed by all of the key social actors involved. We can only say that this generative spirit derived from head taking is transferable, from the wife to the warrior and back to the wife. We also posit that this generative sequence is what seems to constitute the basic rules of *ayni* (composed of *aya* = a cadaver + the possessive suffix *–ni*) as reciprocal exchange in the Andean region, where the power derived from possessing *aya*, a cadaver, is converted into this more dispersed sense of alliance in warfare, relations between family groups, marriage relations, and so on, called in the broadest sense *ayni*.

In this context, there is a key relationship between the violence and masculinity of head taking, and the female creative processes of head regeneration into the pending productive forces of a harvest of new babies (plants, vegetables, animals, and humans). This key relationship is obviously widespread, and has been remarked on in the ethnographies of head taking in many parts of the world (see, for example, Hoskins 1996a on Indonesia). In these wider comparisons, we also suggest that the male aspect of this generative power or agency is similar to the premodern notion of *enjundia* as described by Jean Robert in her classic article on the rural production of maize in the *milpa* family fields of parts of Mexico (1997:277–81). There, male work does not produce things in and of itself. Rather, male toil and sweat impel nature to bring into being (in the way of "emanations") what is already there, but hidden from view. That is, production is still viewed as a pending and potential force of creation and not as something given, to be manipulated technically and measured economically.

It would be a mistake to view the transformations undergone by heads, as well as those impelled by the power of heads, simply in regenerative terms. Obviously, the power of these transformations derives from the way that death is converted into life, and this involves all the stages of decomposition and putrefaction involved in the processes of head metamorphosis. These secondary stages of head taking and head regeneration seem to give rise to the ideas around heads as "fetishes," as one step removed from the normal processes of growth or as ritual inversions of these. They would also seem to shape the instruments of thought at the heart of the practices of documenting and augmenting the productive yield generated by heads, in the more quantitative aspects of warfare and its aftermath, in the calculations of booty, territorial equivalences, and pending tax dues in peacetime. There, the calculations of the value equivalence of commodities in warfare, worked out in the play of quantities and the states of mind that characterize a tournament economy and what we call the "spirit of calculation," become autonomous substitutes for the flow of booty, while adding cultural value to them.

In the iconography of conquest, the powers gained from taking heads on the ayllu frontiers is then carefully replicated across the ayllu territory, from the center outward, in the geo-onotological enactment of head taking, for example in the *willja* rituals of agricultural production. Here again, the making of an offering in a new site serves as an opening deposit or gambit in a new sequence of productivity that expands across ayllu terrain. These activities are first suggested in the early Middle Formative burial offerings at Chiripa.

3. Heads, Violence, and Fertility

In the twofold sequence of head taking, we explored further gendered aspects. One was the way in which head taking and other warfaring acts facilitate the vocal power of men, especially in political oratory, and the control through speech of subordinate populations in a conquered territory. We identified the creative power of women, particularly in weaving and childbirth, as parallel female activities to the warfare of men. The ideal couple in Qaqachaka is still a warrior and a weaver.

This is not to say that women do not participate in the violent deeds of warfare and its aftermath. We saw how many weaving practices still act out in the loom space the suffering of the spirit of a captured prisoner before its powers are appropriated and the spirit reborn into the weaver's group. And we saw how the Coya in many colonial *qeros* is the one who holds a head. This is reinforced by modern-day practices. For example, it is still mainly women who keep skulls in boxes of one kind or another in La Paz and who may even engage in ritual dialogues with them.

In relation to this trapping and taming of enemy spirits to benefit from their powers, we suggested that rituals centered in suffering and sacrifice in the past were ultimately instruments of calling up the rains in a period of drought. It is as if the tears of the victims in these rituals were thought to stimulate the rains. This would seem to be confirmed by the fact that a specific iconography of "crying" is found throughout the Andean region. For example, tears run down the cheeks of the carved and painted front-faced deities at Pukara, Wari, and Tiwanaku, and evidence that the meaning of these images of tears, at least for speakers today, is held to help stimulate agricultural production. In fact, throughout the book, we mention numerous examples where rituals centered on the dead, whether the ancestral dead or the enemy dead, seem to seek the control of water and rains in hard times and difficult environments.

Another important dimension of these more bellicose practices was how they became transformed with the Spanish conquest. It is well documented how, as a strategy, the Spanish legitimated rival groups and encouraged the fragmentation of opposing political forces. This resulted in the contingent historical circumstances of destabilization throughout the Andean region. One aspect of these consequences of conquest is the transformation of political systems.

For example, there is much to suggest that the Inka and other contemporary incipient state formations were characterized by a warrior leader status based on achievements in combat. But after conquest and pacification, the end to raiding resulted in the greater importance of female ritual authority over the management of agriculture and generalized and shared links to the land.[2]

4. The Language of Heads

This same gendered parallelism, first configured in head taking and its aftermath, is echoed in many other settings. One of these is language itself, although the archaeological record can tell us little here. Nevertheless, from an ethnographic stance, we mentioned in Chapter 4 that many Andean language genres (songs, speech making, advice giving), as in other parts of the world, are composed of couplets, with various forms of parallelism: musical, grammatical, semantic, and so on, through which gendered differences are expressed.[3] The formal aspects of music and song also lend themselves to the expression of gendered differences, in real and metaphoric ways. Female song making, in particular, as in the songs to the animals of Qaqachaka, is said to replicate the female notion of "wrapping" as a key semantic domain. Just as women wrap and unwrap trophy heads during the rituals of curation and appropriation, so they wrap their newborn animals metaphorically in song. In this sense, the songs to the animals are described as wrappings of placenta-like sound that transform the animals born in the hills (and the realm of the dead ancestral spirits) into a more human and domestic setting. More work needs to be done here on the prayers offered by women to the trophy heads when they are under their care, to see if other comparisons can be made.

The wedding songs of contemporary Qaqachaka, on the other hand, with their constant allusions to new saplings or *mallki*, echo what McWilliam (1996) has called a "trunk language" elsewhere, in the sense of describing the trunk-like political origins of certain groups that subsequently branch out. Here, we argue that the new household of married life has been founded on the bellicose act of head taking and that the trophy head guarded in the house subsequently provides and nurtures the root, seed, and sapling (*mallki*) that will grow in this new fertile environment and flower with the birth of a crop of new babies. We suggest that the visual language of early stelae, such as the sprouting heads of the Formative times imagery in the Titicaca Basin, might be an early example of these kinds of botanical and zoological metaphors, centered on heads, whose contemplation and associated cultural practices might have included similar forms of verbal art.

The study of visual languages, too, is pertinent to the interpretations of Andean systems of meanings, in the past and the present. We posited throughout this book that textual authority in the Andes was not based in writing, but in weavings, in the practices of knotting threads in *kipus*, and formerly in the practices common to both of these, of head curation. Two other possibilities warrant comment here. One is that evidently the "social life" of material objects expresses this long-lasting relationship between political authority, heads, and speech. This seems to be the case with reference to the woven "head-bags" of office still used today by the male ayllu authorities in Qaqachaka and their counterparts in the female coca cloths, each held to speak at the opening of their administrative periods of office. Another is the way in which the insistent practice of "memory pathways," in Qaqachaka and its neighbors such as K'ulta, seem to harken back constantly to the origins of things, as if to emphasize that the causative agency of head taking is the root of all created things in the social world.

We also considered the iconography of heads, in the designs of these "memory pathways" on the drinking cups called *qiru*, that expressed in visual form the centripetal (inward-directed) and centrifugal (outward directed) patterns of associated polities. According to Jorge Flores Ochoa, these designs transformed the narrative forms of orality into vision and action. In a more corporal sense, the inscribed or painted designs on skull-like drinking vessels were read in an opposed fashion, but according to a common semantic domain, by victor and vanquished alike while drinking and speaking libations together.

Also in the domain of drinking and head taking, we argue that the important Andean notion of *jucha* in the sense of obligation, duty, or debt derives from the original sucking of the brains out of skulls in warfare, and that this is why *jucha*, in the sense of "carrying a head" from the past, is such a key notion today in the sense of personal service in the carrying out of the obligations of ayllu office. We further argue that feasting and drinking are components of the intense victorious celebration of war domination over an adversary, their lands, and products. These feasts often have an aspect of competition.

At the heart of this common visual language of drinking vessels and even cooking pots were the images of felines as the primary warriors and head takers, whether on the periphery or in the very center of Andean polities. These fierce images are then counterbalanced by the accompanying images of flowers and shoots, as if to acknowledge the future of the victim as head giver to participate in a wider sequence of generative growth.

The transformation of heads into other material objects, such as the woven bags of office of ayllu authorities, still held to have the power of speech, or the *vara* staffs of office, often decorated with heads and other vegetative imagery, also considered to be endowed with the powers of speech, seem to confirm the primacy of this generative complex of warfare and head curation, celebrated in the carrying out of ayllu office and feasting.

5. The Body Politic

The study of the power of the head as a symbol in these sequences of head taking and head curation also underlines the interrelations between bodily, political, and moral domains in a premodern world. We have illustrated various cases (Qaqachaka, Jesús de Machaqa, and Cusco) in which body parts constitute metaphors of group and political formation. And we alluded to the way that the Inka had a bodily presence in the territories under his domain through weavings, images, and icons.

There is also a way in which the ongoing geopolitical territorial enactments of the memory of warfare and head taking, and their appropriation to re-create regional or ayllu identity, draw on this sense of a body politic. If the part of the cycle associated with warfare focuses on the destruction and dismantling of body parts, the following, more creative and fertilizing parts of this cycle are concerned with reconstituting the parts of the dismembered dead into a newly functioning whole.

This is the case in ayllu narrative histories, which recount tales of the dismemberment and reconstitution of the ayllu ancestors, as well as in the cultural practices of, say, *wayñu* performance, where the same process is carried out through verbal arts and music. At stake in these practices is the conscious reconstruction of individual powers gained in warfare, whether body strength and essence or the engendering of other individuals, into a much larger conceptual and unifying domain. Hence, individual power becomes changed into household power, kin group power, or even ayllu power. At the same time, the notion of "power over" a common enemy is transposed into the group energy of "power to" continue dominating that enemy or reconstitute one's own ayllu drawing on the energy of that enemy.

Another way in which the geopolitics of head taking is expressed culturally is in architectural form. We suggested that the early ceremonial enclosures and mound of Chiripa, as well as the later Middle Horizon mounds of Tiwanaku, are nested elaborations on the bodies of dead ancestors, in architectonic form, comparable with nested territories within a larger body politic. Here, the dead ancestor also serves as a kind of seed-*illa* within a pyramidal mountain chest, whose architectonic wrappings and ritual accompaniments help sprout into new life.

The same kinds of processes are at work in the rituals that take place in the modern ayllu plazas of today, such as in Qaqachaka, where the layout of buried heads, and the drawing on their power to reconstitute the larger ayllu polity consciously recreate ayllu identity from the powers of the dead (see again Figure 4.3).

We mentioned how in these more generalized cases, as well as in female weaving practices, the head acts as the primordial template that structures other domains. At one level, we saw how the origins of weaving may have derived from creating in the loom space the cultural medium for appropriating the energies of the trophy head of a dead enemy, and reintegrating its spirit into the own group. At a wider level, similar cultural practices serve in times of peacemaking to weave the head seeds captured in warfare into the greater territorial alliances of geopolitical relations. This was illustrated in the dances that take place on the ayllu boundaries between young people of neighboring ayllus now at peace, when the trophies of the aftermath of war are also danced into new forms and structures of cloth.

6. Heads and Political Systems

Throughout, we have developed various models of the relationship between practices concerning heads and political systems.

We considered the center-periphery relations that derive from a world-systems approach, reworked in the Andes by La Lone (2000) and colleagues, but introducing internally generated changes as well as externally generated ones. We also considered the structural approaches of Jonathan Friedman and his argument that societies that might seem quite different in their political systems, might in fact be structural transformations of each other. Friedman found this in Burma, where societies practicing headhunting, competitive feasting, and continual warfare were, in his opinion, structural transformations of societies based on large-scale politically expansive theocratic chiefdoms that took slaves instead of heads, maintained a system of strictly aymmetrical marriage, and tended via the extension of tributary relations toward state forms of organization. Friedman summarized this difference in terms of head takers seeking out an accumulation of soul force. These head takers later converted the heads to ancestors, in an attempt to siphon off ancestral force from their neighbors in a struggle to restore declining fertility. The slave takers, on the other hand, emphasized an accumulation of labor. We concluded that these differences are not so marked in the Andes, where slave taking often accompanied head taking.

Another axis to the study of Andean political systems is the way that the generally dispersed nested and segmentary societies that we see today became hierarchically ordered and even centralized periodically in the past as a result of an overlaying series of unifying features (moiety systems, gendered parallelism, and so on). This debate about the degree of political centralization of different polities is ongoing. Although the general tendency has been to see hierarchy increasing in a diachronic sequence, archaeologists also find evidence for "heterarchy" in the sense of multiple centers of power within the growth of larger polities or even long-term segmentation.

We also drew on Carlos Fausto's distinction in Amazonian societies between overtly expanding, more warlike (including head taking), and centrifugal political systems, as compared to more pacific and centralized centripetal systems that focus on ancestral and family identities (2001:399, 466, 533). The former practice what Viveiros de Castro calls "ontological depredation" to appropriate forces from the outside and so replenish one's own. The latter are characterized by rituals of descent that reproduce one's own group, although the initial rituals in these contexts may also prepare warriors for their intermittent skirmishes on the frontiers of the polity. Contemporary and historical Qaqachaka seem to be examples of the former centrifugal political system, whereas the archaeological example of Chiripa seems to be one of a pacific centripetal system focusing its ritual energies on the maternal kin lines.

However, there are also examples in the Andes that combine both centripetal and centrifugal forms. The Inka state, for example, was evidently an expansive centrifugal polity practicing head taking on its frontiers with other ethnic groups. But these were accompanied by equally centripetal tendencies in Cusco, the center of the empire, where ceremonial and ritual practices were concerned with the mummies of the ruling Inka lines, while bellicose rites of passage for Inka nobles prepared them to go out to the conquering periphery again.

These opposing forces of integration and disintegration seem to be everpresent, as witnessed by the incessant splitting of major ayllu units into their constituent parts, noted by Albó and many others today. Yet, there is an accompanying tendency toward unity, for example, through the unifying notions of body symbolism and the rotational practice of office taking. We also see this process at work in some Late Intermediate Period sites, such as the Upper Mantaro Valley, where previous groups split up while at the same time reformed into two moieties, clearly present in the larger aggregated settlements toward the end of that time phase.

Other tendencies seem directed toward the greater complexity of organizational forms. For example, in Nasca, an earlier and more pacific society cedes to a later and more bellicose one. The earlier matrilineal focus at Chiripa cedes at some point to a more male-based centrifugal political hierarchy. In other cases (as in Wari), former ancestor-based systems of ritual and political practice give way to later military power possibly in the hands of elite families. Similarly, in the developments at Wari, practices that were once more group based seem to become transformed into the more individualized practices of a developed military polity. Could this have been the cause of the demise of Tiwanaku, namely that it did not shift to a more centrifugal form of political hierarchy? Did the Titicaca Basin have to await that development later on, in the more menacing context of Late Intermediate Period aggressive groups?

One of the common themes in these developments is the greater complexity and centralization of systems of tribute and recompense, often within the guise of largesse, propitiation, and offerings.

We referred to "heterarchy" as the heterogeneous and entangled articulation of multiple hierarchies at play in any one historical moment to understand better the complexity of historical and archaeological systems. According to heterarchy, head taking would seem to characterize a "core power matrix" as an organizing principle that reshapes economic, political, and gender relations as well as institutional and household structures in the centers of power, while also articulating peripheral locations within the hierarchies so established. Heterarchy allows us to abstract certain processes, such as head taking, that once integrated—or entangled—in a concrete historical process acquire different structural effects and meanings.[4]

7. Heads as Constructors of Social and Cultural Identity and Difference

In our focus on heads as constructors of social and cultural identity and difference, we had to consider the more generalized notions of the dead in Andean societies. Hastorf has emphasized here the importance of relational identity and meaning in the construction of self-other boundaries, whether at the heart of ancestor-centered rituals or in the bellicose excursions of the periphery.

A key interest of ours was the source of the heads, whether they were ancestral or enemy and what kinds of transformations might have taken place between them. In Arnold's studies of Qaqachaka, the main focus seems to be on enemy heads, and although trophy heads are converted ritually into kin, there still seem to be some differences in focus on these different kinds of heads. For example, ancestral heads are viewed more in terms of the hard ancestral line of bone skulls, rather than in terms of eating the soft brains of enemy heads. The scale of activity may also be a factor here, in the sense that perhaps smaller groups in the past would have used the enemy dead as well as the ancestral dead perhaps in different ways.

Nevertheless, contemporary evidence of head curation in the practices centered on the cherished *ñatita* skulls in La Paz, Bolivia, where the skulls tend to be selected from those who had violent deaths or persons who were thieves or dealt in contraband, points to an association with the enemy dead rather than the ancestral dead. This might also explain why the skulls are considered potentially dangerous, possibly turning against their owners at any time if not attended properly.

In general, though, the evidence seems to weigh in favor of the constant presence of the ancestral dead, from Paracas textiles onward, and the presence of trophy heads seems to be a more exceptional case.

8. Heads as Part of Economic Transactions

The common practices of head taking and head curation found in the Andes as well as in the Amazon Basin suggests that in the past these were part of more generalized circuits of exchange (of heads, objects, souls, names, and body parts), whereby head taking, cannibalism, and regeneration formed a continuum of practices that might have included related activities such as slavery, slave raiding, and coerced or obligatory trade. Although this is easier to trace in the historical literature of the northern Andes, it is equally necessary to develop more historical and ethnographic studies to trace these links in the south-central regions.

There is a wide anthropological debate concerning the role of head taking, and even ear taking, as a part of exchange relations between groups, in which head taking and head caching can be understood as primitive forms of accumulation. Head taking has also been posited in indigenous theory as an idealized vision of exchange relations. In our contribution to this debate, we have referred particularly to Viveiros de Castro's work on "ontological depredation" and Fausto's work on "productive consumption" or its more Amerindian form of "consumptive production" (which we interpret as the producing of objects and people, or kin from heads, through head curation), as aspects of lowland economic circuits that might be equally pertinent to highland studies. We also took into account the more generalized lowland idea that the reproduction of persons is more important to indigenous circuits of production and exchange, rather than things. And we noted above how we were aware that "production" in a premodern context does not refer so much to the creation of finished products as commodities as to the agency of humans in facilitating the generative sequences of making visible the emanations (and energy) already present in nature, perhaps conceived originally as a generalized result of head taking.

In trying to understand pre-state economies, we considered the hoarding or caching of heads as part of a series of practices that controlled the flows of wealth, while at the same time increasing the value of heads as symbolic goods. Thus, the caching (or banking) of both ancestral and enemy heads might stand in for land and water claims over wider territories, also allowing you to speak for these. In this sense, the accumulation of heads was a form of wealth finance. Drawing on Weiner's work in her book *Inalienable Possessions* (1992), we proposed that heads guarded were enclaved, curated commodities, whose controlled distribution and restricted flow, at the service of elite monopolies, defined the values across exchange circuits, authenticating subjective value above exchange value, while practices centered on heads also define the value transformations that might take place. For example, there seems to be value added during the head curating practices that transform enemies into kin.

In these wider economic debates, we reconsidered Marx's notion of commodity fetishism, whereby the commodity represents social relations, and the fetish is only a disguised form of the power of yield. In the exchange circuits based on head taking, we proposed that the series of metamorphosis that Marx sees in terms of "money" and "capital," and the transformations between them, could perhaps be reconsidered in terms of the transformations or metamorphosis between the "heads" taken by men in warfare and the "babies" generated by women as a consequence of this. We proposed that exchange value enters into the head-taking cycle as the added female value of having transformed the head into kin.

We also noted the apparent change of emphasis in the Inka state, where the combination of head taking on the periphery of the empire, as well as the veneration of ancestral heads at its center, seemed to accompany a "specific form of intentional economic rationality," which sought more consciously the production and reproduction of its own form of organization. We suggest that the generating yield obtained from this statewide scale of head taking and head management might even have triggered the initial stage of a differentiated economic domain, with certain elements in common to an incipient form of capitalism.

The testing of these ideas can only be done with further case studies. We have simply looked at the practices surrounding the early forms of accumulation of heads, as in the Nasca Valley, and proposed that these are early forms of head management or emerging bureaucracies ("headocracies"). Only with the later development of state-like polities, do we witness the emergence of systems of tribute and recompense, calculated in the aftermath of warfare. Here, the state becomes the ultimate head taker, as the language of heads becomes more widely disseminated in the "head count" tax systems, or the heads on coinage of more modern examples. In the earlier forms, we witness the emergence of the first bureaucratic instruments for counting the forms of booty taken and tribute owed, accompanied by the tournament logic of the spirit of calculation (in wood and wool).

9. The Guarding and Maintenance of Heads

Finally, the early management of heads evidently gave rise to many of the specific and unique material and textual forms of the Andean region. From the earliest niches at Chiripa, the places for depositing, curating, and managing heads in general became elaborated into the "mountain chests" we find in Moche even today, and then into the chests of rawhide and wood of the colonial, republican, and modern periods.

We argue that these management practices centered in heads became the basis for the early "bureaucratic" systems of the region, such as the knotted threads called *kipu* in Quechua and *chinu* in Aymara, which have their precursors in Wari and Tiwanaku. We further argue that the terminology and practices of knot keeping derived from head taking, whereby the main *kipu* thread was once the skull itself and the pendant threads, human hair.

The *kipu* practices of recent times in ayllus such as Qaqachaka give us further clues to the continuity between head curation practices, the later bureaucratic forms of knot keeping, and the keeping of written documents in the same kinds of enclosed spaces today. We suggest that the origin of these practices derived from warfare and the necessity to keep captive enemy heads safe in contained spaces. Trapped in these chambers, whether mountain chests, or their rawhide counterparts, the sacrificial offerings therein gave off dangerous emanations as they decomposed first into their constituent elements and finally into rain clouds. Death in this context, certainly of the softer tissues, appears to be conceived as "shadow" substance, while the hard bone remains as seed substance waiting for renewal. In this sense, the range of boxed containers used to concentrate the powers of the items contained therein, whether the stone-lined mountain chests or the rawhide chest with its hard wooden base, act as if they were simply the hard bone skulls or crania surrounding the transforming energies inside.

At the same time, the buried skull caches at sites such as the mountain chests were evidently key sites for rainmaking, as a result of the decompositions that took place. And, in turn, these fertilizing rainmaking functions became disseminated with the promotion of wider social relations, such as marriage, exchange, military service, and so on.

Here, the added value of ritual activity surrounding death converts the subjective value of heads taken to the exchange value of wider social relations as well as regeneration. And, as part of the implicit contractual procedures, *degeneration* serves as a vital part of the process of regeneration. Thus, these mountain sites, as the guarding places for skulls, were sites of the emerging practices of focusing value and organized forms of control over accumulation. The expenditure of human energy as strength (Aym. *ch'ama*), accompanied by the more capricious practices of desire and luck making (Aym. *surti*) added value, just as the ongoing deposits of new ritual offerings added value and stimulated growth.

* * * *

We present these preliminary conclusions about the possible role of heads in the constitution and consolidation of social and political power in the Andes in the hope that others will elaborate on the models presented here and help us understand better these processes in Andean political settings and beyond.

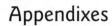

Appendixes

Sites and Toponyms Mentioned in the Text

The Central and North-Central Andes (mainly archaeological sites)

Áspero (coastal Supe Valley), 74, 75, 119, 201
Cali (Colombia), 122
Callejón de Huaylas, 205
Caral (Supe Valley), 119
Cerro Sechín (Casma Valley), 48, 75, 201, 209
Chan Chan (Moche River Valley), 82, 139
Chavín de Huántar, 55, 61, 64, 67, 77, 119, 167, 200, 217
Chicama Valley (Northern Peru), 86
Chordeleg (Cuenca Prov., Ecuador), 83, 85, 90
Chucana ruins (Department of Ancash, Peru), 85
Cuchana (apacheta pass on Mount Huauyan)
Huaca de la Luna (Moche Valley), 74, 90, 211
Huaca de los Reyes (Casma Valley), 200, 209
Huamachuco (Peru), 86
Huandobal (Peru), 85
Kotosh (Huallaga Valley), 75, 200, 201, 205
La Galgada (off the Callejón de Huaylas), 75, 79, 200, 201, 207
Llamas de Moxeke (Casma Valley)
Moche River Valley, 74. *See also* Huaca de la Luna, Chan Chan.
Pacopampa, 200
Pampa de las Llamas–Moxeke (Casma Valley), 74, 200, 209
Pasao (Ecuadorian coast), 179
Sechín Alto (Casma Valley)
Sicán (north coast of Peru), 150

The South-Central Andes (mainly archaeological sites)

Acari Valley (Nasca), 178

Apurímac (southern Peru), 158

Arequipa region, 215

Asia (coast), 162

Cahuachi (Qawachi, Nasca Valley), 74, 75, 119, 122, 171, 174, 177, 180, 182

Cavernas (Paracas Peninsula), 172

Cerro Carapo (Nasca Valley), 64, 74, 178

Cerro de la Cruz (Paracas Peninsula), 171

Cerro del Plomo (Chile), 137

Chanka territory, 92

Chaviña (Nasca Valley), 64

Chinchorro (northern Chile coast), 50, 171, 178, 179

Chiripa (Taraco Peninsula; Lake Titicaca), 71, 75, 79, 183, 201

Ch'isi (Lake Titicaca), 189

Choquecancha (Cusco region), 67

Conchapuquio (near Wari)

Conchopata (Ayacucho Valley), 197, 198

Copacabana Peninsula, 185

Coricancha (Qurikancha, Cusco), 72, 75, 188

Cusco, 67, 72, 79, 98, 137, 228

Estaquería (Nasca Valley), 64

Huarochirí (Waruchiri, Pacota), 88

Huarpa territory (Ayacucho Valley), 197

Ica River Valley, 61, 171, 174, 176–177

Kala Uyuni (Qala Uyuni), 99, 162, 189

Khonko Wankanke (Qunqu Wankanki), 118

La Barca (near Oruro), 72

Llave River (west of Lake Titicaca), 183

Mantaro Valley (Upper, Peru), 89, 92, 155, 212, 228

Nasca (Cerro Carapo, Chaviña, Estaqueria, Nazca River, Palpa, and Tambo Viejo), 27, 51, 91, 114, 122, 162, 171, 176–182, 219

Ocucaje (Ica Valley), 171

Pachacamac (Pachaqamaq), 78, 119

Pacota (Huarochirí), 88, 160

Palpa (Nasca Valley), 178

Paracas (Necropolis), 50, 51, 55, 67, 122, 169–176

Pikillacta (Wari), 201, 202

Pukara (Titicaca Basin), 57, 63–64, 75, 119, 201.

Qala Uyuni. *See* Kala Uyuni (Taraco Peninsula).

Qeros (Qirus, Cusco region), 67, 140
Qunqu Wankanki. *See* Khonko Wankanke.
Qurikancha. *See* Coricancha (Cusco).
Santiago de Huata Peninsula (Titicaca Basin), 162, 185
Sonqo (Peru), 30, 156
Tambo Viejo (Nasca Valley), 64
Taraco Peninsula, 16, 71, 99, 185
Tawantinsuyu
Titicaca Basin, 30, 33, 67, 74, 98, 124, 157,182–196
Titimani (Lake Titicaca), 162, 189
Tiwanaku (Tiahuanaco), 72, 119, 150, 217, 219
Topará (Ica Valley), 122, 169, 171
Vilcashuaman, 205
Wanka and Sausa, 151; territories, 92
Wari (Ayacucho Valley), 72, 79, 99, 122, 139, 150, 219
Xauxatambo (Inka), 152

The South-Central Andes (contemporary sites)

Aguas Calientes, 42
Aiquile (Cochabamba, Bolivia), 37
Ayllu Milma (Aymaya valleys, northern Potosí), 57, 64
Carangas (Karankas, Oruro), 73, 77–79, 83
Challapata, 115–116
Charazani, 160–161
Charkas federation, 40–4, 125
Charkas-Qharaqhara, 37, 41–43, 125, 217
Condocondo, 40, 133
Cordillera de los Frailes, 37
Guapay River, 41
Jesús de Machaca, 111, 118
Jukumani, 42, 64, 125, 132, 134
Killakas-Asanaqi, 37, 42–43, 125
K'ulta, 29, 93
Lake Poopó, 37
Lake Titicaca (Lake Chucuito and *Wiñay marka*), 30, 33, 67, 182
La Paz, 163–166
Lauca River, 100
Laymi, 42, 125, 132, 158
Lima, 119

Macha, 93, 125, 132
North Condo, 42
Northern Potosí, 107, 121
Pukuwata ayllu, 40, 132
Pilcomayo River, 41
Pukuwata ayllu, 40, 132
Qachaja (Carangas, Oruro)
Qaqachaka, 37, 46, 64, 67, 83, 101, 115, 143–144, 159, 176
Qharaqhara, 40

Lowland Groups

Achuar (Ecuador), 117
Amazonian region, 46
Barasana (Columbian Amazon), 153, 207
Bororo (Brazilian lowlands), 152
Caviña groups (Vilcanota River), 103
Chaco (Bolivia), 88
Chichas, 40
Chiriguanos, 40–43
Diaguitas, 40
Ecuadorean lowlands, 47
Ge (Xingu region), 153
Shuar or Jívaro (Ecuador), 47, 49, 65, 123, 179
Tukano (Alto Río Negro and Vaupés), 153
Tupi-Guaraní, 25, 40, 43, 68
Warí (Western Brazil), 51
Xingo, 23

Andean Cultural Sequences

Rowe and Menzel (1967)		Lumbreras (1974) / Rick (1990), Peru		Ponce, Bolivia	
AD 1476–1532	Late Horizon	AD 1476–1532	Inka Empire	AD 1450–1532	Inca
AD 900–1476	Late Intermediate	AD 1000–1476	Regional States	AD 1100–1450	Seniorios
AD 550–900	Middle Horizon	AD 500–1000	Wari Polity	AD 800–1100 AD 475–800	Tiwanaku V Tiwanaku IV
400 BC-AD 550	Early Intermediate	200 BC-AD 500	Regional Development	AD 100–400 100 BC-AD 100	Late Formative II Late Formative I
1400–400 BC	Early Horizon	800–200 BC	Formative	1500–100 BC	Middle Formative
2200–1400 BC	Initial Period	2000–1000 BC	Late Archaic	1500–1000 BC	Early Formative
		8000–2000 BC	Middle Archaic	10,000–1500 BC	Archaic (Preceramic)
		10,000–8000 BC	Early Archaic/ PaleoIndian		

Glossary

Aym. = Aymara
Lit. = literally
Qu. = Quechua
Sp. = Spanish

Achak k'illpha   (Aym.) Lit. "mouse marking." A dance to promote peace time performed by young people on the boundaries between ayllus in dispute.

Ajayu   (Aym.) One of the human souls. A term for the spirit of a regional *wak'a* deity.

Akilla   (Aym. and Qu., Hispanicized as *aquilla*) Colonial silver *qiru* or drinking cup.

Alcalde mayor   (Sp.) Lit. "Greater mayor, Lord mayor." The main authority of a major ayllu such as Qaqachaka.

Alma uru   (Aym.) Lit. "Day of the dead." Monday.

Animu   (Aym. from the Sp. *ánimo*) One of the human souls. The animus. A term for one of the souls that resides in a trophy head. A name for the spirit of a regional *wak'a* deity.

Apacheta   (Aym.) Mountain pass, mountain shrine.

Apu   (Qu.) Guardian mountain. Quechua equivalent to the Aymara *uywiri*.

Awayu   (Aym.) Woman's mantle.

Aya   (Qu.) Cadaver.

Ayllu   (Qu.) Andean communities that claim descent from putative ancestors in common and have common territories.

Ayni   (Qu. and Aym.) Reciprocal support; for example, alliances in warfare, and labor exchange.

Aysiri   (Qu.) Specialist shamans able to speak to trophy heads and the dead.

Baúl	(Sp.) Chest made of wood or rawhide, when it is more usually called *petaca*.
Chachapuma	(Aym.) Lit. "man-puma." A being or ritual office considered to be half man and half puma, who frequently holds a trophy head.
Ch'ama	(Aym.) Strength, force.
Ch'amakani	(Aym.) Specialist shamans able to speak to trophy heads and the dead.
Chakit'aqlla	(Qu.) Foot plow used for farming.
Chhiphiña	(Aym.) Former obligatory period of service to the community, in the Jesús de Machaca region of La Paz.
Chicha	(Qu.) Beer, usually of maize.
Ch'iwu	(Aym.) Shadow. Name for an offering as a whole. Twigs interred in offering sites that symbolize the clouds.
Chinu	(Aym.) Knotted threads used in documenting and planning productive activities in the Andes. Aymara equivalent to *kipu*.
Chonta	(Sp.) The hard dark palm wood from the Amazon (lat. *Bactris gasipaes*).
Chuño	(Aym. *ch'uñu*) Freeze-dried potatoes.
Ch'uqi	(Aym.) Raw.
Comunario	(Sp.) Lit. "commoner." Ayllu member.
El Niño	(Sp.) Lit. "The Boy." Also called ENSO, or *El Niño Southern Oscillation*. Term for cyclic periods of unusual weather, most often torrential rains where usually there is none. Caused by an ocean water-atmospheric phenomenon associated with changes in water temperature in the Pacific Ocean off the west coast of South America. La Niña ("The Girl") is the opposite, a time of drought.
Fardo	(Sp.) Mummy bundle.
Hau	(Maori) The spirit of a gift. We interpret this as a measure of the radiating yield of guarded valuable possessions.
Heterarchy	The heterogeneous articulation of multiple hierarchies at play in any one historical moment. For example, the multiple centers of power within the growth of larger polities.
Illa	(Aym. and Qu.) The essence of something. Often a colored or strangely formed stone or a bezoar.
Inkuña	(Aym.) Woven cloth used by women for coca leaves.
Inqa	(Qu.) Essence, life force.
Invidia	(Sp.) Envy.
Ipala	(Aym.) Aunt. Sisters on the male side.
Ispiritu	(Aym. from Sp. *espíritu*) Spirit. Spiritual energies.

Istalla	(Aym.) Woven cloth used by women for coca leaves.
Jaqi	(Aym.) Person, human. Married person. Personhood in a juridical sense.
Jilanqu	(Aym.) Ayllu leader, sometimes called the "head" or *p'iqi*. Equivalent to the *jilaqata* in other regions.
Jira mayku	(Aym.) Lit. "turning lords, or war lords." The turning spirits of the dead and the vegetation.
Jucha	(Aym. and Qu.) Duty, obligation. Debt, sin.
Jucha p'iqi	(Aym.) Lit. "head carrier." A person who passes a feast.
Juchjaña	(Aym.) The verb "to suck."
Jula jula	(Aym.) Panpipes.
Jump'i	(Aym.) Sweat.
Kharisiri	(Aym.) Lit. "one who cuts, cutter." The "grease-suckers" who drain their victims of energy. Quechua equivalent to *ñaqaq*.
Khuyaq	(Qu., Hispanicized as *cuyac*) Cared for. The material support of the Inka Empire engendered by the circulation of tribute.
Khuyay	(Qu.) Lit. "to care for." The protection and care that a curated skull might provide in a household.
K'illpha	(Aym.) The ceremony of marking the animals. The border of the weft in a woven cloth.
Kipu	(Qu.) Knotted threads used in documenting and planning productive activities in the Andes. Quechua equivalent to *chinu*.
Kipukamayuq	(Qu.) Administrator of the information documented on *kipu* threads.
Kuraji	(Aym. from the Sp. *coraje*) Lit. "courage." A term for the spirit of a regional *wak'a*.
Liwaña	(Aym.) Family or communal offering place on a hillside.
Machay	(Qu.) Cave.
Makana	(Qu.) Pointed lance, often formed from chonta palm wood and used as stakes with trophy heads impaled on top.
Mallki	(Qu.) A sacred ancestor, a mummified ancestral body. A sapling.
Mallku	(Aym.) Noble title. A traditional ayllu authority.
Mana	Pan-pacific notion of a special quality of people, animals, or objects that extends its aura to other possessions.
Manqhasaya	(Aym.) Lower moiety, considered to be feminine.
Manta	(Aym.) Arable land of individual family plots, held and managed in common. The Spanish term refers to a woman's mantle.
Marka	(Aym.) Jurisdiction of a major ayllu, and the name for its central town.

Maskay paycha (Qu.) The Inka's royal fringe, of fine red wool.

Mitimae (Qu.) Families taken from their communities by the Inka State and transferred to conquered districts to perform political, cultural, social, and economic functions.

Mujuna (Aym. from Sp. *mojón*) Boundary marker, boundary stone.

Muyu (Aym.) A drinking round or a concentric design that guides the pattern of remembering, for example, in libation making.

Ñaqaq (Qu.) Lit. "one who cuts, cutter." The "grease-suckers" who drain their victims of energy. Equivalent to the Aymara *kharisi*.

Ñatita (Aym.) Lit. "little turned-up noses." The curated skulls of modern day La Paz, which tend to be kept by women.

Nuwasi (Aym.) Fight. Ontological depredation. A term coined by the Brazilian anthropologist Viveiros de Castro to describe the appropriation of forces from the outside to replenish one's own.

Pachamama (Qu.) The Virgin Earth, also called *Tira wirjina*.

Paititi (Qu.) The lost Inka city, thought to be situated in the rainforest to the east of the Andes.

Pajcha or *phajcha* (Aym. and Qu.) A cascade. A form of *qiru* drinking cup with a long stem and spout, used for making libations.

Patrón (Sp.) An owner of a large landed estate called hacienda in the Andes during the Colonial and Republican periods.

Patxasaya (Aym.) Upper moiety, considered to be masculine.

Pinkillu (Aym. and Qu.) Wooden duct flutes played traditionally in the rainy season.

P'iqi (Aym.) Head.

Pulu (Aym.) The border threads of the warp in a woven cloth.

Puraka (Aym.) Belly.

Qamaqi (Aym.) Name for the spirit that dwells in a trophy head.

Qanchi (Qu.) Lit. "the llama huckle bone." Game of chance played at the Feast of the Dead.

Qarwa (Aym.) Llama.

Qarw katuri (Aym.) Lit. "the one who grasps llamas." Name for a reconstituted carcass used as an offering.

Qarw uywirpa (Aym.) Lit. "the llamas' carer." Name for a reconstituted carcass used as an offering.

Qhati (Aym.) Raw, uncooked.

Qiru (Qu. often Hispanicized as *qero* or *kero*) Drinking cup made of wood, ceramic, or metal, and often fashioned around the form of a skull.

Riwutu	(Aym. from Sp. *devoto*) Lit. "devoted ones." Name for the curated skulls of modern-day La Paz and the surrounding region.
Runa	(Qu.) Person, human. Married person. Personhood in a juridical sense.
Samanchi	(Aym.) Lit. "the air sender." Term for an offering hole on mountainsides.
Samaña	(Aym.) The verb "to breathe."
Sami	(Aym. and Qu.) Breath. Essence. Life force.
Samiri	(Aym.) Lit. "the one who breathes." Breath spirit found on mountainsides.
Sawu tila	(Aym.) Lit. "weaving loom." A dance to promote peace performed by young people on the boundaries between ayllus in dispute.
Siqi	(Aym. and Qu., Hispanicized as *ceque*) Something straight: a straight line, or a straight path. The system of ritual straight paths radiating from Cusco.
Surti	(Aym. from the Sp. *suerte*) Lit. "luck." The sense of luck that generates production and productive activities.
Tambo	(Sp. from Qu. *tampu*) Way-station. Stopping place on the road system.
Taptana	Andean game of chance often played in wakes. Gaming board for playing this game.
Taqawa	(Aym.) Large piles of stones where trophy heads were traditionally displayed.
Taypi	(Aym.) The middle or center.
Tinku	(Qu.) Ritual battle.
Tira wirjina	(Aym.) The Virgin Earth, sometimes called *Pachamama*.
Tocapu	(Aym. and Qu.) Probably written as *thuqapu*. Boxed regular designs found on weavings and *qiru* drinking cups and on textiles.
Tronco	(Sp.) Tree trunk. Name for the dice used to play *pichca* or "fives."
Tsantsa	(Shuar) Shrunken heads of the Shuar (Jívaro) of lowland Ecuador.
Tullqa	(Aym.) Son-in-law.
Tumi	(possibly Mochica) Stone or metal ceremonial knife used in the ancient Andes with a half moon–shaped cutting edge.
T'uxlu	(Aym.) Skull.
T'uxu	(Aym.) Niche, within the walls of house structures or in ceremonial enclosures. Hole for offerings on a mountainside.

Uma	(Qu.) Head.
Uma	(Aym.) Water.
Uma turkaña	(Aym.) Lit. "to change the water." A rainmaking ritual, when water from different sources is mixed to stimulate the circulation of waters through a particular territory.
Unku	(Aym.) Woven tunic.
Upani	(Qu.) Ancestral spirit.
Uru	(Aym.) Day.
Uruyaña	(Aym.) Lit. "making his day." A family ceremony of return to the community in rural areas, after obligatory military service.
Uywiri	(Aym.) Guardian mountain.
Vara	(Sp., written *wara* in Aym.) Staff of office of ayllu authorities.
Wak'a	(Aym. and Qu., Hispanicized as *huaca*) Sacred site, often an important mountain or rocky outcrop.
Wak'a achachila	(Aym.) Lit. the "sacred grandfathers." Powerful masculine deities that control power in determined territories.
Walura	(Aym. from Sp. *valor*) Lit. "value." Name for the stone that covers an offering hole on a hillside.
Wallqipu	(Aym.) Woven bag used mainly by men for coca leaves.
Wanka	(Qu.) A highland dance of victory.
Wawa	(Qu. and Aym.) Baby. Offspring in a generic sense.
Wayñu	(Qu. and Aym.) Song and dance form, performed traditionally in the rainy season.
Wayru	(Qu.) Game of chance played with *wayruru* seeds that generally precedes sacrifices.
Wayruru	(Aym.) Red and black seeds used as counters in the game of *taptana*.
Wijsa	(Qu.) Belly.
Wila	(Aym.) Blood.
Wila thakhi	(Aym.) Lit. "red pathway." The warpath.
Willja	(Aym.) An agricultural ritual concerned with expanding fertilizing power outward.
Willjaña	(Aym.) The verb "to spread out."
Wincha	(Qu. and Aym.) Woven or braided headband.
Yatiri	(Aym.) Lit. "the one who knows." Wise one.
Yupana	(Qu.) Checkered counting board.

Notes

Introduction

1. See Arnold (In press); cf. Hoskins (1996b:1).
2. See, for example, Barzel (2002).
3. See Fried (1967), Marx (1973 [1894]), and McGuire (1992).
4. These power strategies are examined by Earle (1997), Chase-Dunn and Jorgenson (2001), and La Lone (2000).
5. See, for example, D'Altroy (2001, 2002).
6. These factors are considered by Alcock et al. (2001) and by Miller, Rowlands, and Tilley (1989:5).
7. See, for example, Wallerstein (1988) for a summary of the debates around this theory.
8. This range of views can be found in La Lone (2001:68) and Kolata (1996).
9. On this enabling concept of power, see again Miller and Tilley (1989).
10. See, for example, Atkinson (1989) and Pauketat (2000).
11. Here we might also refer to the agency-based models of political discussion (see Dobres and Robb 2001 and Pauketat 2001).
12. See, for example, Métraux (1949), Browne et al. (1993), Carmichael (1994), Chávez (2002), DeLeonardis (1997, 2000), Donnan (1978, 2004), Neira Avedaño and Coehlo (1972), Proulx (1971, 1989, 1999), Tello (1918), Verano (1995), Verano et al. (1999), and Bourget (2001a, 2001b).
13. For an ethnographic view, see Platt (1987a, 1987b), Arnold and Yapita (1996, 2000, 2006), Arnold and Espejo (2004), and Weismantel (2005), among others.
14. See Engel (1963), Wheeler and Mujica (1981), and Hastorf (2003), among others.
15. See Rendón (2000) and Arnold (In press).
16. On lowland headtaking, see Murphy (1958), Harner (1978), Menget (1993), Taylor (1993), Viveiros de Castro (1994), B. Conklin (2001), and Fausto (1999).
17. See Caillavet y Pachón (1996), Arnold (2001), and Weismantel (2005), among others.
18. See also the more recent thesis by David Kojan (2002) on historical narratives from the Bolivian eastern Andes.
19. See, for example, Cook (2001), Bourget (2001a), Browne et al. (1993), and Arnold and Yapita (1996).
20. See Dobres and Robb (2000:10) and Bourdieu (1977:52, 65).

21. See, for example, Parker Pearson (1993).
22. See, for example, Flores Ochoa (1977), Catherine Allen (1988), and Inge Bolin (1998).
23. The debates in Conrad and Demarest (1984), Demarest (1981), Flores Ochoa (1977), and Rowe (1946, n.d.) illustrate these uncertainties.
24. See, for example, Strathern (1988).
25. See, too, Marcus and Flannery (1996:157) and Redmond (1994).
26. Cf. Caillavet and Pachón (1996:97).

Part I: The Ethnography of Andean Head Taking and Power

1. On ayllu communities, see, for example, Godoy (1986), Allen (1988:257), and Zuidema (1973:19).

Chapter 1: Heads in Pre-State Economies

1. On land fights in the Andes in general, see Platt (1987a, 1987b, 1996) and Picht (1995), and concerning the region of Qaqachaka, see Arnold and Yapita (1996), Molina Rivero (2006), Arnold (In press), among others.
2. See especially questions 4 to 6 in the 1575 *Información* by Colque Guarache, cited in Espinoza Soriano (1981:197).
3. This *Probanza* is examined by Saignes (1985:12–13) and by Renard-Casevitz-Saignes and Taylor (1988:35–36).
4. See Saignes (1985:14–17) for an account of these Inka incursions into lowland territory.
5. (Saignes 1985:14–17) On these Chiriguano incursions and the corresponding Inka defensive measures, see also Platt, Bouysse-Cassagne, and Harris (2006:23–132), Del Río (1995), and Barragán (1994:93–119).
6. *Documento 20* cited in Platt, Bouysse-Cassagne, and Harris (2006:841–42) as f.45 of the original *Memorial de los Mallku y principales de la provincia de los Charcas*.
7. See Arnold and Yapita (1996:339–50) and Molina (2006:277–82). For a comparative view, see Picht (1995).
8. Cf. Descola (1993b:184).
9. Cf. McWilliam (1996:129).
10. See the debate in Arkush and Stanish (2005); cf. Platt (1987a) and Arnold and Yapita (1996:352–53).
11. See, for example, Downs (1956:64).
12. Cf. George (1991:557).
13. In recent years, the concepts of heirlooms, memorial, and "keeping while giving" have each become rich sources with which to discuss ethnographic and archaeological material (see also Hendon 2000 and Joyce 2000).
14. See, for example, Taylor (1985).
15. On the Inka's headdress, see Cieza de León (1985 [1553] Chap. 8:19) and Arnold and Yapita (2000:344).
16. See Freeman (1979:241–42) on Indonesia and Onians (1951) for a more general account centered in the classical world.

17. On the Andes, see Browne et al. (1993), Tello (1918), Hocquenghem (1987:116–70, Peters (1991:311), and Arnold and Yapita (1996:355–61), among others.
18. See, for example, the account in Bandelier (1910:114).
19. See also Hutton (1921:165).
20. On these differences between Shuar warfare and feuds, see, for example, Karsten (1935:275), Harner (1972:182–83), and Wall Hendricks (1993:16–17).
21. Dransart (2002) described this process at length.
22. Other scholars, such as Naváez (2003), view this ambiguity as simply another aspect of Andean duality, this time between head and tail.
23. On the Nasca examples, see also Narváez (2003:27), who, citing Kauffmann (2001: 153, Photo 219) and Lyon (1978:106), describes the central feline head whose rays culminate in volutes and whose tongue approaches both the vagina and anus on some ceramics. Images of trophy heads can be seen below the feline head, on either side of the tongue.
24. On Middle America, see Brotherston (1997:102), which refers in one case to a period of nine moons: the *tonalámatl*, common to human cycles, work, and the construction of society, and in another to the *teoamoxtli* (Féjérváry), which contrasts tribute in things, to birth, growth, and the obligations of citizens. In the Andean case, see Arnold and Yapita with Tito (1999:40).
25. See, for example, Arnold and Yapita (1996:368, 2000:191–92).
26. Among the Warí, see Conklin (1996), among the Araweté, a group of Tupi-Guaraní, see Viveiros de Castro (1992), and among the Pano, Cashibo, and Matses, see Wistrand (1967) and Romanoff (1984), cited in Erikson (1986).
27. Harris (1983:147–48) first described similar ideas in neighboring Laymi. On Qaqachaka, see Arnold (1992:26) and Arnold and Yapita (2001:Chap. 1). See Bolin (1998) for similar ideas elsewhere.
28. Cf. Paul (2000b:163).
29. See Zuidema (1989a) and Arnold and Yapita (2000:301–02).
30. A comparative view of this idea is found in Borneo, in, for example, Drake (1991: 284).
31. On the importance of the head in ancient Andean cultures, see Forgerty and Williams (2001). On this importance in other parts of the world, see, for example, Bloch (1992).
32. See also DeLeonardis (1997, 2000:371, Fig. 9).
33. On domestic burials, see Earle et al. (1987), Hastorf (2003), and Dean (2005).
34. On this association, see D'Altroy and Hastorf (2001) and Dean (2005).
35. On eating brains, see Arguedas and Izquierdo Riós (1970:209–10), cited in Naváez (2003:15). Naváez (2003) describes the added potential of head excretions.
36. The Quechua term *kamaqi* is described in the historical literature as "life force," with an additional creative or animating sense. This term has pertinent ramifications that extend into related terms for communal obligations (*kama*) that are similar to those of *jucha* and seem to have had a similar change in meaning in colonial times skewed toward the Christian sense of "sin." See, for example, Gerald Taylor (1976, 2001:438).
37. See Arnold and Yapita (2000:197–98) and Arnold (2000:18) for this attribution of the hair to think and act in a contemporary setting.

38. The collected papers in Ossio (1973) are a key reference on the myth of Inkarriy.
39. On the Inkarriy designs of Qeros, see Silverman (1994); on the designs of Choquecancha, see Seibold (1992).

Chapter 2: The Captured Fetish, the Mountain Chest, Offerings and Sacrifice

1. See, for example, Browne, Silverman, and García (1993), Wheeler and Mujica (1981:29), and Feldman (1980).
2. For further insights on these niches, see Mohr Chávez (1988) and Chávez (1992).
3. For details of these niches and their contents, see Wheeler and Mujica (1981:29). Even earlier, at the Formative site of Kotosh, multiple small chambers built on a platform mound each have walls surrounded by small niches at shoulder height. Later, in the Middle Horizon Wari polity, there are walls filled with niches, often associated with the clearly ceremonial D-shaped structures that occur at most important Wari sites (Cook 2001a).
4. Anita Cook, personal communication.
5. Various authors suggest that this might have been the case: see, for example, Doyle (1988), Chessen (1999), Isbell (1997), and Parker Pearson (1993).
6. On rainmaking rituals and mountain sacrifice, see López García (1999) Arnold and Yapita (2000:328–33), and Doutriaux (2001), among others.
7. Contemporary references to similar places can be found in Bolin (1998); also see Guaman Poma de Ayala (*ca.* 1615:f.239–40) for colonial references to this kind of site.
8. See also Hocquenghem (1987:80, Figs. 33a and 33b).
9. These kinds of contractual arrangements have been described (and debated) in other parts of the Andes by Platt (1982a:132ff., 1982b:39) and Bolin (1998), among others.
10. See Ziólkowski (1996:36) and López García (1999:64) for comparative examples of these practices.
11. Zuidema (1989d:275) mentions other aspects of this process of reconsidering *wak'a* status under the Inkas.
12. For a colonial description of rituals to these mummy bundles, see Betanzos (1996 [1557]), and Rowe (1946); for those to their saint equivalents, see Arnold (2007: 193–200).
13. See Arnold and Yapita (2000:Chaps. 6, 10, 11) for an extended account of this process in relation to weaving.
14. On the notion of "tournament economy," see Appadurai (2000 [1986]:50).
15. On Andean wooden staffs, see Radicati di Primeglio (1984), and more recently Salomon (2004:Chap. 4).
16. Salomon (2002a:310) notes that these interpretations take too literally a remark by Leland Locke (1923:32) that the *kipu* was not adapted for calculations.
17. See Hocquenghem (1989:142–56) for a detailed review of this ample literature.
18. Interestingly, Laurencich Minelli (2003: Fig. 3) gives a similar definition of this checkered design from the controversial Clara Miccinelli documents found in Naples, attributed to the Jesuit, Blas Valera.

19. See Arnold (1988:66).
20. See, for example, Zuidema (1989c), Ziólkowski (1997), Gentile (1998), Salomon (2002b), Arellano (2003), and Castro Rojas and Uribe Rodríguez (2004).
21. See also Ziólkowski (1997), Zuidema (1989c, 1995), Gentile (1998:114), and Cobo 1968 [1653] 2:86–87).
22. See, for example, Gentile (1998:112) and Salomon (2002b:3ff.).
23. Cited in Radicati di Primeglio (1990:220).
24. See Engl (1967:Plate 15 and p. 200).
25. Cf. Hocquenghem (1989:144–56).
26. Hastorf field notes.
27. See Karsten (1935:Chap. 12).

Chapter 3: Drinking the Power of the Dead

1. On Inka customs of drinking from skulls, see, for example, Cieza de León (1985 [1553]:210), Platt (1987a), Abercrombie (1998), and Cummins (1988:214–16, 2002:94).
2. See Cabello Balboa (1945 [1586]:288) and Murúa (1946 [1615]:46).
3. For accounts of this, see Pedro Pizarro (1986 [1571]:210), Cieza de León (1985 [1553]), Mena (1534), and Ogburn (2007), among others.
4. For an ethnographic account of this, see Abercombie (1993) on K'ulta, and Arnold, Jiménez, and Yapita (1992), and Arnold, Yapita, and López García (2001) on Qaqachaka and other ayllus.
5. See, for example, Zuidema's essay on "Burocracia y conocimiento" (1989b), which examines the religious and economic aspects of *jucha*, in the sense of redeeming faults and maintaining health and communal wellbeing, and Zuidema (1992:32–38) on comparisons between *jucha* and *khuyaq* (or *cuyac*), the latter in the sense of the complementary material support of the Inka Empire engendered by the circulation of tribute.
6. For a historical study of drinking practices, see Saignes (1993); on K'ulta, see Abercrombie (1993, 1998); and on Qaqachaka, see Arnold (1991, 1992) and Arnold, Yapita, and López García (2001).
7. Among the many studies on *qiru*, see Rowe (1961), Cummins (1988, 1998, 2002), Flores Ochoa (1998), Flores Ochoa et al. (1999), and Allen (2002).
8. See, for example, Schultes (1972). A popular account of Schultes's work, can be found in Wade Davis's book *One River* (1996:215–19). On the importance of certain flowers in Andean symbolism, see Mulvany (2004). See also Knobloch (2000) for an interpretation of *Anadenanthera colubrina* iconography.
9. See Arnold and Yapita (2001:111–13) and Arnold, Yapita, and López García (2001:144).
10. On *qiru* history, see Conklin (1990) and Flores Ochoa (1998:161), among others.
11. That colonial *qiru* might have formed part of an Inka art of resistance is supported by the recent debates around the Clara Miccinelli documents, described in Laurencich Minelli (2003).
12. Karsten (1968:267–68), cited in Saunders (1998:32), mentions the particular fear of some highland Quechua speakers concerning the jaguar, because some are thought to be *uturuncus*: men who have changed into jaguars.

13. See, for example, Cordy-Collins (1998:166) on the feline-shaman association in the Andes.
14. On these rituals, see Molina del Cusco (1943 [1573]:80) and Cieza de León (1945 [1551]:Chap. 97). See also Zuidema (1982:99) and Arnold and Yapita (2001:136).
15. On the Inka *maska paycha* and its relation to warfare, see also Arnold and Yapita (2000:343) and Cummins (1998:115, Fig. 14).

Chapter 4: The Nested Power of Modern Andean Hierarchies

1. The Africanist influence of, say, Fortes (1965), is evident in the widely cited article by Platt (1978).
2. See, for example, Albarracín-Jordán (1996).
3. Luykx (1999:113–18) describes more generally the way that rural men are required to prove their bravery through military service before being accepted as a spouse.
4. For similar examples from other parts of the world, see Monnas and Granger-Taylor (1989).
5. On this idea in Qaqachaka, see Arnold (1991); for similar ideas elsewhere, see Ackerman (1985).
6. In the archaeological record, see McEwan (1998) on the use of niched walls in Wari architecture.
7. On lowland groups, Caillavet (1996:77) cites Diego de Ortegón (1577), in Pedro de Aguado's *Recopilación historial* (1568:385) and Oberem's *Relación de Ortegón* ... (1958 [1577]:235).
8. On the historical record in the Andes, see Caillavet (1996:69–70, 74–75), citing Cieza de León, among others.
9. See, for example, Browne, Silverman, and García (1993:291).
10. See Janusek, Ohnstad, and Roddick (2003) for archaeological work on the Khonkho Wankane (Qunqu Wankani) site.
11. See also Héritier-Augé (1986:164) for a similar study of agnatic power and its relationship to speech.
12. See also Arnold and Yapita (1996:362).
13. For other references to these ritual dialogues, see López García (1999) and Arnold and Yapita (2000:298–99).
14. On these oracular sites, see Burger (1988:114, 1992).
15. Reflections on these former state relations can be found in Arnold and Yapita (2000: 150–54).
16. On the concept of *jucha*, cf. Zuidema (1989b).
17. See Soukup (1970:37), cited in Mannheim (1999).
18. See Caillavet (1996:89), citing Anónimo, "Espejo de Variedades" (1936–38 [1575]: 180).
19. See Beresford-Jones (2005), Peters (2000), and Silverman (1988), among others.
20. See Paul and Turpin (1986) and Silverman (1993).
21. Don Domingo Jiménez described in Aymara how in his ayllu, *Uka kunturiw utji, ukata iñchhi uka awil achach p'iqiña yaqhipan utji ... uka alma t'uxlulu, alma p'iqi*: "It has a condor, and mm ... others have the heads of the ancestors ... those skulls of the ancestral dead, heads of the ancestral dead."

22. See also Shortland (1882:29) on these weaving pole-like staffs.
23. In Aymara, *Taqi kunani ukax waraxa, taqi kunatxay yatixa.*
24. Rowe (1946) and Zuidema (1989b) have examined this idea in relation to Cusco (Peru); Albó et al. (1972) and Asvaldsson (1994) in the case of Jesús de Machaqa (Bolivia).
25. See, for example, Schobinger (1966), Medina Rojas (1958), Ramos Gavilán (1976 [1621]:26), Doutriaux (2001), and Arnold and Yapita (2000:329–33).
26. The account by the cacique Luís Capoche, in *Relación general de la Villa Imperial de Potosí* (1959 [1585]:40), makes this case.
27. On narrative *kipus*, see, for example, Conklin (1990), Arnold and Yapita (2000: Chaps. 10 and 11), Urton (2003), Salomon (2004).

Part II: The Archaeology of Andean Head Taking and Power

1. On the relation between archaeological and contemporary practices concerning heads, see Rendón Lizarazu (2000).

Chapter 5: Heads and the Consolidation of Andean Political Power

1. For descriptions of these court proceedings, see, for example, Salomon (1995) and Doyle (1988).
2. On the ancestral *mallki*, see Arriaga (1968 [1621]), Doyle (1988), Rowe (1946, 1995), Salomon (1995), and Bolin (1998), among others.
3. Salomon (1991), Arnold (1993, 2007), and Arnold and Yapita (1996:322–23) all describe these kinds of ayllu ancestors and their journeys through the local territory.
4. Hastorf and Johannessen (1991) discuss his use of imagery in Andean social structures. On "trunk speech," see McWilliam (1996:139–42).
5. For more detailed descriptions of these ayllu obligations, see Rowe (1946), Spalding (1984), and Salomon (1991).
6. On these miniature stones, see also Doyle (1988:66) (cf. Asvaldsson 1994).
7. See Kolata (1996:56), Proulx (2001:135), and Browne, Silverman, and García (1993).
8. But see, for example, Rösing (1996:427–31) on the region of Charazani.
9. See Bandy et al. (2004), Bennett (1936), Lemuz Aguirre (2001), Portugal Ortíz (1981, 1988), and Portugal Ortíz et al. (1993).
10. See Wheeler and Mujica (1981).
11. See Browne (n.d.).
12. Thanks to Alison Spedding for calling our attention to this detail.
13. On the *wayñu* and *wanka* as dances to the dead, see Arnold (1992) and Cornejo Polar (1994:71ff.) respectively.

Chapter 6: Heads and Andean Political Change from an Archaeological Perspective

1. On the irrigations systems of the Ica and Nasca valleys, see Schreiber and Lancho Rojas (2003).
2. See also Paul (2000c:69).

3. See also Coelo (1972:134–43).
4. On the *huarango* staffs in Nasca Cahuachi, see Silverman (1993); on those throughout the Ica Valley, see Beresford Jones (2005).
5. Schreiber and Lancho Rojas (2003) and Vaughn (2004) are key references on the Nasca desert societies and their political formations.
6. See also Browne (2000).
7. Proulx (1999, 2001) describes these portable Nasca heads.
8. See Neira Avedaño and Coelho (1972–73), Carmichael (1988), Proulx (1989), and DeLeonardis (1997, 2000:375), among others.
9. Tello (1918: Figs. 9.12–9.16), cited in Vreeland and Cockburn (1980:154), makes this comparison.
10. See also DeLeonardis (1997, 2000:381).
11. Aldenderfer, personal communication.
12. See works by Bandy (1999), Hastorf (1999), and Whitehead (1999).
13. On the Yayamama or Pa'ajano tradition in general, see Mohr Chávez (1988) and Browman (n.d.).
14. See Bennett (1936, 1948) and Kidder (1956) on the results of earlier excavations at the site.
15. On Ch'isi, see Chávez and Mohr Chávez (2001); on Titimani, see Portugal Ortíz (1988, 1989, 1992).
16. See again Paul and Turpin (1986).
17. See, for example, Janusek (1994, 2004) and Kolata (2001, 2003).
18. See also Blom and Janusek (2004) and Blom, Janusek, and Buikstra (2003).
19. On interpretations of the stone-carved tenon heads at Chavín, see Burger (1988, 1992), Cordy-Collins (1977), Lumbreras (1989), and Rick (2000), among others.
20. See especially Arnold and Yapita (1996:369–70).
21. Leonardo Benitez, personal communication.
22. Concerning heads painted onto Tiwanaku ceramics, see Alconini (1995), Cook and Benco (2000), and Janusek (1994, 2004).
23. For a more detailed analysis of the Wari face-neck urns, see Menzel (1976) and Cook and Benco (2000).
24. On the more general power relations of ceremonial drinking, see again Saignes (1993) and Abercrombie (1993).
25. On D-shaped structures elsewhere, see Cook (2001a), Meddens and Cook (2001), and Williams (2001).
26. Interestingly, Campana (1995:151–73), taking his cue from Pozorski (1980) and Watanabe (1979), proposes that the primary sacrificial space of these D-shaped temples was the enclosed buildings on the east-west-facing axis and that this axis would now express the death-regeneration theme in public architectonic form.
27. See also Topic (1991).
28. See also Whitley (2002).
29. See Kolata (1996) on *yatiris* and rainmaking around Tiwanaku.

Chapter 7: Central Andean Political Developments

1. On the use of chile peppers in initiation rituals, see Stephen Hugh-Jones (n.d. and personal communication) and Smith in Grieder et al. (1988).

2. On the use of chile peppers in suffocation, Denise Y. Arnold (personal communication); on their use in malefic witchcraft, Alison Spedding (personal communication).
3. See Vreeland and Cockburn (1980:145).
4. See the description of an Inka burial in Arnold and Yapita (2000:301–05).
5. The site of Chavín de Huántar is examined in Burger (1988, 1992), Lumbreras (1989), and Rick (2000).
6. For a comparative view, see Verano (2001).
7. The original is as follows:

   ¡Oh, Viracocha! ... y ... vuestro hijo el Inca,
   a quien diste de señor;
   Mientras este reinare, multipliquen y sean guardados a salvo;
   los tiempos sean properados, las chácaras y las gentes y el Ganado todo vaya en aumento.

8. See, for example, Ogburn (2007).
9. See again Ogburn (2007:2).
10. See Arguedas and Duviols (1966:24), cited in Ogburn (2007).
11. See, for example, Caillavet (1996).

Chapter 8: Conclusions

1. See, for example, Alconini (2002) and Salomon (1986).
2. This diarchic theory of power has already been put forward for the Andean region in the work of the Bolivian psychologist Fernando Montes Ruíz, especially in his book *La máscara de piedra* (1986:257–59).
3. On *parallelism* in the Andes, see Mannheim (1987); in other parts of the world, see James Fox (1974), for example, on Rotinese views of language.
4. We draw here on some insights in Grosfoguel (forthcoming).

References

Abercrombie, Thomas Alan. 1993. Caminos de la memoria en un cosmos colonizado: Poética de la bebida y conciencia histórica en K'ulta. In *Borrachera y memoria. La experiencia de lo sagrado en los Andes*, pp. 139–70. Comp. Thierry Saignes. La Paz: Hisbol and IFEA.

———. 1998. *Pathways of memory and power: Ethnography and history among an Andean people*. Madison: University of Wisconsin Press.

Ackerman, Raquel. 1985. The muleteer of the mountain gods: Eschatology and social life in a south-central Andean community. Unpublished Ph.D. thesis. Cambridge: University of Cambridge.

Aguado, Pedro de. 1956–1957 [1568]. *Recopilación historial*, 4 vols. Bogota: Biblioteca de la Presidencia de la República.

Albarracín-Jordan, Juan. 1996. Tiwanaku settlement system: The integration of nested hierarchies in the lower Tiwanaku Valley. *Latin American Antiquity* 7(3):183–210.

Albó, Xavier. 1977. *La paradoja aymara: Solidaridad y faccionalismo*. La Paz: Centro de Investigación del Campesinado (CIPCA), Cuadernos de Investigación 8.

Albó, Xavier and CIPCA team. 1972. Dinámica en la estructura inter-comunitaria de Jesús de Machaqa. *América Indígena* (Mexico) 32(3):773–816.

Alborñoz, Cristóbal de. 1989 [*ca.* 1530–1603]. *Fabulas y mitos de los Incas*. Edition by C. de Molina and C. de Alborñoz. Eds. Henrique Urbano and Pierre Duviols. Madrid: Historia 16.

Alcock, Susan E., Terence N. D'Altroy, and Katerina Schreiber, eds. 2001. *Empires: Perspectives from archaeology and history*. Cambridge: Cambridge University Press.

Alconini, Sonia. 1995. *Rito, símbolo e historia en la pirámide de Akapana, Tiwanaku: Un análisis de cerámica ceremonial prehispánica*. La Paz: Editorial Acción.

———. 2002. Prehistoric Inka frontier structure and dynamics in the Bolivian Chaco. Ph.D. dissertation. Pittsburgh: University of Pittsburgh. Ann Arbor, MI: UMI.

Allen, Catherine J. 1982. Body and soul in Quechua thought. *Journal of Latin American Lore* 8(2):179–96.

———. 1988. *The hold life has*. Washington, DC: Smithsonian Institution Press.

———. 2002. The Incas have gone inside. Pattern and persistence in Andean iconography. *Res: Anthropology and Aesthetics* 42 (Autumn):180–204.

Anónimo. 1936–1938 [1575]. "Espejo de variedades." In *Sebastián de Benalcázar*. Ed. Jacinto Jijón y Caamaño. 2 vols. Quito, Ecuador: Editorial Imprenta del Clero. Editorial Ecuatoriana.

Appadurai, Arjun. 2000 [1986]. Introduction: Commodities and the politics of value. In *The social life of things. Commodities in cultural perspective*, pp. 3–63. Ed. Arjun Appadurai. Cambridge: Cambridge University Press.

Arellano Hoffmann, Carmen. 2003. El juego de chuncana entre los chimú. Un tablero de madera que prueba la hipótesis de Erland Nordenskiöld. *Bulletin de l'Institut Français d'Études Andines* 32(2):317–45.

Arguedas, J. M. and Pierre Duviols. 1966. Dioses y hombres de Huarochiri: Narración quechua recogida por Francisco de Avila [1598?]. Lima: Instituto Francés de Estudios Andinos.

Arguedas, J. M. and Francisco Izquierdo Ríos. 1970. *Mitos, leyendas y cuentos peruanos.* Lima: Casa de la Cultura del Perú.

Arnold, Denise Y. 1988. Matrilineal practice in a patrilineal setting. Metaphors and rituals of kinship in an Andean ayllu. Unpublished Ph.D. thesis. London: University of London.

———. 1991. The house of earth-bricks and Inka-stones: Gender, memory and cosmos in ayllu Qaqachaka. *Journal of Latin American Lore* 17(1):3–69.

———. 1992. At the heart of the woven dance-floor: The wayñu in Qaqachaka. *Iberoamericana* (Frankfurt) 3/4(47/48):21–66.

———. 1993. Adam and Eve and the red-trousered ant: History in the southern Andes. *Travesía, Journal of Latin American Cultural Studies* 2(1):49–83.

———. 1994. Reseña del libro *Borrachera y memoria: La experiencia de lo sagrado en los Andes*. Comp. Thierry Saignes. La Paz. Eds. Hisbol and IFEA. *Revista Unitas* (La Paz) (13–14):193–99.

———. 1998. Introducción. In *Gente de carne y hueso. Las tramas de parentesco en los Andes*, pp. 15–66. Comp. D. Y. Arnold. La Paz: CIASE and ILCA.

———. 2000. "Convertirse en persona" el tejido: La terminología aymara de un cuerpo textil. In *Actas de la 1 Jornada Internacional sobre Textiles Precolombinos*, pp. 9–28. Ed. Victòria Solanilla Demestre. Barcelona: Servei de Publicacions de la UAB.

———. 2004. Midwife singers: Llama-human obstetrics in some songs to the animals by Andean women. In *Quechua verbal artistry: The inscription of Andean voices*, pp. 145–79. Eds. Guillermo Delgado and John Schechter. Bonn, Germany: Estudios Americanistas de Bonn, BAS 38.

———. 2005. The social life of a communal chest: Hybrid characters and the imagined genealogies of written documents and their woven ancestors. In *Remembering the past, retrieving the future: New interdisciplinary contributions to the study of colonial Latin America*, pp. 92–131. Ed. Verónica Salles. Bogota: Pontificia Universidad Javeriana.

———. 2007. El camino de Tata Quri: Historia, hagiografía y las sendas de la memoria en Qaqachaka. In *Hilos sueltos. Los Andes desde el textil*, pp. 181–240. By Denise Y. Arnold, with Juan de Dios Yapita and Elvira Espejo. La Paz: Plural and ILCA.

———. In press. *Warriors and weavers: Gender and interethnic violence in the Andes.* Under consideration in Narrating Native Histories series. Eds. Florencia Mallon and Joanne Rappaport. Durham, NC: Duke University Press.

Arnold, Denise Y. and Elvira Espejo A. 2004. Las cabezas de la periferia, del centro y del mundo interior: Una comparación de la iconografía bélica en los textiles arqueológicos de Paracas-Topará y del ayllu Qaqachaka (Bolivia) contemporánea. In *Tejiendo sueños en el Cono Sur: Textiles andinos: Pasado, presente, futuro*, pp. 348–64. Ed. Victòria Solanilla Demestre. Barcelona: Servei de Publicacions de la UAB.

Arnold, Denise Y. and Juan de Dios Yapita. 1996. La papa, el amor y la violencia. La crisis ecológica y las batallas rituales en el linde entre Oruro y Norte de Potosí. In *Madre melliza y sus crías. Antología de la papa*, pp. 311–71. Comps. Denise Y. Arnold and Juan de Dios Yapita. La Paz: ILCA and Hisbol.

———. 1999. La trama revitalizante de los rezos de *paskusay* (Pascuas) en Qaqachaka, Bolivia. Formaciones textuales de las interpretaciones religiosas. In *La lengua de la cristianización en Latinoamerica: Catequización e instrucción en lenguas amerindias*, pp. 277–312. Eds. S. Dedenbach and L. Crickmay. Bonn, Germany: Verlag, Anton Sauerwein, BAS 32 and CIASE, Occasional Papers 29.

———. 2000. *El rincón de las cabezas. Luchas textuales, educación y tierras en los Andes*. La Paz: ILCA and UMSA.

———. 2001. *River of fleece, river of song. Singing to the animals. An Andean poetics of creation*. La Paz: ILCA, Serie Etnografías No. 2 and University of Bonn: BAS 35.

———. 2004. K'ank'isi: The braiding of words, music, and families in the wedding songs from Qaqachaka, Bolivia. In *Quechua verbal artistry: The inscription of Andean voices*, pp. 415–80. Eds. Guillermo Delgado-P. and John Schechter. Bonn, Germany: Estudios Americanistas de Bonn, BAS 38.

———. 2006. *The metamorphosis of heads. Textual struggles, education and land in the Andes*. Pittsburgh: University of Pittsburgh Press, Illuminations series.

Arnold, Denise Y., with Juan de Dios Yapita and Cipriana Apaza. 1996. Mama Trama y sus crías: Analogías de la producción de la papa en los textiles de Chukiñapi, Bolivia. In *Mama Melliza y sus crías: Antología de la papa*, pp. 373–411. Comps. Denise Y. Arnold and Juan de Dios Yapita. La Paz: Hisbol and ILCA.

Arnold, Denise Y. with Juan de Dios Yapita and Ulpián R. López García. 2001. La chicha: Lubricante por excelencia de la sociedad andina. In *Perú: El legado de la historia*, pp. 129–51. Eds. Luís Millones and José Villa Rodríguez. Seville, Spain: Prom Perú, Universidad de Sevilla and Fundación El Monte, Colección América.

Arnold, Denise Y. and Juan de Dios Yapita, with Margarita Tito. 1999. *Vocabulario aymara de la vida reproductiva de la mujer*. La Paz: Family Health International and ILCA.

Arriaga, Father Pablo Joseph de. 1968 [1621]. *The extirpation of idolatry in Peru*. Trans. L. Clark Keating. Lexington: University of Kentucky Press.

Ascher, Marcia and Robert Ascher. 1981. *Code of the quipu*. Ann Arbor: University of Michigan Press.

Assadourian, Carlos Sempat. 1982. *Sistema de la economía colonial: Mercado interno, regiones y espacio económico*. Lima: Instituto de Estudios Peruanos.

Astvaldsson, Astvaldur. 1994. Wak'a: An Andean religious concept in the context of Aymara social and political life. Unpublished Ph.D. thesis. London: King's College London.

———. 1996. Socio-political organization, authority, gender and kinship in the Bolivian Andes. Research Paper 19. Liverpool: University of Liverpool.

———. 1998. The powers of hard rock: Meaning, transformation and continuity in cultural symbols in the Andes. *Journal of Latin American Cultural Studies* 7(2):203–23.

———. 2000. *Las voces de los wak'a*. La Paz: CIPCA Cuadernos de Investigación 54, Serie Jesús de Machaqa: La marka rebelde.

Atkinson, Jane Monnig. 1989. *The art and politics of Wana shamanship*. Berkeley: University of California Press.

Bandelier, Adolph F. A. 1910. *The islands of Titicaca and Koati*. New York: Hispanic Society of America.

Bandy, Matthew S. 1999. History of investigations at the site of Chiripa. In *Early settlement in Chiripa, Bolivia: Research of the Taraco archaeological project*, pp. 9–16. Ed. C.A. Hastorf. Archaeological Research Facility Monograph Publications, No. 57. Berkeley: University of California.

———. 2001. Population and history in the ancient Titicaca Basin. Unpublished Ph.D. dissertation. Berkeley: University of California.

———. 2004. Fissioning, scalar stress, and social evolution in early village societies. *American Anthropologist* 106(2):322–33.

Bandy, Matthew, Christine Hastorf, Lee Steadman, Katherine Moore, Melissa Goodman Elgar, William Whitehead, Jose Luís Paz, Amanda Cohen, Maria Bruno, Andrew Roddick, Kirk Frye, María Soledad Fernández, Jose Capriles Flores, and Mary Leighton. 2004. Taraco Archaeological Project Report on the 2003 Excavations at Kala Uyuni, Submitted to the National Directorate of Archaeology, La Paz, Bolivia.

Barnes, Ruth. 1997. Women as headhunters. The making and meaning of textiles in a Southeast Asian context. In *Dress and gender. Making and meaning*, pp. 29–343. Eds. Ruth Barnes and Joanne B. Eicher. Oxford: Berg, Cross-Cultural Perspectives on Women, vol. 2.

Barragán, Rossana. 1994. *¿Indios de arco y flecha?* Sucre, Bolivia: Ediciones ASUR 3.

Barrett, John. 2000. A thesis on agency. In *Agency in archaeology*, pp. 61–68. Eds. Marcia-Anne Dobres and John Robb. London: Routledge.

Barzel, Yoram. 2002. *A theory of the state: Economic rights, legal rights, and the scope of the state*. Cambridge: Cambridge University Press.

Bennett, W. C. 1936. Excavations in Bolivia. *Anthropological Papers of the American Museum of Natural History* 35(4):329–507.

———. 1948. A revised sequence for the south Titicaca Basin, in a reappraisal of Peruvian archaeology. *Memoirs of the Society for American Archaeology* 13(4):90–93.

Beresford-Jones, D. G. 2005. Pre-Hispanic prosopis-human relationships on the south coast of Peru: Riparian forests in the context of environmental and cultural trajectories of the Lower Ica Valley. Unpublished Ph.D. dissertation. Cambridge: University of Cambridge.

Betanzos, Juan de. 1996 [1557]. *Narrative of the Incas*. Trans. and ed. Roland Mailton and Dana Buchanan. Austin: University of Texas Press.

Bloch, Maurice and Jonathan Parry, eds. 1982. *Death and the regeneration of life*. Cambridge: Cambridge University Press.

Blom, Deborah E. and Matthew S. Bandy. 1999. Human remains and mortuary practices. In *Early settlement in Chiripa, Bolivia: Research of the Taraco Archaeological Project*, pp. 117–22. Ed. Christine A. Hastorf. Archaeological Research Facility Monograph Publications, No. 57. Berkeley: University of California.

Blom, Deborah E. and John W. Janusek. 2004. Making place: Humans as objects of dedication in Tiwanaku society. *World Archaeology* 36(1):123–41.

Blom, Deborah E., John W. Janusek, and Jane E. Buikstra. 2003. A re-evaluation of human remains from Tiwanaku. In *Archaeology and paleoecology in the Tiwanaku heartland*, vol. 2, *Rural and urban archaeology*, pp. 435–48. Ed. Alan L. Kolata. Washington, DC: Smithsonian Institution Press.

Bolin, Inge. 1998. *Rituals of respect. The secret of survival in the high Peruvian Andes*. Austin: University of Texas Press.

Bourdieu, Pierre. 1977. *Theory of an outline of practice*. Cambridge: Cambridge University Press.

Bourget, Steven. 1998. Pratiques sacrificielles et funéraires au site moche de la Huaca de la Luna, Côte Norte du Pérou. *Bulletin de l'Institute Français d'Études Andines* 27(1):41–74.

———. 2001a. Children and ancestors: Ritual practices at the Moche site of Huaca de la Luna, North Coast of Peru. In *Ritual sacrifice in ancient Peru*, pp. 93–118. Eds. E. P. Benson and A. G. Cook. Austin: University of Texas Press.

———. 2001b. Rituals of sacrifice: Its practice at Huaca de la Luna and its representation in Moche iconography. In *Moche art and archaeology*, pp. 88–109. Ed. Joanne Pillsbury. Studies in the History of Art, Center for Advanced Study in the Visual Arts. Washington, DC: National Gallery of Art.

———. 2005. *Sex, death, and sacrifice*. Austin: University of Texas Press.

Brotherston, Gordon. 1997. *La América indígena en su literatura: Los libros del cuatro mundo*. Mexico City: Fondo de Cultura Económica.

Browman, David. n.d. Asiruni, Pukara-Pokotia and Pajano: Pre-Tiahuanaco south Andean monolithic stone styles. Manuscript in author's possession.

———. 1978. The temple at Chiripa. In *III congreso peruano, el hombre y la cultura andina*, pp. 807–13. Ed. Ramiro Matos M. Lima: Universidad Nacional de San Marcos.

Browne, David H. n.d. Nasca civic-ceremonial center at Llapata, Palpa. Manuscript in author's possession.

Browne, David H., H. Silverman, and Rubén García. 1993. A cache of 48 Nasca trophy heads from Cerro Carapo, Peru. *Latin American Antiquity* 4(3):274–94.

Burger, Richard L. 1988. Unity and heterogeneity within the Chavín Horizon. In *Peruvian prehistory*, pp. 99–144. Ed. Richard W. Keatinge. Cambridge: Cambridge University Press.

Bustillos, Martha Sandra and others. 2005. Las cabezas de Todos Santos. Presentation of group work for the course "Duke in the Andes: Visual Languages," directed by Denise Y. Arnold, with Juan de Dios Yapita and Elvira Espejo.

Butler, Judith. 1993. *Bodies that matter*. London: Routledge.

Cabello Balboa, Miguel. 1945 [1586]. *Obras*, vol. 1. Quito: Editorial Ecuatoriana.

Caillavet, Chantal. 1996. Antropofagia y frontera: el caso de los Andes septentrionales. In *Frontera y poblamiento: Estudios de historia y antropología de Colombia y Ecuador*, pp. 57–109. Comps. Chantal Caillavet and Ximena Pachón. Santafé de Bogotá, Colombia: IFEA, Instituto de Investigaciones Amazónicas, Sinchi, and Departamento de Antropología, Universidad de Los Andes.

Campana, Cristóbal. 1995. *Arte chavín. Análisis estructural de formas e imágenes*. Lima: Universidad Nacional Federico Villarreal.

Capoche, Luís. 1959 [1585]. *Relación general de la Villa Imperial de Potosí*. Madrid: Biblioteca de Autores Españoles, vol. 122.

Carmichael, Patrick H. 1988. Nasca mortuary customs: Death and ancient society on the south coast of Peru. Ph.D. dissertation. Ann Arbor, MI: UMI.

———. 1994. The life from death continuum in Nasca imagery. *Andean Past* 4:81–90.

Carneiro, Roberto. 1970. A theory of the origin of the state. *Science* 169(3947):733–38.

Castro Rojas, Victoria and Mauricio Uribe Rodríguez. 2004. Dos "pirámides" de caspana. El juego de la Pichica y el dominio Inka en el loa superior. *Chungará* (Arica), 36, supplement (September):879–91.

Cereceda, Verónica. 1978. Semiologie des tissus andins. *Annales* (Paris) 33(5–6): 1017–35.

Chase-Dunn, Christopher and Thomas D. May. 1997. *Rise and demise, comparing world systems*. Boulder, CO: Westview Press.

Chase-Dunn, Christopher and Andrew Jorgenson. 2001. Regions and interaction networks: A world-systems perspective. *Institute for Research on World Systems (IROWS) Working Paper # 3.* Paper presented to the UC World History Workshop, University of California, Riverside, February 3.

Chávez B., Sergio J. 1992. The conventionalized rules in Pucara pottery technology and iconography: Implications for socio-political developments in the northern Lake Titicaca Basin. Ph.D. dissertation. East Lansing: Michigan State University. Ann Arbor, MI: UMI.

———. 2002. Identification of the camelid woman and feline man themes, motifs, and designs in Pucara style pottery. In *Andean Archaeology II*, pp. 35–69. Eds. Helaine Silverman and W. H. Isbell. New York: Kluwer Academic/Plenum Publishers.

Chávez B., Sergio J. and Karen Mohr Chávez. 1975. A carved stela from Taraco Peru, and the definition of an early style of stone sculpture from the altiplano of Peru and Bolivia. *Ñawpa pacha* (Berkeley: Institute of Andean Studies) 13:45–83.

———. 2001. The Formative Ch'isi sunken enclosure. Presented at the symposium "The Formative in the Titicaca Basin," at the 66th annual meeting of the Society for American Archaeology, New Orleans, April 19.

Chesson, Meridith S. 1999. Libraries of the dead, early Bronze age charnel houses and social identity at Urban Bab edh-Dhra', Jordan. *Journal of Anthropological Archaeology* 18(2):137–64.

Cieza de León, Pedro de. 1945 [1551]. *La crónica del Perú*. Buenos Aires: Espasa-Calpe Argentina, S.A.

———. 1985 [1553]. *La crónica del Perú. Segunda parte (El señorio de los Incas)*. Lima: Pontificia Universidad Católica del Perú, Fondo Editorial.

Cobo, Father Bernabé. 1968 [1653]. *Historia del nuevo mundo*, vol. 3. Madrid: Ediciones Atlas, Biblioteca de Autores Españoles.

———. 1988 [1653]. *History of the Inca Empire: An account of the Indians customs and their origin together with a treatise on Inca legends, history and social institutions*. Trans. and ed. Roland Hamilton. Austin: University of Texas Press.

Coelho, Vera Penteado. 1972. Enterramiento de cabeças de cultura Nasca. Unpublished doctoral thesis. São Paolo, Brazil: Universidade de São Paolo.

Colque Guarache, Juan. 1575. Primera información hecha por don Juan Colque Guarache, cerca de sus predecesores y subcesión en el cacicazgo mayor de los Quillacas, Asanaques, Sivaroyos, Uruquillas y Haracapis, y de sus servicios a favor de su magestad en la conquista, allanamiento y pacificación desde reino del Pirú. Año 1575, AGI, Seville, Spain. *Revista del Museo Nacional de Lima* (1981) 45:237–51.

Conklin, Beth A. 1993. Hunting ancestor: Death and alliance in Wari' cannibalism. *Latin American Anthropology Review* 5(2):65–70.

———. 1995. "Thus are our bodies, thus was our custom": Mortuary cannibalism in an Amazonian society. *American Ethnologist* 22(1):75–101.

Conklin, Beth A. 1996. Women's blood, warrior's blood, and the conquest of vitality in Amazonia. Paper for the Wenner Gren Symposium for Anthropological

Research, International Symposium 121, "Amazonia and Melanesia: Gender and Anthropological Comparison," September 7–15, Mijas, Spain.

——. 2001. *Consuming grief. Compassionate cannibalism in an Amazonian society.* Austin: University of Texas Press.

Conklin, William J. 1990. El sistema informativo de los quipus del horizonte medio. In *Quipu y Yupana. Colección de escritos*, pp. 21–38. Eds. Carol Mackey, Hugo Pereyra, Carlos Radicati, Humberto Rodríguez, and Oscar Valverde. Lima: CONCYTEC.

——. 1999. Structure as meaning in Andean textiles. *Revista Chungará* (Arica, Chile) 29(1):109–31.

Conrad, Geoffrey W. and Arthur A. Demarest. 1984. *Religion and empire: The dynamics of Aztec and Inca expansionism.* Cambridge: Cambridge University Press.

Connerton, Paul. 1989. *How societies remember.* Cambridge: Cambridge University Press.

Cook, Anita. 2001a. Huari D-shaped structures, sacrificial offerings and divine rulership. In *Ritual sacrifice in ancient America*, pp. 127–63. Eds. E. P. Benson and A. G. Cook. Austin: University of Texas Press.

——. 2001b. Los nobles ancestros de piedra: El lenguaje de la vestimenta y rango imperial entre las figurilla Huari. In *Wari, el primer estado imperial andino*, pp. 229–71. Eds. Luís Millones and Enrique González Carré. Seville, Spain: Fundación El Monte.

——. 2002. Las deidades huari y sus orígenes altiplánicos. In *Los dioses del antiguo Perú*, vol. 2, pp. 39–65. Ed. Cristóbal Makowski. Lima: Banco de Crédito.

Cook, Anita and Nancy Benco. 2000. Vasijas para la fiesta y la fama: Producción artesanal en un centro urbano Huari. In *Huari y Tiwanaku: Modelos y evidencias*, pp. 489–504. Eds. Peter Kaulicke and W. H. Isbell. Lima: Pontificia Universidad Católica del Perú, Fondo Editorial.

Cordero Miranda, Gregorio. 1977. Descubrimiento de una estela lítica en Chiripa. In *Jornadas*, vol. 2, pp. 229–32. La Paz: Franz Tamayo.

Cordy-Collins, Alana. 1977. Chavin art: Its shamanic/hallucinogenic origins. In *Precolumbian art history*, pp. 353–62. Eds. A. Cordy-Collins and J. Stern. Palo Alto, CA: Peek Publications.

——. 1998. The jaguar of the backward glance. In *Icons of power. Feline symbolism in the Americas*, pp. 155–70. Ed. Nicholas J. Saunders. London: Routledge.

Cornejo Polar, Antonio. 1994. *Escribir en el aire. Ensayo sobre la heterogeneidad socio-cultural en las literaturas andinas.* Lima: Editorial horizonte.

Costin, Cathy L. 1986. From chiefdom to empire state: Ceramic economy among the prehispanic Wanka of highland Peru. Unpublished Ph.D. dissertation. Los Angeles: University of California.

Couture, Nicole, 2002. The construction of power: Monumental space and elite residence at Tiwanaku, Bolivia. Unpublished Ph.D. dissertation. University of Chicago, Department of Anthropology.

——. 2005. Monumental space, courtly style and elite life at Tiwanaku. In *Tiwanaku ancestors of the Inca*, pp. 126–35. Ed. Margaret Young-Sanchez. Lincoln: University of Nebraska Press.

Cummins, Tom. 1988. Abstraction to narration: Kero imagery of Peru and the colonial alteration of native identity. Ph.D. dissertation. Los Angeles: University of California. Ann Arbor, MI: UMI.

——. 1993. La representación en el siglo XVI: La imagen colonial del Inca. In *Mito y simbolismo en los Andes. La figura y la palabra*, pp. 87–136. Comp. H. Urbano. Cusco, Peru: Centro de Estudios Regionales Andinos "Bartolomé de Las Casas."

——. 1998. Let Me See! Reading is for them: Colonial Andean images and objects "como es costumbre tener los caciques señores". In *Native traditions in the postconquest world*, pp. 91–148. Eds. Elizabeth Hill Boone and Tom Cummins. Washington, DC: Dumbarton Oaks Research Library and Collection.

——. 2002. *Toasts with the Inca: Andean abstractions and colonial images in Qero Vessels*. Ann Arbor: University of Michigan Press.

D'Altroy, Terence N. 1992. *Provincial power in the Inka Empire*. Washington, DC: Smithsonian Institution Press.

——. 2002. *The Incas*. Malden, MA: Blackwell.

D'Altroy, Terence N. and Christine A. Hastorf. 2001. *Empire and domestic economy*. New York: Plenum.

Davis, Wade. 1996. *One River. Explorations and discoveries on the Amazon rain forest*. New York: Simon and Shuster.

Dean, Carolyn. 2001. Andean androgyny and the making of men. In *Gender in pre-Hispanic America*, pp. 143–82. Ed. Cecelia F. Klein. Washington, DC: Dumbarton Oaks Research Library and Collection.

Dean, Emily. 2005. Ancestors, mountains, shrines, and settlements: Late Intermediate Period landscapes of the Southern Vilcanota River Valley, Peru. Ph.D. dissertation. Berkeley: University of California. Ann Arbor, MI: UMI.

DeLeonardis, Lisa. 1997. Paracas settlement in Callango, Lower Ica Valley, first millennium BC, Peru. Unpublished Ph.D. dissertation. Washington, DC: Catholic University of America.

——. 2000. The body context: Interpreting early Nasca decapitated burials. *Latin American Antiquity* 11(4):363–86.

Del Río, Mercedes. 1995. Estructuración étnica Qharaqhara y su desarticulación colonial. In *Espacio, etnias, frontera*, pp. 3–47. Comp. Ana María Presta. Sucre, Bolivia: Ediciones ASUR 4.

Demarest, Arthur Andrew. 1981. *Viracocha: The nature and antiquity of the Andean High God*. Cambridge, MA: Peabody Museum of Archaeology and Ethnology, Peabody Museum monographs, No. 6, Harvard University.

Descola, Philippe, 1989. *La selva culta. Simbolismo y praxis en la ecología de los Achuar*. Quito: Abya-Yala-MLAL.

——. 1993a. Les affinités sélectives. Alliance, guerre et predation dans l'ensemble jívaro. *L'Homme* (Paris) 126(8):171–90.

——. 1993b. *Les lances du crépuscule. Relations Jivaros, Haute-Amazonie*. Paris: Plon.

Desrosiers, Sophie. 1982. *Métier à tisser et vêtements andins ou le tissu comme être vivant*. Paris: Ceteclam.

——. 1997. Lógicas textiles y lógicas culturales en los Andes. In *Saberes y memorias en los Andes. In Memoriam Thierry Saignes*, pp. 325–49. Comp. T. Bouysse-Cassagne. Lima: CREDAL-IFEA.

Dillehay, Tom D., ed. 1995. *Tombs for the living*. Washington, DC: Dumbarton Oaks Research Library and Collection.

Dobres, Marcia-Anne and John Robb, eds. 2000. *Agency in archaeology*. London: Routledge.

Donnan, Christopher B. 1978. *Moche art of Peru: Pre-Columbian symbolic communication*. Los Angeles: Museum of Cultural History, University of California.

———. 2004. *Moche portraits from ancient Peru*. Austin: University of Texas Press.

Donnan, Christopher B. and Donna McClelland. 1979. The burial theme in Moche iconography. In *Studies in pre-Columbian art and archaeology*, No. 21, pp. 5–65. Washington, DC: Dumbarton Oaks Research Library and Collection.

Douglas, Mary. 1967. Primitive rationing: A study in controlled exchange. In *Themes in economic anthropology*, pp. 119–47. Ed. R. Firth. London: Tavistock.

Doutriaux, Miriam. 2001. Power, ideology and ritual: The practice of agriculture in the Inca empire. In *Past ritual and the everyday*, pp. 91–108. Ed. Christine A. Hastorf. Berkeley: University of California Press.

Downs, R. E. 1956. *The religion of the Bare's speaking Toradja of central Celebes*. The Hague: Uitgiverij Excelsior.

Doyle, Mary. 1988. The ancestor cult and burial ritual in seventeenth and eighteenth century central Peru. Ph.D. dissertation. Los Angeles: University of California. Ann Arbor, MI: UMI.

Drake, Richard Allen. 1991. The cultural logic of textile weaving practices among the Ibanic peoples. In *Female and male in Borneo: Contributions and challenges to gender studies*, pp. 271–93. Ed. Vinson H. Sutlive, Jr. Borneo Research Council, Monograph Series, vol. 1. Shanghai, VA: Ashkey Printing Services, Inc.

Dransart, Penelope. 2002. *Earth, water, fleece and fabric: An ethnography and archaeology of Andean camelid herding*. London: Routledge.

Drusini A. G. and J. P. Baraybar. 1991. Anthropological Study of a Nasca Trophy Head *Homo* 43(3):251–265.

Duverger, Christian. 1979. *La fleur létale, économie du sacrifice aztèque*. Paris: Editions Le Seuil/Recherches anthropologiques. Paris: Editions Le Seuil.

Duviols, Pierre. 1971. *La lutte contre les religions autochtones dans le Pérou colonial*. Lima: Institut Français d'Études Andines.

———. 1976. La Capacocha. Mecanismo y función del sacrificio humano, su proyección geométrica, su papel en la política integracionista y en la economía redistributiva del Tawantinsuyu. *Allpanchis phuturinqa* (Cusco, Peru) 9:11–56.

Earle, Timothy K. 1997. *How chiefs come to power: The political economy in prehistory*. Stanford, CA: Stanford University Press.

Earle, Timothy K., Terence N. D'Altroy, Christine A. Hastorf, Catherine Scott, Cathy Costin, Glenn Russell, and Elsie Sandefur. 1987. *Archaeological field research in the Upper Mantaro, Peru, 1982–1983 Investigations of Inka expansion and exchange*. Monograph 28. Los Angeles: Institute of Archaeology, University of California.

Ehrenreich, Barbara. 1997. *Blood rites. Origins and history of the passions of war*. New York: Henry Holt and Co., Metropolitan Books.

Ehrenreich, Robert M., Carole L. Crumley, and Janet E. Levy, eds. 1995. *Heterarchy and the analysis of complex societies*. Arlington, VA: American Anthropological Association.

Engel, Fréderic André. 1963. A preceramic settlement on the central coast of Peru: Asia, unit I. *Transactions of the American Philosophical Society*. Philadelphia: American Philosophical Society.

Engl, Lieselotte y Theo. 1967. *Glanz und Untergang des Inkareiches. Conquistadoren—Mönche—Vizekönige*. Munich: Callwey.

Erikson, P. 1986. Altérité, tatouage et anthropologie chez les Pano: La belliqueuse quête du soi. *Journal de la Société des Américanistes* 72:185–210.

Espinoza Soriano, Waldemar. 1981. El reino aymara de Quillaca-Asanaque, siglos XV y XVI. *Revista del Museo Nacional de Lima* 45:175–274.

Estete, M. de. 1938 [1535]. Noticia del Perú. In *Los cronistas de la Conquista*, pp. 195–251. Ed. H. Urteaga. Paris: Biblioteca de Cultura Peruana.

Fausto, Carlos. 1999. Of enemies and pets: Warfare and shamanism in Amazonia. *American Ethnologist* 26(4):933–56.

———. 2001. *Inimigos fiéis. História, guerra e xamanismo na Amazônia*. São Paolo, Brazil: Editoria da Universidade de São Paolo.

Feldman, Robert. 1980. Áspero, Peru: Architecture, subsistence economy, and other artifacts of a preceramic maritime chiefdom. Unpublished Ph.D. dissertation. Cambridge, MA: Harvard University.

Flores Ochoa, Jorge. 1977. Aspectos mágicos del pastoreo: *Enqa, enqaychu, illa y khuya rumi*. In *Pastores de puna: Uywamichiq punarunakuna*, pp. 211–38. Comp. J. Flores Ochoa. Lima: IEP.

———. 1990. Arte de resistencia en vasos ceremoniales Inka siglos XVII–XVIII. In *El Cuzco: resistencia y continuidad*, pp. 15–72. Ed. J. Flores Ochoa. Cuzco, Peru: Editorial Andina S.R. Ltda.

———. 1998. Imagen y memoria colectiva en qeros incas de los siglos XVII y XVIII. In *XII reunión anual de etnología* 26 al 29 de agosto de 1999, pp. 161–65. La Paz: MUSEF.

Flores Ochoa, Jorge, Elizabeth Kuon Arce, and Roberto Samanez Argumedo. 1999. *Qeros: Arte Inca en vasos ceremoniales*. Lima: Banco del Crédito del Perú, Colección Arte y Tesoros del Perú.

Forgerty, Kathleen and Sloan Williams. 2001. The Nasca trophy heads: Warfare trophies or revered ancestors? Paper presented in the symposium "Interacting with the Dead: Secondary Burial and Cultural Modification of Human Remains" (organized by S. Williams and Lane Beck) at the 66th annual meeting of the Society of American Archaeology, New Orleans, April 18–22.

Fortes, M. 1965. Some reflections on ancestor worship in Africa. In *African systems of thought*, pp. 122–44. Eds. Meyer Fortes and Germaine Dieterlen. Oxford: Oxford University Press.

Foucault, Michel. 1980. *Power/Knowledge*. Sussex, UK: Harvester Press.

Fox, James. 1974. "Our ancestors spoke in pairs": Rotinese views of language. In *Explorations in the ethnography of speaking*, pp. 65–85. Eds. R. Bauman and Joel Sherzer. New York: Cambridge University Press.

Frame, Mary. 1991. Structure, image, and abstraction: Paracas Necrópolis headbands as system templates. In *Paracas art and architecture. Object and context in south coastal Peru*, pp. 110–71. Ed. Anne Paul. Iowa City: University of Iowa Press.

Freeman, Derek. 1979. Severed heads that germinate. In *Fantasy and symbol: Studies in anthropological interpretation*, pp. 233–46. Ed. R.H. Hook. London: Academic Press.

Fried, Morton H. 1967. *The evolution of political society: An essay in political anthropology*. New York: Random House.

Friedman, Jonathan. 1985. Post structuralism and the new moon. *Ethnos* 50(1–2): 123–33.

Fung P., Rosa. 1988. The late preceramic and initial period. In *Peruvian prehistory*, pp. 67–81. Ed. Richard W. Keatinge. Cambridge: Cambridge University Press.

Gentile, Margarita E. 1998. La *pichca*: Oráculo y juego de fortuna (su persistencia en el espacio y tiempo andinos). *Bulletin de l'Institut Français d'études andines* 27(1): 75–131.

George, Kenneth. 1991. Headhunting, history and exchange in Upland Sulawesi. *Journal of Asian Studies* 50(3):536–64.

Gisbert, Teresa. 1999. La serpiente Amaru y la conquista del Antisuyu: Una historia alternativa. In *El paraíso de los pájaros parlantes. La imagen del otro en la cultura andina*, pp. 85–95. Ed. Teresa Gisbert. La Paz: Plural y Universidad Nuestra Señora de La Paz.

Gisbert, Teresa, Juan Carlos Jemio, Roberto Montero, Elvira Salinas, and María Soledad Quiroga. 1996. Los chullpares del río Lauca y el parque Sajama. La Paz: *Revista de la Academia Nacional de Ciencias de Bolivia* 70:1–81.

Glasser B. and A. Strauss. 1967. *The discovery of grounded theory: Strategies for qualitative research*. New York: Aldine.

Glowacki, Mary and Michael Malpass. 2003. Water, huacas, and ancestor worship: Traces of a sacred Wari landscape. *Latin American Antiquity* 14(4):431–48.

Gluckman, Max. 1983. Essays on Lozi land and royal property. In *Research in Economic Anthropology*, pp. 1–94. Ed. George Dalton. Greenwich, CT.: JAI Press.

Godelier, Maurice. 1971. L'anthropologie économique. In *L'Anthropologie, science des sociétés primitives?*, pp. 225–37. Eds. J. Copans J., S. Tornay, M. Godelier, and C. Backès-Clément. Paris: Denoël.

Godoy, Ricardo. 1986. The fiscal role of the Andean ayllu. *Man* N.S. 21(4):723–41.

Goldstein, Paul. 2005. *Andean diaspora: The Tiwanaku colonies and the origins of South American empire*. Gainesville: University of Florida Press.

González Holguín, Diego. 1952 [1608]. *Vocabulario de la lengua general de todo el Perú llamada lengua quichua o del Inca*. Lima: Universidad Nacional Mayor de San Marcos.

Gose, Peter. 1994. *Deathly waters and hungry mountains: Agrarian ritual and class formation in an Andean town*. Toronto: University of Toronto Press.

Grieder, Terence, Alberto Bueno Mendoza, C. Earle Smith, and Robert Malina. 1988. *La Galgada: A preceramic culture in transition*. Austin: University of Texas Press.

Grosfoguel, Ramón. Forthcoming. Decolonizing political-economy and post-colonial studies: transmodernity, border thinking, and global coloniality. In *Unsettling postcoloniality: Coloniality, transmodernity and border thinking*. Eds. R. Grosfoguel, José David Saldívar, and Nelson Maldonado Torres. Durham, NC: Duke University Press.

Guaman Poma de Ayala, don Felipe. ca. 1615. *El primer nueva corónica y buen gobierno*. Copenhagen: Det Kongelige Bibliotek, GKS 2232 4to.

Guaman Poma de Ayala, don Felipe. 2005, orig. 1993 [ca. 1615]. *Nueva corónica y buen gobierno*. Ed. Franklin Pease G. Y., vocabulary and translation from the Quechua by Jan Szemiński. 3 volumes. Lima: Fondo de Cultura Económica.

Harner, Michael J. 1972. *The Jívaro: People of the sacred waterfalls*. New York: Doubleday/ Natural History Press.

———. 1978. *Shuar: Pueblo de las cascadas sagradas*. Quito: Ediciones Mundo Shuar.

Harris, Olivia. 1983. Los muertos y los diablos entre los laymi de Bolivia. *Revista Chungará* (Arica, Chile) 11:135–52.

Harrison, Simon. 2006. Skull trophies of the Pacific War: Transgressive objects of remembrance. *Journal of the Royal Anthropological Institute* 12(4): 817–36.

Hastorf, Christine A. 1999. *Early settlement in Chiripa, Bolivia: Research of the Taraco Archaeological Project*, No. 57, Archaeological Research Facility Monograph Publications. Berkeley: University of California.

———. 2003. Community with the ancestors: Ceremonies and social memory in the Middle Formative at Chiripa, Bolivia. *Journal of Anthropological Archaeology* 22(4):305–332. Available online at http: //authors.elsevier.com/sd/article/ S0278416503000291

Hastorf, Christine A. and Sissel Johannessen. 1991. Expanding perspectives on prehistoric people/plant relationships. In *Processual and postprocessual archaeologies, multiple ways of knowing the past*, pp. 140–55. Ed. R.W. Preucel. Carbondale: Center for Archaeological Investigations, Southern Illinois University.

Hendon, Julia A. 2000. Having and holding: Storage, memory, knowledge and social relations. *American Anthropologist* 102(1):42–53.

Héritier-Augé, Françoise. 1986. Semen and blood: Some ancient theories concerning their genesis and relationship. In *Fragments for a history of the human body*, Part 3, pp. 159–75. Eds. Michel Feher with Ramona Naddaff and Nadia Tazi. New York: Zone.

Hocquenghem, Anne Marie. 1987. *Iconografía Mochica*. Lima: Pontificia Universidad Católica del Perú, Fondo Editorial.

Hoskins, Janet, ed. 1996a. *Headhunting and the social imagination in Southeast Asia*. Stanford, CA: Stanford University Press.

———. 1996b. Introduction. In *Headhunting and the social imagination in Southeast Asia*, pp. 1–49. Ed. Janet Hoskins. Stanford, CA: Stanford University Press.

Huanca, Tomás. 1989. *El yatiri en la comunidad aymara*. La Paz: CADA.

Hubert, Henri, and Marcel Mauss. 1964 [1898]. *Sacrifice, its nature and function*. Trans. W. D. Halls. Chicago: University of Chicago Press.

Hugh-Jones, Stephen. n.d. The gender of some Amazonian gifts: An experiment with an experiment. Amazonia and Melanesia: Gender and anthropological comparison. Paper for the Wenner Gren Symposium for Anthropological Research, International Symposium 121, "Amazonia and Melanesia: Gender and Anthropological Comparison," September 7–15, Mijas, Spain.

Hutton, J. H. 1921. *The Angami Nagas*. London: Macmillan.

Isbell, W. H. 1997. *Mummies and mortuary monuments: Post-processual prehistory of central Andean social organization*. Austin: University of Texas Press.

Isbell, W. H. and G. F. McEwan. 1991. A history of Huari studies and introduction to current interpretations. In *Huari administration structures*, pp. 1–17. Eds. W. H. Isbell and G. McEwan. Washington, DC: Dumbarton Oaks Research Library and Collection.

Isbell, W. H. and A. Vranich. 2004. Experiencing the cities of Wari and Tiwanaku. In *Andean Archaeology*, pp. 167–82. Ed. Helaine Silverman. Oxford: Blackwell Publishing.

Izikowitz, Karl. 1967. Berattelze for 1966. In *Etnografiska musset. Gotenborg. Arstryck 1963–1966*, pp. 78–79. Ed. Ethnography Museum. Goteborg, Sweden: Ethnography Museum.

Izumi, S. and K. Terada. 1972. *Andes 4: Excavations at Kotosh, 1963 and 1966*. Tokyo: University of Tokyo Press.

Janusek, John W. 1994. State and local power in a pre-Hispanic Andean polity; changing patterns of urban residence in Tiwanaku and Lukurmata, Bolivia. Ph.D. dissertation. Chicago: University of Chicago.

———. 2004. *Identity and power in the ancient Andes: Tiwanaku cities through time*. New York: Routledge.

Janusek, John W., Arik Ohnstad, and Andrew P. Roddick. 2003. Khonko Wankane and the rise of Tiwanaku. In *E-ntiquity*, vol. 77.

Jennings, Jesse. 1978. *Ancient Native Americans*. San Francisco: Freeman.

Joyce, Rosemary. 2000. Heirloom and houses, materiality and social memory. In *Beyond kinship: Social and material reproduction in house societies*, pp. 189–212. Eds. Rosemary A. Joyce and Susan D. Gillespie. Philadelphia: University of Pennsylvania Press.

Karsten, R. 1935. *The head-hunters of western Amazonas. The life and culture of the Jíbaro Indians of eastern Ecuador and Peru*. Helsingfors, Finland: Societas Scientiarum Fenniga.

———. 1968. *The civilization of the South American Indians*. London: Dawsons of Pall Mall.

Kauffmann Doig, Federico. 2001. *Sexo y magia sexual en el antiguo Perú*. Lima: Quebecor World Peru, S.A.

Kidder, II, A. V. 1956. Digging in the Titicaca Basin. *University of Pennsylvania Museum Bulletin* 20(3):16–29.

Knobloch, Patricia J. 1993. Who was who in the Huari empire. Paper presented at the 33rd Annual Meeting of the Institute of Andean Studies, Berkeley, California, January 8–9. Available online at http://www-rohan.sdsu.edu/~bharley/WWWIAS93Paper.html

———. 2000. Wari ritual power at Conchopata. An interpretation of *Anadenanthera colubrina* iconography. *Latin American Antiquity* 11(4):387–402.

Kojan, David. 2002. Cultural identity and historical narratives of the Bolivian eastern Andes: An archaeological study. Unpublished Ph.D. dissertation. Berkeley: University of California. Ann Arbor, MI: UMI.

Kolata, Alan L. 1996. *Valley of the spirits*. New York: John Wiley & Sons.

———., ed. 2001. *Tiwanaku and its hinterlands*, vol. 1. Washington, DC: Smithsonian Institution Press.

———. 2003. Tiwanaku ceremonial architecture and urban organization. In *Tiwanaku and its hinterland: Archaeology and paleoecology of an Andean civilization*, vol. 2, *Urban and rural archaeology*, pp. 175–201. Ed. A. Kolata. Washington, DC: Smithsonian Institution Press.

Kontopoulos, Kyriakis M. 1993. *The logic of social structures*. Cambridge: Cambridge University Press.

Kowta, Makoto. 1987. *An introduction to the archaeology of the Acarí Valley in the south coast region of Peru*. Sacramento: California Institute for Peruvian Studies. Referenced in Browne et al. 1993.

Kroeber, Alfred L. 1944. *Peruvian archaeology in 1942*. Viking Fund Publications in Anthropology, No. 4. New York: Viking Fund.

———. 1956. Toward definition of the Nazca style. *University of California Publications in American Archaeology and Ethnology* 43(4):327–432.

Kruyt, Albert C. 1906. *Het Animisme en den Indischen Archipel*. The Hague: Mantinus Nijhoff.

La Lone, Darrell. 2000. Rise, fall, and semiperipheral development in the Andean world system. *Journal of World-Systems Research* 6(1):68–99.

Lathrap, Donald W. 1977. Our father the cayman, our mother the gourd: Spinden revisited, or a unitary model for the emergence of agriculture in the New World. In *Origins of Agriculture*, pp. 713–51. Ed. Charles A. Reed. The Hague: Mouton.

Laurencich Minelli, Laura. 2003. Nuevas perspectivas sobre los fundamentos ideológicos del Tahuantinsuyu: Lo sagrado en el mundo Inca de acuerdo a dos documentos jesuíticos secretos. *Espéculo. Revista de estudios literarios*, No. 25. Madrid: Universidad Complutense. Available online at http: //www.ucm.es/info/especulo/numero25/tahuan.html

Lavalle, José Antonio de and José Alejandro González García. 1991. *The textile art of Peru*. Lima: Industria Textil Piura, S.A.

Lemuz Aguirre, Carlos. 2001. Patrones de asentimiento arqueológico en la Peninsula de Santiago de Huata, Bolivia. Unpublished Lic. dissertation. La Paz: Universidad Mayor de San Andrés.

Lévi-Strauss, Claude. 1967. *Structural anthropology*. Trans. Claire Jacobson and Brooke Grundfest Schoepf (original in French, 1958). New York: Anchor Books.

Llanos, David. 2004. Ritos para detener la lluvia en una comunidad de Charazani. In *Gracias a Dios y a los achachilas. Ensayos de sociología de la religión en los Andes*, pp. 159–84. Comp. Alison Spedding P. La Paz: Plural and ISEAT.

Locke, L. Leland. 1923. *The ancient quipu or Peruvian knot record*. New York: American Museum of Natural History.

López García, Ulpián R. 1999. *El rito de Qachaj Mallku*. Unpublished B.A. dissertation. Oruro, Bolivia: Universidad Técnica de Oruro.

Lumbreras, Luís G. 1989. *Chavín de Huántar en el nacimiento de la civilización andina*. Lima: Ediciones INDEA, Instituto Andino de Estudios Arqueológicos.

Luykx, Aurolyn. *1999. The citizen factory. Schooling and cultural production in Bolivia*. Albany: State University of New York Press.

Malinowski, W. 1935. *Coral gardens and their magic*. New York: American Book Company.

Mannheim, Bruce. 1987. Couplets and oblique contexts: The social organization of a folksong. *Text* (Amsterdam) 7(3):265–88.

———. 1999. El arado del tiempo: Poética quechua y formación nacional. *Revista Andina* (Cusco: BLC) 17(1):15–63.

Marx, Karl. 1973 [1894]. *Capital*. Buenos Aires: Editorial Cartago.

McEwan, Gordon F. 1998. The function of niched walls in Wari architecture. *Latin American Antiquity* 9(1):68–86.

McGuire, Randall H. 1992. *A Marxist archaeology*. San Diego, CA: Academic Press.

McWilliam, Andrew. 1996. Severed heads that germinate the state. History, politics and headhunting in southwest Timor. In *Headhunting and the social imagination in Southeast Asia*, pp. 127–66. Ed. Janet Hoskins. Stanford, CA: Stanford University Press.

Meddens, Frank and Anita Cook. 2001. La administración Wari y el culto a los muertos: Yako los edificios en forma "D" en los Andes sur central del Peru. In *Wari, arte precolumbino peruano*, pp. 212–28. Ed. Luís Millones. Seville, Spain: Fundación El Monte.

Medina Rojas, A. 1958. Hallazgos arqueológicos en el Cerro El Plomo. In *Arqueología chilena*. Santiago: Centro de Estudios Antropológicos, Universidad de Chile.

Mejía Xesspe, Toribio and Julio C. Tello. 1959. *Paracas*. New York: Institute of Andean Research.

———. 1979. *Paracas II*. Lima: Universidad Nacional Mayor de San Marcos.

Mena, Cristóbal de. 1534. *La conquista del Perú llamada la Nueva Castilla*. Lima: Editores Técnicos Asociados.

Menzel, Dorothy. 1976. *Pottery style and society in ancient Peru: Art as a mirror of history in the Ica Valley, 1350–1570*. Berkeley: University of California Press.

Métraux, A. 1949. Warfare, cannibalism, and human trophies. In *Handbook of South American Indians*, vol. 5, pp. 383–409. Ed. Julian H. Steward. Bureau of American Ethnology, Bulletin 143. Washington, DC: Government Printing Office.

Miller, Daniel, Michael J. Rowlands and Christopher Y. Tilley. 1989. *Domination and resistance*. London: Unwin Hyman.

Mohr Chávez, Karen. 1988. The significance of Chiripa in Lake Titicaca Basin developments. *Expedition* 30(3):17–26.

Molina del Cusco, Cristóbal. 1943 [*ca.* 1573]. Fábulas y ritos de los Incas. In *Los pequeños grandes libros de la historia Americana*. Ed. Francisco A. Loayza. Series 1, vol. 4. Lima: Editorial Domingo Miranda.

Molina Rivero, Ramiro. 2006. Entre fuego y sangre: Violencia entre Qaqachakas y Laymis. In *De memorias e identidades. Los aymaras y urus del sur de Oruro*, pp. 257–82. Comp. Ramiro Rivero Molina. La Paz: Asdi, Instituto de Estudios Bolivianos y Fundación Diálogo.

Monnas, Lisa and Hero Granger-Taylor, eds. 1989. Ancient and medieval textiles. Studies in honour of Donald King. *Textile History* 20(2):283–307.

Montes Ruíz, Fernando. 1986. *La máscara de piedra. Simbolismo y personalidad aymaras en la historia*. La Paz: Editorial Quipus, Comisión Episcopal de Educación, Secretario Nacional para la Acción Social.

Moore, Jerry. 1996. *Architecture and power in the ancient Andes*. Cambridge: Cambridge University Press.

Moseley, Michael E. 1992. *The Incas and their ancestors*. London: Thames and Hudson.

Mulvany, Eleanora. 2004. Motivos de flores en qeros coloniales: Imagen y significado. *Chungará, Revista de Antropología Chilena* 36(2):407–19.

Murúa, Martín de. 1946 [1590]. Los orígenes de los Inkas, crónica sobre el antiguo Perú. In *Los pequeños grandes libros de la historia Americana*. Ed. Francisco A. Loayza. Series 1, vol. 11. Lima: Editorial Domingo Miranda.

Narváez Vargas, Alfredo. 2003. Cabeza y cola: Expresión de dualidad, religiosidad y poder en los Andes. In *Tradición popular. Arte y religión de los pueblos del norte del Perú*, pp. 5–43. Eds. Luís Millones, Hiroyasu Tomoeda, and Tatsuhiko Fujii. Osaka, Japan: National Museum of Ethnology.

Needham, Rodney. 1976. Skulls and causality. *Man* 11:71–88.

Neira Avedaño, M. and V. P. Coehlo. 1972. Enterramientos de cabezas de la cultura Nasca. *Revista do Museu Paulista* n.s. 20:109–42.

Oberem, Udo. 1958. Diego de Ortegón's Beichreibung der "Gobernación de los Quijos, Zumaco y la Canela. Ein Ethnographischer Bericht aus dem Jahre 1577. *Zeitschrift für Ethnologie* (Braunschweig, Germany) 83:230–51.

Ochatoma Paravicino, José. 1999. Recientes descubrimientos en el sitio Huari de Conchopata, Ayacucho. Paper presented at the 64th annual meeting of the Society for American Archaeology, Chicago, Illinois.

Ogburn, Dennis. 2007. Human trophies in the Late Pre-Hispanic Andes. In *The taking and displaying of human body parts as trophies by Amerindians*, pp. 501–18. Eds. Richard J. Chacon and David H. Dye. New York: Springer.

Onians, R. B. 1951. *The origins of European thought*. Cambridge: Cambridge University Press.

Ortegón, Diego de. 1577. *Descripción de la gobernación de los Quijos*. Manuscript, February 1, conserved in the Real Archivo de Indias in Seville, Spain.

Ossio A., Juan M., ed. 1973. *Ideología mesiánica del mundo andino*. Lima: Ignacio Prado Pastor.

Parker Pearson, Mike. 1993. The powerful dead: Archaeological relationships between the living and the dead. *Cambridge Archaeological Journal* 3(2):203–29.

Pärsinnen, Martti and Antti Korpisaari, comps. 2003. *Western Amazonia—Amazônia Ocidental. Multidisciplinary studies in ancient expansionistic movements, fortifications and sedentary life*. Helsinki: Renvall Institute Publications 14, University of Helsinki.

Pauketat, Timothy. 2000. The tragedy of the commoners. In *Agency in archaeology*, pp. 113–29. Eds. M.-A. Dobres and J. Robb. London: Routledge.

———. 2001. *The archaeology of traditions: Agency and history before and after Columbus*. Gainesville: University Presses of Florida.

Paul, Anne. 1982. The symbolism of Paracas turbans. A consideration of style, serpents and hair. *Ñawpa Pacha* (Berkeley: Instituto de Estudios Andinos) 20:41–60.

———. 1986. Continuity in Paracas textile iconography and its implications for the meaning of linear style images. In *The Junius B. Bird Conference on Andean Textiles*, pp. 81–99. Ed. Ann P. Rowe. Washington, DC: The Textile Museum.

———. 1992. Paracas necropolis textiles: Symbolic visions of coastal Peru. In *The ancient Americas: Art from sacred landscapes*, pp. 279–88. Ed. Richard Townsend. Chicago: The Art Institute of Chicago.

———. 2000a. The configuration and iconography of borders on Paracas Necrópolis ponchos. In *Lisières et bordures*, pp. 101–15. Eds. F. Cosin, S. Desrosiers, D. Beirnaeret, and N. Pellegrin. Poitiers, France: Editions Les Gorgones.

———. 2000b. Protective perimeters: The symbolism of borders on Paracas textiles. *Res: Anthropology and Aesthetics* 38 (Autumn):144–68.

———. 2000c. Bodiless human heads in Paracas Necropolis textile iconography. *Andean Past* 6:69–94.

Paul, Anne and Solveig A. Turpin. 1986. The ecstatic shaman theme of Paracas textiles. *Archaeology*, special edition, 39(5):20–27.

Peters, Ann. 2000. Funerary regalia and institutions of leadership in Paracas and Topará. *Chungará* (Arica, Chile) 32(2):245–52.

Pezzia Assereto, Alejando. 1968. *Ica y el Perú precolombino*, vol. 1, *Arqueología de la Provincia de Ica*. Ica, Peru: Editorial Ojeda, S.A.

Picht, Hans-Joachim. 1995. Conflictos intercomunales en los Andes centrales. *Debate Agrario, Análisis y Alternativas* 23:37–50.

Pizarro, Pedro. 1986 [1571]. *Relación del descubrimiento y conquista de los reinos del Perú*, 2nd ed. Lima: Pontificia Universidad Católica del Perú, Fondo Editorial.

Platt, Tristan. 1978. Symètries en miroir: Le concept de yanantin chez les Macha de Bolivie. *Annales* (Paris) E.S.C. 33(5–6):1081–107.

———. 1982a. *Estado boliviano y ayllu andino: tierra y tributo en el Norte de Potosí*. Lima: Instituto de Estudios Peruanos.

Platt, Tristan. 1982b. Dos visiones de la relación ayllu-estado: La resistencia de los indios de Chayanta a la Revisita General (1882–1885). *Historia Boliviana* (La Paz) 2(1):33–46.

———. 1986. Mirrors and maize, the concept of yanantin among the Macha of Bolivia. In *Anthropological history of Andean polities*, pp. 229–59. Eds. J. V. Murra, N. Wachtel, and J. Revel. Cambridge: Cambridge University Press.

———. 1987a. Entre *ch'axwa* y *muxsa*. Para una historia del pensamiento político aymara. In *Tres reflexiones sobre el pensamiento andino*, pp. 61–132. Ed. Javier Medina. La Paz: Hisbol.

———. 1987b. The Andean soldiers of Christ. Confraternity organization, the mass of the sun and regenerative warfare in rural Potosí. *Journal de la Société des Américanistes* 73:139–91.

———. 1996. *Guerreros de Cristo*. La Paz: ASUR and Plural Editores.

———. 2001. El feto agresivo. Parto, formación de la persona y mito-historia en los Andes. *Anuario de Estudios Americanos* (Seville) 57(2):633–78.

Platt, Tristan, Thérèse Bouysse-Cassagne, and Olivia Harris. 2006. *Qaraqara-Charka. Mallku, Inka y Rey en la provincia de Charcas (siglos XV–XVIII). Historia antropológica de una confederación aymara.* La Paz: IFEA, University of St. Andrews, University of London, Inter-American Foundation, and Fundación Central del Banco Central de Bolivia.

Ponce Sanginés, Carlos. 1957. Una piedra esculpida de Chiripa. In *Arqueología boliviana*, pp. 119–38. Ed. C. Ponce Sanginés. La Paz: Biblioteca Paceña.

———. 1970. Las culturas Wankarani y Chiripa y su relación con Tiwanaku. *Academia Nacional de las Ciencias* (La Paz), publication 25.

———. 1990. *Descripción sumaria del templete semisubterráneo de Tiwanaku*, 6th rev. ed. La Paz: Juventud.

Portugal Ortíz, M. 1981. Expansión del estilo escultórico Pa-Ajanu. *Arte y arqueología* 7:149–59.

———. 1988. Excavaciones arqueológicas en Titimani, 2nd part. *Arqueología Boliviana* 3:51–81.

———. 1989. Estilo escultórico Chiripa en al Peninsula de Santiago de Huata. *Textos Anthropológicos* (La Paz) 1(1):45–78.

———. 1992. Aspectos de la cultura Chiripa. *Textos Antropológicos* (La Paz) 3:9–26.

Portugal Ortíz, M., H. Catacora, J. Inchuasti, A. Murillo, G. Suñavi, R. Gutiérrez, V. Plaza, W. Winkler, S. Avilés, and J. Portugal. 1993. Excavaciones en Titimani (Temporada II). *Textos Antropológicos* (La Paz) 5:11–191.

Pozorski, Shelia and Thomas Pozorski. 1986. Recent excavations at Pampa de las Llamas-Moxeke. *Journal of Field Archaeology* 13(4):381–401.

Pozorski, Thomas. 1980. The Early Horizon site of Huaca de los Reyes. *American Antiquity* 45:100–10.

Proulx, Donald A. 1971. Head hunting in ancient Peru. *Archaeology* 24(1):16–21.

———. 1989. Nasca trophy heads: Victims of warfare or ritual sacrifice? In *Cultures in conflict: Current archaeological perspectives*, pp. 73–85. Eds. Diana C. Tkaczuk and Brian C. Vivian. Calgary, Canada: University of Calgary Archaeological Association.

———. 1999. Nasca headhunting and the ritual use of trophy heads. Trans. from Kopfjagd und rituelle Verwendung von Trophäenköpfen in de Nasca-Kultur. In *Nasca, geheimnisvolle Zeichen im Alten Peru*, pp. 79–87. Ed. Judith Rickenbach. Zurich: Museum Rietberg.

Proulx, Donald A. 2001. Ritual uses of trophy heads in ancient Nasca society. In *Ritual sacrifice in ancient Peru*, pp. 119–36. Eds. E. P. Benson and A. G. Cook. Austin: University of Texas Press.

———. 2006. *A sourcebook of Nasca ceramic iconography*. Iowa City: University of Iowa Press.

Radicati de Primeglio, Carlos. 1979. *El sistema contable de los Incas. Yupana y quipu*. Lima: Librería Studium.

———. 1984. El secreto de la quilca. *Revista de Indias* (Madrid) 44(173):11–62.

———. 1990. Tableros de escaques en el antiguo Perú. In *Quipu y Yupana. Colección de escritos*, pp. 219–34. Eds. Carol Mackey, Hugo Pereyra, Carlos Radicati, Humberto Rodríguez, and Oscar Valverde. Lima: CONCYTEC.

Ramirez, Susan E. 1996. *The world upside down: Cross-cultural contact and conflict in sixteenth century Peru*. Stanford, CA: Stanford University Press.

———. 2005. *To feed and be fed: The cosmological bases of authority and identity in the Andes*. Stanford, CA: Stanford University Press.

Ramos Gavilán, A. 1976 [1621]. *Historia de nuestra señora de Copacabana*. La Paz: Academia Boliviana de la Historia.

Renard-Casevitz, France-Marie, Thierry Saignes, and Ann Christine Taylor. 1985. *L'Inca, l'Espagnol et les sauvages*. Paris: Editions de l'Association pour la Diffusion de la Pensée Française.

———. 1988. *Al este de los Andes. Relaciones entre las sociedades amazónica y andina entre los Siglos XV y XVII*, vol. 1. Quito: Ediciones Abya-Yala e IFEA.

Rendón Lizarazu, Pablo M. 2000. El culto de las cabezas trofeo. In *XIV Reunión Annual de Etnología. Aportes indígenas: Estados y democracia*, vol. 1, pp. 171–78. La Paz: MUSEF.

Rick, John. 2000. Chavín. Lecture at the Department of Anthropology, University of California-Berkeley, Spring.

Robert, Jean. 1997. Producción. In *Diccionario del desarrollo. Una guía del conocimiento como poder*, pp. 277–98. Ed. Wolfgang Sach. Cochabamba, Bolivia: Centro de Aprendizaje Intercultural, CAI.

Rodriguez Kembel, Silvia and John Rick. 2004. Building authority at Chavín de Huántar: Models of social organization and development in the Initial period and early Horizon. In *Andean Archaeology*, pp. 51–76. Ed. Helaine Silverman. Oxford: Blackwell Publishing.

Roe, P. 1982. *The cosmic zygote*. New Brunswick, NJ: Rutgers University Press.

Romanoff, Steven A. 1984. Matses adaptations in the Peruvian Amazon. Unpublished Ph.D. dissertation. New York: Colombia University.

Root, Deborah. 1996. *Cannibal culture*. Boulder, CO: Westview Press.

Rosaldo, Renato. 1989. Introduction: Grief and the headhunter's rage. In *Culture and truth: The remaking of social analysis*, pp. 1–21. Ed. R. Rosaldo. Boston: Beacon Press.

Rose, Courtney E. 2001. Household and community organization of a formative period, Bolivian settlement. Unpublished Ph.D. dissertation. Pittsburgh: University of Pittsburgh.

Rösing, Ina. 1996. *Rituales para llamar la lluvia: Rituales colectivos de la región kallawaya en los Andes bolivianos*. Cochabamba, Bolivia: Los Amigos del Libro.

Rowe, John H. 1946. Inca culture at the time of the Spanish conquest. In *Handbook of South American Indians*, vol. 2, pp. 183–330. Ed. Julian Steward. Washington, DC: Bureau of American Ethnology, Bulletin 143.

Rowe, John H. 1961. The chronology of Inca wooden cups. In *Essays in Pre-Columbian art and archaeology*, pp. 317–41. Eds. S. Lothrop, Doris Stone, Junius Bird, Gordon Ekholm, and Gordon Willey. Cambridge, MA: Harvard University Press.

———. 1967. Form and meaning in Chavin art. In *Readings in Peruvian archaeology*, pp. 72–104. Eds. John Howland Rowe and Dorothy Menzel. Palo Alto, CA: Peek Publishers.

———. 1995. Behavior and belief in ancient Peruvian mortuary practice. In *Tombs for the living; Andean mortuary practices*, pp. 24–27. Ed. T. D. Dillehay. Washington, DC: Dumbarton Oaks Research Library and Collection.

———. n.d. Origins of creator worship among the Incas. Manuscript stored at the University of California libraries.

Saignes, Thierry. 1985. *Los Andes orientales: Historia de un olvido*. Cochabamba, Bolivia: CERES and IFEA.

———. 1993. Estar en otra cabeza: Tomar en los Andes. In *Borrachera y memoria: La experiencia de lo sagrado en los Andes*, pp. 11–12. Comp. Thierry Saignes. La Paz: Hisbol and IFEA.

Salomon, Frank. 1986. *Native lords of Quito in the age of the Incas*. Cambridge: Cambridge University Press.

———. 1991. *The Huarochiri manuscript: A testament of ancient and Colonial Andean religion*. Austin: University of Texas Press.

———. 1995. "The beautiful grandparents": Andean ancestor shrines and mortuary ritual as seen through colonial records. In *Tombs for the living*, pp. 315–53. Ed. T. D. Dillehay. Washington, DC: Dumbarton Oaks Research Library and Collection.

———. 2002a. Patrimonial khipu in a modern Peruvian village: An introduction to the "quipocamayos" of Tupicocha, Huarochirí. In *Narrative threads. Accounting and recounting in Andean khipu*, pp. 293–319. Eds. Jeffrey Quilter and Gary Urton. Austin: University of Texas Press.

———. 2002b. "*¡Huara huayra pichcamanta!*": Augurio, risa y regeneración en la política tradicional (Pacota, Huarochirí). *Bulletin de l'Institut français d'études andines* 31(1):1–22.

———. 2004. *The cord keepers: Khipus and cultural life in a Peruvian village*. Durham, NC: Duke University Press.

Saunders, Nicholas J., ed. 1998. *Icons of power. Felines symbolism in the Americas*. London and New York: Routledge.

Sawyer, Alan. 1979. Painted Nasca textiles. In *The Junius B. Bird pre-Columbian textile conference*, pp. 129–59. Eds. A. P. Rowe, E. P. Benson, and A. Schaffer. Washington, DC: The Textile Museum and Dumbarton Oaks Research Library and Collection.

Schaedel, Richard P. 1988. Andean world view: Hierarchy or reciprocity, regulation, and control? *Current Anthropology* 29(5):768–75.

Schobinger, J. 1966. La momia del Cerro El Toro. *Anales de arqueología y etnología* (Nacional University of Cuyo, Mendoza, Argentina), supplement, 21:89–96.

Schreiber, Katharina Jeanne. 1992. *Wari imperialism in Middle Horizon Peru*. Anthropological papers No. 87. Ann Arbor: Museum of Anthropology, University of Michigan.

Schreiber, Katharina Jeanne and Josué Lancho Rojas. 2003. *Irrigation and society in the Peruvian desert: The puquios of Nasca*. Lanham, MD: Lexington Books.

Schultes, Richard E. 1972. Hallucinogens of the Western Hemisphere. In *Flesh of the Gods: The ritual use of hallucinogens*, pp. 3–54. Ed. P. T. Furst. New York: Praeger.

Seibold, Katherine E. 1992. Textiles and cosmology in Choquecancha, Cuzco. In *Andean cosmologies through time. Persistence and emergence*, pp. 166–201. Eds. R.V.H. Dover, Katherine E. Seibold, and John H. McDowell. Bloomington: Indiana University Press.

Shortland, Edward. 1882. *Maori religion and mythology*. London: Longmans Green and Co.

Sikkink, Lynn. 1997. El poder mediador del cambio de aguas: Género y el cuerpo político condeño. In *Más allá del silencio. Las fronteras de género en los Andes*, pp. 94–122. Comp. D. Y. Arnold. La Paz: CIASE and ILCA.

Silverman, Helaine. 1988. Cahuachi: Non-urban cultural complexity on the south coast of Peru. *Journal of Field Archaeology* 15(4):403–30.

———. 1993. *Cahuachi in the ancient Nasca world*. Iowa City: University of Iowa Press.

Silverman, Gail P. (formerly Silverman-Proust). 1994. *El tejido andino. Un libro de sabiduría*. Lima: Fondo Editorial, Banco Central de Reserva del Perú.

Smith, C. Earle. 1988. Floral Remains. In *La Galgada: A preceramic culture in transition*, pp. 123–151. Eds. Terence Grieder, Alberto Bueno Mendoza, C. Earle Smith, and Robert Malina. Austin: University of Texas Press.

Soukup, Jaroslav. 1970. *Vocabulario de los nombres vulgares de la flora peruana*. Lima: Colegio Salesiano.

Spalding, Karen. 1984. *Huarochiri, an Andean society under Inca and Spanish rule*. Stanford, CA.: Stanford University Press.

Spedding, Alison. 1993. Gótico americano: Una notas sobre las cabezas cortadas en el imaginario boliviano. Manuscript in author's possession.

Stanish, Charles. 2001. The origin of state societies in South America. *Annual Reviews in Anthropology* 30:41–64.

———. 2003. *Ancient Titicaca*. Berkeley: University of California Press.

Steadman, Lee and Christine A. Hastorf. 2001. Construction for the ancestors: The creation of territory and society in the Middle formative at Chiripa. In "Symposium: The Formative in the Titicaca Basin," organized by A. Plourde and C. Stanish, at the 66th annual meetings of the Society for American Archaeology, New Orleans, April 19.

Stobart, Henry. 1996. Los wayñus que salen de las huertas: Música y papa en una comunidad campesina del Norte de Potosí. In *Madre melliza y sus crías: Antología de la papa*, pp. 413–30. Comp. D. Y. Arnold and Juan de Dios Yapita. La Paz: Hisbol e ILCA.

Strathern, Marilyn. 1988. *The gender of the gift*. Berkeley: University of California Press.

Szemiñski, Jan. 1987. *Un kuraka, un dios y una historia* ("Relación de antigüedades de este reyno del Perú" por don Joan de Santa cruz Pacha cuti yamqui Salca Maygua). Monograph series. San Salvador de Jujuy, Argentina: Social Anthropology Section (ICA), Faculty of Philosophy and Letters (UBA/MLAL).

Tantalean Arbulu, Javier. 1998. El circuito macroeconómico incaico. In *Pueblos de indios, economía y relaciones interétnicas en los Andes, Anuario de Historia Regional y de las Fronteras*, nos. 2, 3, and 4, pp. 233–57, 1996, 1997, 1998; *Anuario de Historia Regional y de las Fronteras*, nos. 2, 3, and 4, 1996–1997. Bogota: Universidad Industrial de Santander, Escuela de Historia.

Taylor, Anne Christine. 1985. L'art de la réduction. *Journal de la Société de Américanistes* 71:159–73.

Taylor, Anne Christine. 1993. Les bons ennemis et les mauvais parents. Le traitment de l'alliance dans les rituals de chasse aux têtes des Shuar (jívaro) de l'Ecuateur. In *Les complexités de l'alliance*, vol. 4, *Symbolisme et fondement économique et politiques de l'alliance matrimoniales*, pp. 73–105. Eds. E. Copet-Rougier and F. Héretier-Augé. Paris: Éditions des Archives Contemporains ("Ordres sociaux").

Taylor, Gerald. 1976. Camac, camay et camasca dans le manuscrit quechua de Huarochirí. *Journal de la Société des Américanistes* (Paris) 63:231–44.

———. 2001. La platica de fray Domingo de Santo Tomás (1560). *Bulletin de l'Institut français d'études andines* (Lima) 30(3):427–53.

Tello, Julio C. 1918. El uso de las cabezas humanas artificialmente momificadas y su representación en el antiguo arte peruano. *Revista Universitaria* (Lima) 13(1): 478–533.

Tilly, Charles. 1992. *Coercion, capital, and European states, AD 990–1992*. Cambridge MA: Blackwell.

Topic, John R. 1991. Huari and Huamachuco. In *Huari administrative structures: prehistoric monumental architecture and state government*, pp. 141–64. Eds. W. H. Isbell and G. McEwan. Washington, DC: Dumbarton Oaks Research Library and Collection.

———. 2003. From stewards to bureaucrats: Architecture and information flow at Chan Chan, Peru. *Latin American Antiquity* 14(3):243–74.

Torrico, Cassandra. 1989. Living weavings: The symbolism of Bolivian herders' sacks. Mimeo in author's possession.

Uhle, Max. 1901. Die deformierten Köpfe von peruanischen Mumin und die Uta-Krankheit. *Verhandlungen der Berliner Bessellschaft für Anthropolgie, Ethnologie und Urgeschichte* (Berlin) 33:404–48.

———. 1918. El uso de las cabezas humanas artificiales. *Revista Universitaria* 13(1): 478–533.

———. 1922. Influencias mayas en el alto Ecuador. *Boletín de la Academia Nacional de Historia de Ecuador* (Quito) 4:205–41.

Urton, Gary. 1994. A new twist in an old yarn: Variation in knot directionality in the Inka khipus. *Baessler-Archiv*, new series, 42:271–305.

———. 1997. *The social life of numbers. A Quechua ontology of numbers and philosophy of arithmetic*. Austin: University of Texas Press.

———. 2003. *Signs of the Inka kipu. Binary coding in the Andean knotted-string records*. Austin: University of Texas Press.

Valcárcel, L. E. 1932. El personaje mítico de Pukara. *Revista del Museo Nacional* (Lima) 4:18–30.

———. 1935. Litoesculturas y cerámica de Pukara. *Revista del Museo Nacional* (Lima) 4:25–28.

Vaughn, K. J. 2004. Households, crafts and feasting in the ancient Andes: The village context of early Nasca craft consumption. *Latin American Antiquity* 15(1):61–88.

Verano, John. 1995. Where do they rest? The treatment of human offerings and mummies in ancient Peru. In *Tombs for the living*, pp. 189–227. Ed. Tom D. Dillehay. Washington, DC: Dumbarton Oaks Research Library and Collection.

———. 2001. The physical evidence of human sacrifice in ancient Peru. In *Ritual sacrifice in ancient Peru*, pp. 165–84. Eds. E. P. Benson and A. G. Cook. Austin: University of Texas Press.

Verano, John, Santiago Uceda, Claude Chapdelaine, Richardo Tello, María Isabel Paredes, and Víctor Pimente. 1999. Modified human skulls from the urban sector of the pyramids of Moche, northern Peru. *Latin American Antiquity* 19(1):59–70.

Viveiros de Castro, Eduardo. 1992. *From the enemy's point of view. Humanity and divinity in an Amazonian society*. Trans. Catherine V. Howard. Chicago: University of Chicago Press. Original 1986.

———. 1998. Cosmological deixis and Amerindian perspectivism. *The Journal of the Royal Anthropological Institute* (London) 4(3):469–88.

Vreeland, James M. Jr. and Aidan Cockburn. 1980. Mummies of Peru. In *Mummies, disease and ancient cultures*, pp. 135–74. Eds. Aidan and Eve Cockburn. Cambridge: Cambridge University Press.

Wall Hendricks, Janet. 1993. *To drink of death. The narrative of a Shuar warrior*. Tucson: University of Arizona Press.

Wallace, Dwight T. 1991. A technical and iconographic analysis of Carhua painted textiles. In *Paracas art and architecture: Object and context in south coastal Peru*, pp. 61–109. Ed. Anne Paul. Iowa City: University of Iowa Press.

Wallerstein, Immanuel Maurice. 1988. *Revolution in the world-system: Theses and queries*. Binghamton: State University of New York at Binghamton.

Watanabe, Luís. 1979. Arquitectura de la Huaca de los Reyes. In *Arqueología peruana: Investigaciones arqueológicos en el Perú, 1976*, pp.17–35. Ed. Ramiro Matos. Lima: Centro de Proyección Cristiana.

Weiner, Annette B. 1992. *Inalienable possessions. The paradox of keeping-while-giving*. Berkeley: University of California Press.

Weismantel, Mary. 2004. Moche sex pots: Reproduction and temporality in ancient South America. *American Anthropologist* 106(3):495–505.

———. 2005. Two heads are better than one. Paper presented in symposium "Between the Living and the Dead," organized by Izumi Shimada, Society for American Archaeology 70th annual meetings, Salt Lake City, March 30–April 3.

Wheeler, Jane, and Elías Mujica. 1981. Prehistoric pastoralism in the Lake Titicaca Basin, Peru, 1979–1980 field season. Final report to the National Science Foundation, Washington, DC.

Whitehead, William T. 1999. Dating at Chiripa. In *Early settlement in Chiripa, Bolivia: Research of the Taraco archaeological project*, pp. 17–21. Ed. C. A. Hastorf. No. 57, Archaeological Research Facility Monograph Publications. Berkeley: University of California.

Whitley, James. 2002. Too many ancestors. *Antiquity* 76(291):119–26.

Wickler, Wolfgang and Uta Steibt. 1982. Toad spawn symbolism suggested for Sechin. *American Antiquity* 47(2):441–44.

Wiener, Charles. 1879. *Pérou et Bolivie, récit de voyage suivi d'études archéologiques et ethnographiques et de notes sur l'écriture et les langues des populations indiennes*. Paris: Hachette.

Williams, P. Ryan. 2001. Cerro Baúl: A Wari center on the Tiwanaku frontier. *Latin American Antiquity* 12(1):67–83.

Wistrand, L. 1967. Cashibo kinship system and social relationship. Series CENDIE 00178, I.C. No. 171. Buenos Aires: Centro de Documentación e Información Educativa (CENDIE).

Young, Michael W. 1971. *Fighting with food: Leadership, values and social control in a Massim society*. Cambridge: Cambridge University Press.

Ziólkowski, Mariusz S. 1996. *La guerra de los Wawqi. Los objetivos y los mecanismos de la rivalidad dentro de la élite inka, S. XV–XVI*. Quito: Biblioteca Abya-Yala.

———. 1997. Los juegos y las apuestas o "del origen de la propiedad privada." In *Arqueología, antropología e historia en los Andes, Homenaje a María Rostworowski*, pp. 301–19. Eds. R. Varón and J. Flores Ochoa. Lima: IEP.

Zuidema, R. Tom. 1972. Meaning in Nazca art: Iconographic relationships between Inca- Huari- and Nazca cultures in southern Peru. *Annual report for 1971, Goteborgs Ethnografiska Museum*, pp. 35–54. Arstryck, Sweden: Goteborgs Ethnografiska Museum.

———. 1973. Kinship and ancestor cult in three Peruvian communities: Hernández Príncipe's account of 1622. *Bulletin de l'Institute Français d'Études Andines* 2(1): 16–33.

———. 1982. The sidereal lunar calendar of the Incas. In *Archaeoastronomy in the New World*, pp. 59–106. Ed. Anthony F. Aveni. Cambridge: Cambridge University Press.

———. 1989a. Significado en el arte Nasca. Relaciones iconográficas entre las culturas Inca, Huari y Nasca en el sur del Perú. In *Reyes y guerreros. Ensayos de cultura andina*, pp. 386–401. Comp. Manuel Burga. Lima: FOMCIENCIAS. Grandes Estudios Andinos series.

———. 1989b. Burocracia y conocimiento sistemático en la sociedad andina. In *Reyes y guerreros. Ensayos de cultura andina*, pp. 488–535. Comp. Manuel Burga. Lima: FOMCIENCIAS. Grandes Estudios Andinos series.

———. 1989c. El juego de los ayllus y del amaru. In *Reyes y guerreros. Ensayos de cultura andina*, pp. 256–72. Comp. M. Burga. Lima: FOMCIENCIAS. Grandes Estudios Andinos series.

———. 1989d. La cuadratura del círculo en el antiguo Perú. In *Reyes y guerreros. Ensayos de cultura andina*, pp. 273–305. Comp. M. Burga. Lima: FOMCIENCIAS. Grandes Estudios Andinos series.

———. 1990. *Inca civilization in Cuzco*. Trans. Jean-Jacques Decoster. Austin: University of Texas Press.

———. 1992. Inca cosmos in Andean context. From the perspective of the Capac Raymi Camay Quilla feast celebrating the December solstice in Cuzco. In *Andean cosmologies through time*, pp. 17–45. Eds. Robert V. H. Dover, Katherine E. Seibold, and John H. McDowell. Bloomington: Indiana University Press.

———. 1995. *El sistema de ceques del Cuzco. La organización social de la capital de los Incas*. Lima: Pontificia Universidad Católica del Perú, Fondo Editorial.

Index

Abercrombie, Thomas A., 29, 93–95, 98
accumulation: control of, 219; generative power and vitality of accumulated heads, 23, 46; of heads, 20, 71, 139, 162; of labor, 24; of soul force, 24; of wives, 220; patterns of accumulating heads, 21; political uses of accumulated heads, 217; power over model and accumulated heads, 23, 226; primitive forms of, 35, 218; theories of, 220
agency. See political agency.
Akapana pyramid (Tiwanaku), 72
Albarracín-Jordan, Juan, 124, 156
Albó, Xavier, 124, 228
Alborñoz, Cristóbal, 155
Alconini, Sonia, 193
Aldenderfer, Mark, 183
Al este de los Andes (Renard-Casevitz, Saignes, and Taylor), 27
Allen, Catherine, 30, 98–105, 114, 156, 159, 178
Alvarado, José de la Vega, 132
Amazon Basin, 20
ancestors, 19–20, 30–31; bones, 156; creation myths and, 155; day of the dead, 30; descent group identities, 153; fertility and, 61; force-feeding of, 30; heads of, 24, 26, 28, 36, 45; Inka use of, 214; male initiation rites and, 153; mallki bundles, 154, 174, 195, 202; mummified, 155; origin routes, 154; Pikillacta figurines of, 202; political manipulation of, 215; souls of, 175; spirit essence of, 175; water and, 159; worship of ancestors in common, 195
Andean history, 20
Anderson, Benedict, 22

androgeny, 180; heads and, 181
Apaza, Cipriana, 54
Appadurai, Arjun, 44
appropriation: of subjectivities, 46–47
Arellano Hoffmann, Carmen, 88
Arnold, Denise, 19, 40, 42–43, 46–48, 50, 54, 57, 72, 73, 78, 79, 83, 93, 98, 108–109, 112, 118, 125, 127, 133–134, 136, 138–139, 142, 155, 158, 159, 167, 186
Arnold, Denise and Espejo, 48, 55, 130, 133–134
Arnold and Yapita, 32, 35, 46–49, 55, 60, 65, 72, 80, 93, 95, 98, 101, 111–113, 121, 136, 138–139, 142, 155, 159; Andean textual-ontological theory, 32, 57; metamorphosis of heads, 49, 54, 64, 110
Arnold, Yapita, and Tito, 109
Ascher, Marcia and Robert, 81
Assadourian, Carlos Sempat, 25
Astvaldsson, Astvaldur, 111, 118–120, 190
Atahualpa, 92
Atoc (Atahualpa's brother), 92
ayllu, 35, 42, 45, 95, 107, 111, 124; boundaries and heads, 132, 135; center, 126; gatherings, 166; identity of, 126–127; landholding groups, 155; mayor and minor, 125–126, 137; narrative histories, 226; nested hierarchies of, 155–156; territorial logic of, 128, 135, 227
ayllu head, 111, 117–121
ayllu Qaqachaka. See Qaqachaka.
Aymara: Colla leaders under the Inka, 214; language, 16; nation, 40; political thought, 120; treatment of the dead, 163
ayni: as exchange of heads, 57, 222

babies, 47, 49; as converted heads, 54; as enemy descendants, 51; as warriors, 52; female authority and rearing, 116; heads and the proliferation of, 50, 78, 114, 221–222; nurture of, 176
Bandelier, Adolph F. A., 157
Bandy, Matthew, 126, 156, 187–189
Barnes, Ruth, 49
Barrett, John, 30
belly: as seat of head metamorphosis to babies, 50–51
Benetiz, Leo, 87
Bennett, W. C., 71, 74
Betanzos, Juan de, 66, 214
black magic, 161
Bloch, Maurice, 29, 60, 89
Blom, Deborah E., 188
Blood Rites (Ehrenreich), 22
Bodies that Matter (Butler), 30
body: body relations and political relations, 166, 226; body parts, 33; body politic, 21; body use in politics, 26, 221; imagery of, 125; Inka body, 150; state formation and, 27
Bolivia, 20
Bourget, Steven, 75, 90, 211
Bouysse-Cassagne, Thérèse, 41
brains: breath or spirit and, 65; eating, 65; generative seed and, 65; gray matter, 46, 220; sucking, 93
Browman, David, 184
Browne, David H., 74, 177, 178, 180, 181
Burger, Richard L., 208
burial chests. *See* mountain chests.
Burma, 24, 54, 227; the Kachin of, 24; the Naga of, 24, 49
Bustillos, Martha Sandra and colleagues, 163–164
Butler, Judith, 30

Cabello Balboa, Miguel, 214
Caillavet, Chantal, 215
cannibalism, 20, 26, 43; attributes of, 154; commodification and, 116; exo-cannibalism, 47; jaguars and, 101; under Spanish rule, 215
capital: headlike, 60; mercantile, 58
cargo: heads and, 93, 113
Carmichael, Patrick H., 61

Carneiro, Robert L., 23, 24
Castro Rochas, Victoria, 83
cemeteries: group, 171
centrifugal: drinking pathways, 94–95; political and economic models, 25, 41, 46, 68, 125, 128, 150
centripetal: drinking pathways, 94–95; political and economic models, 25, 125, 150
Cereceda, Verónica, 54
Cerro Sechín, 48, 75, 201; head imagery at, 209; iconography, 209
chachapumas, 67, 101, 181, 190–191, 193
Chalcochima (Inka general), 92
Chanka, 92
Chase-Dunn, Christopher, 23, 25, 150
Chávez, Sergio, 57, 59, 101, 184, 191; two distinct ritual phases, 58, 158, 221
Chavín de Huántar, 61, 207; Amazonian links, 218; as oracle site, 119–120; cera-mics and metamorphosis images, 64; deities, 208; *kipus*, 143; portable artifacts, 119; rainmaking at, 208; tenon heads, 167, 175, 194, 207–208
ch'axwa, 43
checkered, 82
Chesson, Meredith, 45
chicha, 92
childbirth, as opposed to warfare, 51
chinu: heads and, 47. *See also kipu.*
Chiripa: architecture, 187; as centripetal polity, 228; burial offerings, 223; burials, 77; carved stela, 189; civic core, 188; matri-focus, 187; matri- to patri-focus, 228; niches, 188, 232; platform mound, 188; semi-subterranean enclosures, 188; settlement, 184; stone heads, 162, 184; Upper Houses, 71, 74
Ch'isi (Lake Titicaca), 189
Christian ideas: about heads, 35
chullpa tombs: construction period, 211; rains and, 161
circulation, controlled, 44
Cobo, Bernabé, 155
Coercion, Capital, and European States, AD 990–1992 (Tilly), 22
colonial contact: and destabilization, 223; and heads, 22; centrifugal expansion, 215
Colque Guarache, Juan, 40

CONAMAQ (Consejo Nacional de Ayllus y Markas de Qullasuyo), 40
Conklin, Beth, 51
Conklin, William, 96, 104, 140
Connerton, Paul, 29–30, 152
consumptive production, 230
containers: for heads, 72; sacrifice and, 72; to concentrate power, 72
"contract" theories of state emergence, 22, 219
Cook, Anita, 181–182, 200, 201, 202
Cordero Miranda, Gregorio, 184
Cordy-Collins, Alana, 208
Coricancha (Qurikancha, Cusco), 72; niches, 188, 202
corporeality, 46
Costin, Cathy, 92
counting boards (*yupana*), 80–81, 85, 90, 145
Couture, Nicole, 194, 202
Coya: as head holder, 102, 223; sovereignty, 121; weaving and, 104
crania: contents, 48; corporeal power concentration and, 147; curated, 19–20
criollo culture, 20
Crónica del Perú (Cieza de León), 215
Crumley, Carole L., 24
Culture and Truth (Rosaldo), 21
culture heroes: acts of, 21
Cummins, Tom, 96, 97, 99–102
curatorial practices, 20, 29, 45, 63, 71
Cusco: *ceques*, 96; dominion by, 138; libations that record, 137; *qapaqjucha ritual*, 98; sun religion, 97

D-shaped structures, 195; and rains, 203; and sacrifice, 201; in Wari, 195, 197, 200, 201, 203; niched halls in, 201
D'Altroy, Terence N., 150, 151
dead: ancestral, 163; calling up, 174–175; enemies, 29, 163; kinsmen, 29; recent, 29
Dean, Caroline, 110, 211
deaths: bad, 29; good, 29
Death and the Regeneration of Life (Bloch and Parry), 29
Deathly Waters and Hungry Mountains (Gose), 158
DeLeonardis, Lisa, 33, 179, 181–182
Descola, Philippe, 47, 49, 117, 123

Desrosiers, Sophie, 54, 57
diarchy, 43
disintegrative forces, 43
distribution: controlled, 44
Donnan, Christopher, 74–76, 210
Douglas, Mary, 44, 68
Doyle, Mary, 154, 155, 188, 215
drinking: festive, 94; iconography, 96–99; pathways, 94–96, 98, 225
Drusini, Andrea, 74
duality, 137–138, 144, 152; gendered duality, 125
Duverger, Christian, 103
Duviols, Pierre, 50, 98

Earle, Timothy, 167
economic rationality, 213
economic space, 25; field of forces and, 25; poles of growth and, 25;
economic systems and heads, 212, 230
economy: bellicose, 41; pre-state, 37
Ehrenreich, Barbara, 22
Ehrenreich, Robert M., 24
El Niño, 157
embodiment, 119
enclaved (curated) objects, 44; heads as, 44; heads as heirlooms in, 45
enemies: destructive relations and, 60; heads of, 26
Engel, Fréderic André, 162
Engl, Lieselotte and Theo, 83, 89
Espejo, Elvira, 48, 55, 117, 130, 134; significance of weavings, 133; *wayñu* meanings, 127–128
Estete, M. de, 179
exchange: circuits, 44; of body parts, 33; of heads, 33, 43–44; primitive forms of, 218; raising stakes, 90; reciprocal, 24, 36; restricted, 44, 231; violent, 36

Fausto, Carlos, 25, 27, 33, 36, 43, 46–47, 68, 94, 100, 153–154, 194; model of centrifugal and centripetal tendencies, 36, 153, 228; productive consumption, 36, 230; symbolic efficacy, 46
Feldman, Robert, 74
feasting: competitive, 24
felines: cannibalism and, 101, 154; feline state and hallucinogens, 191, 201; feline warriors, 209; heads and, 101;

iconography of, 184, 191, 225; *qiru* designs of, 100–103; *wak'as* and, 119

fetishism of the commodity, 20, 45, 58–60; and heads, 21, 46, 173, 222, 231

finance: staple, 44; wealth, 44

Flores Ochoa, Jorge, 96–97, 100–104, 225

flying heads, 65–67

force, threat of, 22

Forgerty, Kathleen, 178

Foucault, Michel, 23

Frame, Mary, 55, 132, 133

Friedman, Jonathan, 24, 54, 227

frontiers: bellicose practices on, 40, 215, 219

Fung P., Rosa, 207

games: dice, 80, 83, 145; heads and, 83; Huarona games at New Year, 88; luck, 89; number games, 81; *pichca* (fives), 87–88; *qanchi*, 89; sacrifice and, 89; tournament economy, 81, 222; *wayruru* seed game, 89

gaming boards: iconography, 83; platforms, 86; pyramid form, 83; *taptana*, 81, 88–90, 145

García, Rubén, 74, 177, 178, 180, 181

gender: female weaving and male warfare, 223; relations in Nasca, 180; ritual practice and, 138

gendered: dualism, 137–138, 144; identities, 109, 144; heads, 114–117; parallelism in language, 138, 224

Gentile, Margarita, 83

geoanatomy, 135

geopolitical patterns, 130; and heads, 126–128; and pacification, 133, 227

Gisbert, Teresa, 100; and colleagues, 99

Glasser B. and A. Strauss, 32

Glowacki, Mary, 197, 204

Gluckman, Max, 44

Godelier, Maurice, 213

Goldstein, Paul, 192

González García, José Alejandro, 172

González Holguín, Diego, 88

Gose, Peter, 158–159

grease suckers, 115

Grieder, Terence, 207

Guaman Poma de Ayala, don Felipe, 81, 85, 92, 100, 110, 140, 150, 151, 214

hair: twisted, 55; trophy heads and, 66; thought and, 66

Harner, Michael, 61

Harris, Olivia, 41, 158

Harrison, Simon, 21

Hastorf, Christine, 19, 58, 71, 74, 77, 155, 183, 185, 187–188, 190, 194, 212, 229

hau. *See* Maori *hau*.

head caches, 171–172, 177–179, 201, 231; as concentrations of political power, 219–220; banking of heads, 90, 131, 138, 143, 231; rainmaking and, 232

head capture, 20, 25; from enemy groups, 25

head givers: as peripheral polities, 23; as concentrations of ritual power, 64, 162

Headhunting and the Social Imagination in Southeast Asia (Hoskins), 24

headhunting, 20; interpretations of, 21; practices of, 21; Toraja example of, 27

head management, 27, 232

head raiding: competitive, 22

heads: accumulation of, 20, 179; ancestor, 19, 20, 36, 153; ancestral and enemy head differences, 144, 147–148, 179, 219; as hierarchical religious systems, 35; as power holders, 117–118; body politic and, 21; capture of, 19, 25; carved stone, 19; cigarettes offered to, 20; commodity fetish and, 21; converted to babies, 50; curated crania, 19, 20, 29, 45; difference and, 21; enemy, 19; exchange of, 21; family, 45; fertility and, 21; fetishism of, 43–47; flying, 20, 65–67; geopolitical organization of, 126; guarding of, 21; household, 110–114; human skulls, 19; hunting of, 20; identity and, 21, 229; imagery of, 20; imagined, 20; incense offered to, 20; keeping of, 20; knots as, 20; land titles, and, 45; language of, 21; libations made to, 20; maintenance of, 21; of state, 152–154; on poles, 114, 210; pathways created by, 219; political control over, 22; political economy and, 21; political systems and, 21, 124–126; political uses of, 20–22, 27, 214; powers of, 27, 48, 50; regeneration and, 21, 27; ritual uses of, shamanic uses of, 21, 27; significance of, 20; shapes of, 20; shrunken, 179; slavery and, 21; sprouting, 61; symbolism of, 21, 23, 107, 144; taking of, 20–21, 43; territorial conformation and, 149; territorial power and, 107; theory of, 37–44; trophy, 19, 26, 36; violence and, 21; vital force of soul substance in, 28–29, 220; water and, 203; weaving designs of, 20; wrapping, 20. *See also* regeneration, trophy heads.

head takers: as core polity, 23; state as, 232; status of, 26, 114, 220

head taking, 20–21, 26–27; economic domain of, 231; exchange and, 43; female phase, 221; *jira mayku* and, 136; male phase, 221; regional contextualization of, 21; spiritual explanation for, 64; symbolism of, 43; threats of, 22

Hendon, Julia, 22, 44

heterarchy, 24–25, 33, 228, 229

highland-lowlands: and coastal trading, and heads, 21, 217; comparison, 26; dynamics, 25, 100; ongoing relations between, 27, 217–218

Hobsbawm, Eric, 22

Hocquenghem, Anne Marie, 75

Hoskins, Janet, 24, 29, 222

How Chiefs Come to Power (Earle), 22

How Societies Remember (Connerton), 152

Huaca de la Luna (Moche Valley), 74, 90, 211

Huanca, Tomás, 160

Huascar Inka. *See* Inka Waska.

Hubert, Henri, 45, 220

human sacrifice, 26–27

Iconografía mochica (Hocquenghem), 210

iconography: Chavín, 55, 61; flow of life, 187; Moche war, 48, 74, 83; Nasca, 50, 61; *qiru*, 96–106

identities: centrifugal systems and, 25, 153; centripetal systems and, 25, 153; group, 153; heads and, 153, 162; outside, 25, 153; relational, 31–32; social, 156; vertical perpetuation of, 25, 153–154

illa, 79; ancestral, 156, 202; as seed-like, 79, 203, 226

Inalienable Possessions (Weiner), 44, 231

indigenous: autonomy, 21; people, 20

Inimigos fiéis (Fausto), 27

initiation: cycles of, and male identity, 103, 109, 153

Inka: armies, 151; body, 150; burial position, 207; doubles, 149; flower, 103; head of, 150; itinerant person, 149; miniature heads, 214; mitimae communities, 151; mummies, 214; rebellions against, 151; regenerative powers, 149; rituals, 150; rituals of conquest, 150; sovereignty, 120; use of dead bodies, 214

Inka Pachakuti, 41, 92

Inka Roca, 101

Inka state, 47, 51, 137; as head taker, 51, 214; *ceques*, 96; direct rule, 150; enemy trophy head use, 214; empire, 139; expansion, 120, 212–214; incursion or occupation, 43, 78–79, 138, 143; Inka rituals and rainfall, 72, 137; Qapaq Raymi feast and male initiation, 103; *qiru* tumblers, 91, 99

Inka Topa Yupanki, 41

Inka Tupaq Yupanki, 40

Inka Waska (Huascar), 41, 92, 214

Inka Wayna Qapaq (Huayna Capac), 41, 214

Inkarriy, 67

inqa, 30

integrative forces, 43

interethnic relations: offensive, 25; pacific, 25

Isbell, William H., 194, 197, 211, 212

Izikowitz, Karl, 82

Izumi, S., 207

JAKISA (Jatun Killakas-Asanaqi), indigenous council, 40

Jennings, Jesse, 209

Jesús de Machaqa: authority obligations, 118; ayllu heads, 118; deity heads, 118; marriage obligations, 111; stone heads, 120, 190

Jiménez, Domingo, 57, 64–65, 121, 123–124, 141–143, 157

jira mayku devil spirits, 54–55, 68, 136; heads and, 136; rains and, 158;

Jorgenson, Andrew, 23

Joyce, Rosemary, 22, 202

jucha, 93; duty, 120; heads and, 93; sucking crania and, 93, 225

Kala Uyuni (Qala Uyuni), 99, 162, 189
Kanchi, Ayra, 40
Kapital (Marx), 22
Keeping-while-giving. See Weiner, Annette.
Kidder, II, A. V., 72, 190
kipu: and head curation, 225; as records, 80, 81, 139; bureaucracy development and, 139–143, 232; counting on, 85; division, 80; hair and, 47, 159, 232; heads and, 47, 142–143; *kipukamayuq*, 81, 85, 139, 143; *kipu*-like mnemonics and mapping, 78; luck and, 140; main cord of, 80; mountains and, 159; narrative, 139; numerical, 139; origins in heads, 139; threads of, 90; water and, 159. *See also chinu*.
Knobloch, Patricia J., 201, 202
Kolata, Alan, 72, 137, 191, 193
Kontopoulos, Kyriakis, 24
Korpisaari, Antti, 40
Kotosh, 206–207; Mito culture, 207; niches, 207
Kowta, Makoto, 178
Kroeber, Alfred L., 171, 178
Kruyt, Albert C., 29
K'ulta ayllu, 29, 93; animal marking ceremony, 95; memory pathways, 94

land fights, 133; contemporary, 37
La Lone, Darrell, 25, 27, 119, 227
Lancho Rojas, Josué, 177
Lanzón (Chavín), 77; heads and, 208
Lathrap, Donald, 61, 192
Lavalle, José Antonio de, 172
Leach, Edmund, 24
leadership, 22; heads and, 108, 120, 178; symbols of, 108; turns of office, 121; *wara* staff of office, 112, 121–124
Lemuz Aguirre, Carlos, 185
Lévi-Strauss, Claude, 152
Levy, Janet E., 24
Llanos, David, 157, 160–161
L'Inca, l'Espagnol et les sauvages (Renard-Casevitz, Saignes, and Taylor), 40
Logic of Social Structures, The (Kontopoulos), 24
Los Andes orientales (Saignes), 27

López G., U. R., 73, 77–79
luck, 89, 109; adding value and, 233; and heads, 143; rains and, 160
Lumbreras, Luís G., 197

Macha: *tinku*, 94; warriors, 94
Malinowski, Bronislaw, 117
Malpass, Michael, 197, 204
mana, 45; as difference in potential, 220; compared to Aymara *ch'ama*, 220
Manco Inka, 41
Mannheim, Bruce, 122
Maori *hau*, 20, 50; as radiating yield, 20, 45, 220; and regenerative power, 57; compared to Aymara *ch'ama*, 220
marka, 79, 108, 127; territorial jurisdiction of, 79
marking ceremony (of animals, *k'illpha*), 95
Marx, Karl: fetishism of the commodity, 20, 45, 58–60, 81, 90, 231; *Kapital*, 22, 58; Marxist models of state emergence, 22; Marxist theory, 20; theories of accumulation, 220
Massim (Papua New Guinea), 93
Mauss, Marcel, 20, 45; on Maori *hau*, 20, 220
May, Thomas D., 25
McClelland, Donna, 74–76
McEwan, Gordon F., 197, 201–202
McWilliam, Andrew, 224
Mejía Xesspe, Toribio, 171
memory: pathways of, 29; pathways of heads, 225
metamorphosis: Moche burial theme and, 75; of foe into friend, 49, 144, 219, 229; of heads, 49, 54, 64, 83, 90, 104, 208; of money into capital, 231; sacrifice and, 74, 77–78, 90, 159
Metamorphosis of Heads, The (Arnold and Yapita), 19, 41, 93, 110, 144
Middle America, 51
Moche, 48; burial theme, 74–75; ceramics, 64; feline warriors, 191; iconography, 83; Moche-Chimu, 150; portrait head vessels, 209; warfare imagery, 48
models of state formation: body parts and, 27; centralizing functions, 23; centripetal

and centrifugal forces of, 25–26, 125; combined models, 228; contract theories of, 22, 33, 78, 219; duality, 137–138, 144, 152; environmental and social circumscription theories, 23; heterarchy, 24, 228, 229; increasing complexity, 228; institutional specialization in, 23; internally generated, 24; nested hierarchy, 43, 137; power over, 22–23, 219; predatory theories of, 22, 33; primitive forms of accumulation and, 35; stratification of, 23; theory of heads in, 37; world systems theory, 23

Mohr Chávez, Karen, 74, 184

Molina del Cusco, Cristóbal, 213

monumental architecture, 167; dead and, 167; heads and, 167, 226

Moore, Jerry, 166

Morales, Evo, 109

mountain chests, 73–74, 77, 104, 232; other forms of chest and, 79; sites of transformation, 203; small dark rooms like, 203

mountains: dead and, 159; as guardians, 64, 73, 79–80, 159; rains and, 159

Mujica, Elías, 190

Mulvany, Eleanora, 102

mummy bundles (*fardos*), 154–155, 171, 174, 195, 202; colonial veneration of, 215

Murúa, Martin de, 66, 214

Nasca, 176–182; ceramics, 180; ceremonialism, 61, 63; drought, 197; dualism, 177; emerging bureaucracy and heads, 231; expanding centrifugal system, 177; head taking and, 27; heads with pinned mouths, 181; iconography of heads, 51, 179–180; kin-oriented groups, 177; *kipus*, 143; *qiru*, 91; shrunken heads, 179; skulls with carrying ropes, 171; stone head, 162; textiles, 133; two cranial lines, 178; worldview, 64, 181

ñatitas, 163; form of death, 163, 230; skull bundles, 165; women owners of, 163–164

Needham, Rodney, 28–29, 220

niches: as containers for heads, 71–73, 188, 190, 207

nuwasi, 43–45

Ochotoma, José, 201

Ogburn, Dennis, 27

ontological depredation, 36, 45, 57, 68, 228, 230

oratory: male power and political oratory, 46

Pachaqamaq: as oracle site, 119

Paititi, 100, 104

Paracas, 169–176; heads on textiles, 173; mummy bundles, 171; Necropolis, 173; staffs, 122; textile iconography, 174; textiles, 55, 67, 122, 133, 169, 175, 230

Parry, Jonathan, 29, 60, 89

Pärsinnen, Martti, 40

Pauketat, Timothy, 167

Paul, Anne, 55–56, 67–68, 173–174, 176, 186–187

Pérez Bocanegra, Juan, 122

Pérou et Bolivie (Wiener), 85

Perroux, François, 25; poles of growth, 25

Pezzia Assereto, Alejandro, 171

Pikillacta, 201–202; figurines, 202

platform mounds, 74–75; Chiripa mound, 188, 202; labor concentrated in, 167; Nasca mounds, 177; Pukara mound, 202; Tiwanaku mounds, 193

Platt, Tristan, 41, 52, 94, 120–121, 124

political agency, 26, 30; head and body use and, 26, 221; head taking and, 230; notions of political personhood, 108–109

political development: "contract" theories of, 22; existing models of, 20

political formations: acephalous groups, 137; balanced dualism, 107, 125, 138; body imagery of, 125; center and periphery, 138, 144, 227; centralizing centripetal, 150, 152; complex, 21; constructive and destructive forces, 137; corporate, 153; dispersed centrifugal, 150; evolutionary theories of, 21; duality, 137–138, 144, 152; fissioning of, 126; heads and, 147; heterarchy, 107; hierarchical, 149, 150; incipient political hierarchy, 22; nested hierarchies, 33, 107–108, 144, 147, 155; rotating, 107, 125; segmentary, 107, 124, 149, 150; stratified, 107 political power: consolidation of, 107, 182; expanding outward, 130; female political power and shamanism, 220; heads as symbols of, 218; head taking and, 46, 147

political processes, 125; alliances, 133–135, 152, 220; bipolar dynamics, 198; centrifugal break away tendencies, 152; combined models, 228; descent group celebration through heads, 153; dispersal and disintegration, 43; integration and reintegration, 43, 125, 135; long-lived group identities, 152; predatory and reconciliatory practices, 152

political relations: body relations and, 166; cannibalism and, 26

Ponce Sanginés, Carlos, 184, 192, 194

Popular Participation Law (1994), 42

Portugal Ortíz, M., 184, 189

possessions, alienable, 45

power: channeling, 23, 30; enabling, 23, 80; relations, 20, 153; strategies, 22; to coerce, 23

Pozorski, Shelia and Thomas G., 209

Primera información (Colque Guarache), 40

Probanza (1637), 40

production: control of, 22; household, 47; of objects or persons, 46, 230; productive yields, 80, 139, 222; resources and, 22; symbolism for, 184

productive consumption, 36, 230

Proulx, Donald, 51, 52, 61, 63, 65, 115, 143, 179, 181; metamorphozing plants and heads, 64; two complexes of Nasca, 63, 158

Pukara, 190–192; ceramics and metamorphosis images, 64, 101, 104; ceramics and enemy head capture, 191; *chachapuma*, 190; imagery, 191; niches, 71, 190; *qirus*, 99; sacrifice images, 57

Pukina language, 16

qapaqjucha ritual, 98

Qaqachaka, 20, 37, 40, 53; *achak k'illpha* and *sawu tila* dance, 133–134; animal-marking ceremony, 95; as centrifugal polity, 228; ayllu, 20, 29, 32, 125; caches of heads, 72; Carnival, 118, 135; embalming, 179; enemies of, 64; feast sponsors and heads, 121; game of *taptana*, 89; gender

relations, 109; head taking and, 41, 43, 46, 48; initiation rites, 109; *kipus*, 232; leadership duties, 120; libations, 98; *marka*, 79, 108, 127; marriage obligations, 111; oral history, 41; personhood, 108–109; political organization, 108, 125, 137; power of heads in, 167; power relations, 153; rainmaking, 157; rituals, 80; sacrifices, 75, 77; stone mounds for heads, 72, 136, 183; textual practices, 140–141; toasts, 92; toasts in warfare, 65; warriors, 82, 114–117; warriors of the Inka, 40–42; *wayñu* dance, 126; *willja* ritual, 130–132, 223

qilqa: incised designs, 81

qiru (or *qero*) tumblers, 91–106; belt of, 100; concentric designs, 95–98; feline-rainbow motif, 100; heads and, 91, 94, 99, 106; head shapes, 215; iconography of, 97, 99, 221; memory pathways and, 94–96, 225; outward designs, 95–98; *paccha*, 99; rhomboid designs, 102; semiotic analysis of, 98; sun religion and, 98; waterflow and, 159; wooden, 99; zigzag designs, 102

Quechua: language, 16; poetry and song, 122

radiating yield, 20, 45, 127, 220; and heads, 127, 131, 203, 213; fecund power, 137; of agricultural production, 130–131; of ritual power, 130–132. *See also* Maori *hau*.

Radicati di Primeglio, Carlos, 81, 82, 84, 85, 86, 89

Raimundi stela, 55, 67; heads and, 208

rainbow arch: head recycling and, 103

rainfall: ancestors and, 158; heads and, 104, 157–161; enemies and, 158; Inka rituals and, 72; rainmaking powers, 73; rainmaking rituals, 124, 137, 144; suffering and, 223; uncertainty of, 72

rainmaking rituals: *vara* staffs and, 124

Ramirez, Susan A., 149

redistribution, 90

regeneration: as opposed to destructive warfare, 63; bones and, 156; degeneration and, 233; heads and, 162, 220; identity and, 152; of heads, 21, 27, 36, 47–58

Renard-Casevitz, France-Marie, 27, 40
reproduction: of persons, 45; of things, 45
resources: management of, 22, 83
Rick, John, 119, 208
ritual battles, 46. *See also nuwasi* and *tinku*.
rituals: choreography of, 133–135; of health,
    131; transformative practices, 144; *willja*,
    130–131
River of Fleece, River of Song (Arnold and
    Yapita), 55, 126
Robert, Jean, 222
Rodriguez Kembel, Silvia, 119
Roe, Peter, 187, 192
Root, Deborah, 116
Rosaldo, Renato, 21
Rose, Courtney E., 72
Rowe, John H., 62

sacrifice: for rainfall, 137, 159; niches for,
    73; of animals, 75, 131
sacrificer and regenerator theme, 58, 158,
    207–208, 221
Saignes, Thierry, 27, 40
saints: treated like heads, 114
Salomon, Frank, 80, 81, 87–88, 155, 160,
    174–175, 215
sami, 30–31
Samoa: staffs of office, 123
Santiago de Huata Peninsula, 162, 185
Sawyer, Alan, 61
Schaedel, Richard P., 124, 150
schooling, 47, 144
Schreiber, Katherina Jeanne, 177, 198
Schültes, Richard, 97
seed: and head, 57, 220; and seed-like *mallki*
    bundles, 79, 154, 174, 195, 202, 224;
    disseminating sequence and heads, 221;
    seed imagery of heads, 221
seminal thought, 57
shamans: flying, 67; flying heads and, 66;
    head caches and, 66; speaking to heads,
    66
Shuar: *arutam*, 65; *muisak*, 65; staffs of
    office, 123
Sikkink, Lynn, 159
Silverman, Gail, 140
Silverman, Helaine, 74, 171, 177, 178, 180,
    181
Sistema de la economía colonial (Assadourian),
    25

skulls: ancestral and enemy, 161; Day of
    the Skulls, 164–166; luck and, 160;
    ñatita, 163–166; rainmaking and, 157,
    160; vehicles of ritual power, 158; water
    guardians as, 88; with carrying ropes,
    171
slavery: and heads, 21; male prisoners as
    slaves, 53; slave raiding and heads, 21;
    slave taking and headhunting, 24; slave
    trading and heads, 21
Social Life of Things, The (Appadurai), 44
social power, 20; as enabling or generating
    power, 23
Spedding, Alison, 67, 166
spirit essence, 175
spirit of calculation, 20, 81, 86, 145, 222;
    luck and, 145; tournament economy
    and, 81, 222, 232
Stanish, Charles, 74, 183, 190
state formations: ayllus and, 137; early, 22;
    modern states, 23; state as head taker,
    232; theories of, 22; unifying features
    of, 228
Steadman, Lee, 187
Steibt, Uta, 209
Stobart, Henry, 116
Strathern, Marilyn, 30
Structural Anthropology (Lévi-Strauss), 152
symbols of office, 27
Szemiński, Jan, 78–79

tambos, 138; heads and, 138
Tantalean Arbulu, Javier, 213
Taraco: carved stones, 189; dual images,
    185; group fissioning in, 126; niched
    enclosure, 71
Tawantinsuyu, 40, 41; expansion, 83
Taylor, Ann Christine, 27, 40, 47, 49
Tejido andino, El (G. Silverman), 140
Tello, Julio C., 171, 173, 176, 178
Tello Obelisk, 61–62; heads and, 208
Terada, K., 207
theories of the Andean state, 20
Tilly, Charles, 22
tinku, 43, 93–94
Titicaca Basin: ayllu-like kin groups, 186;
    carved stelae, 192; ceremonial use of
    heads, 183; dualism, 186; feline postures
    in, 192; priestly or military elites, 192;

territorial use of heads, 183; Yayamama tradition, 184

Tiwanaku, 192–196; Akapana platform, 193, 195, 203; Amazonian links, 218; ancestral heads, 195; centralizing tendency, 194; ceramics, 194–195; *chachapumas,* 101, 190; coastal incursion threat, 177; deities, 195–196; demise of, 211, 229; expansion, 197; heads in semi-sunken enclosure, 194; *kipus*, 140, 143; leadership, 195; monumental structures, 192; multiculturalism of, 194; nested center, 192; polity, 139, 156, 182; portrait vessels, 199; Pumapunku, 196; *qiru* tumblers, 91, 192–193; sacrifice, 194; secondary burial, 193; stone heads, 162; stonework, 184; tenon heads, 194, 202; textiles, 194; trophy head imagery, 194; water and heads at, 196

tocapu, 95, 100, 101; trophy head symbolism and, 105

tongue: and speech of souls, 175

Topa Inka, 66; headdress, 47; shamanic powers and, 66

Topic, John R., 201

Torrico, Cassandra, 54

tribute: categories of tributary systems, 22; cycles, 51; extension of and state formation, 227; heads and, 22, 24; Inkas and, 213; in war, 199; obligations, 41; payments, 89, 96; reckoning of, 85; *tasa*, 118; threats for non-payment, 195; tributary groups in Tiwanaku, 194

trophy heads, 26, 36; capture of by married men, 48; founding a household and, 113; men and, 114; three-year cycle of, 113; trophy head taking in World War II, 21; *vara* staffs like, 124; wrapping of, 48

tsantsa heads, 47, 49, 179, 181; compared to Nasca shrunken heads, 181

Turpin, Solveig A., 67–68, 174

twisting: twisted threads and heads, 55

Uceda, Santiago, 211

Uhle, Max, 83, 89, 178, 181

Uribe Rodríguez, Mauricio, 83

Urton, Gary, 60, 81, 139

Urukilla languages, 16

Valcárcel, L. E., 192

value: added value, 77; equivalence, 222; exchange value, 59–60; movement of, 81; of heads, 203; potential, 60; stone called, 77; theories of, 20; transformation of, 60; use value, 59–60, 203

vara staff of office, 112, 121–124; colonial staffs, 122; heads and, 123, 144, 226; *huarango* staffs, 122, 174; loom poles and, 122; of *chonta* wood, 122; of plaza altars, 127; *vara* bearers, 122. *See wara. See also* leadership.

Verano, John, 75, 178, 179, 181, 211

violence: ceremonial, 43

Viveiros de Castro, Eduardo, 36, 43, 46; ontological depredation, 36, 45, 57, 228, 230

Voces de los wak'a, Las (Astvaldsson), 111, 118

Vranich, A., 194

wak'a (huaca), 73, 78–80, 100, 118, 155; and corpses, 155; and heads, 119; rainmaking and, 159; ritual dialogues with, 83

Wallace, Dwight T., 56

Wallerstein, Immanuel, 23

wanka, 168

wara. See vara.

"war of the ayllus" (2000), 20, 42–43; head taking and, 42–43, 92

warfare: Andean and Amazonian connections, 27; as male counterpart to weaving, 49, 57, 144, 223; Aztec, 103; booty, 86; coercion and, 22, 219; continual, 24; economic aspects of, 22; flowers and, 103; forging nation-states and, 22; ideological aspects of, 22; indigenous, 21; internecine, 23; military aspects of, 22; military force and, 22; primitive, 21; seed imagery and, 201; turns of office and, 121; use of indigenous practices by the Spanish, 215

Wari, 196–203; ancestral and enemy heads, 202; and Tiwanaku sister polities, 198; architecture, 200; ceremonial enclosures, 72; city, 197; coastal incursion threat, 177; concern with water, 197, 204; deities, 198; demise of, 211, 229; expansion, 197, 198; face-neck urns, 198; iconography,

202; *kipus,* 140, 143; leadership, 198; lineage halls, 202; Moradchayoc niches, 197; polity, 182, 229; portrait vessels, 199; staffs, 122; state, 196; stone heads, 162; tumblers, 91

Warriors and Weavers (Arnold), 19

water: ancestors and, 159; changing, 160; control of, 74; heads and, 157, 203; owners of, 88; supplication for, 75

wawa. See babies.

wayñu, 126–127, 167; and history, 226; dead and, 128, 167

weaving: as female counterpart to war, 49, 57, 144, 223; as living beings, 54; bags, 140, 144, 225; borders, 55–56, 135, 140; dance choreography and new designs, 135; Coya and, 104; designs and heads, 48; female power and, 46; gyrations of dress, 175; hatbands, 132–133; heads and, 46, 227; in India, 48; interlacing, 135; loom space as site of transformation, 54, 127; macramé, 134; mummy bundles, 171; mourning cloth, 48; over-and-under motif, 96; plaza as loom, 127–128; stripes and quantity, 140; warp and heads, 112

Weiner, Annette, 44–45, 58, 123

Weismantel, Mary, 21, 33, 48, 175, 186, 210

Wheeler, Jane, 190

Wickler, Wolfgang, 209

Wiener, Charles, 85–88

Williams, Sloan, 178

wooden chests, 72; for storing heads, 72; for storing *kipus,* 140

world systems theory, 23; core and peripheral polities, 23

wrapping: female activity of, 49, 224; of heads, 49; of stone heads, 120; ritual bundles, 72

Yapita, Juan de Dios, 32, 35, 46–49, 54, 55, 57, 60, 64–65, 72, 80, 93, 95, 98, 101, 110–113, 121, 136, 138, 142, 155, 159

Yayamama tradition, 184, 187, 198; botanical iconography of, 184, 224; feline iconography of, 184

Young, Michael W., 93; fighting with food, 93

yupana. See counting boards.

Ziólkowski, Mariusz, 79

Zuidema, R. T., 53, 96, 98, 177

About the Authors

Denise Y. Arnold (Ph.D. 1988, University College London) is an Anglo-Bolivian anthropologist who holds postgraduate degrees in architecture and environmental studies. Her interests include kinship and gender, Andean literatures, textual practices and visual languages, methodologies, and data interpretation. She has been Leverhulme Research Fellow and ERSC Senior Research Fellow in England and is currently teaching at the Universidad Mayor de San Andrés and Universidad PIEB in La Paz, Bolivia, and the Universidad de Tarapaca in Chile. She is visiting Research Professor in Birkbeck College London and director of the Instituto de Lengua y Cultura Aymara in Bolivia. Among her recent p0ublications are "The Nature of Indigenous Literatures in the Andes: Aymara, Quechua and Others" in *Literary Cultures of Latin America: A Comparative History* (Oxford University Press, 2004); *The Metamorphosis of Heads: Textual Struggles, Education and Land in the Andes* (University of Pittsburgh Press, 2006); *River of Fleece, River of Song* (Bonn-BAS 35, 2001), and *Hilos sueltos. Los Andes desde el textil* (2007).

Christine A. Hastorf (Ph.D. 1983, University of California–Los Angeles) is Professor in the Department of Anthropology, University of California–Berkeley. Her major interests include paleoethnobotany, food and foodways, meaning in the everyday, Andean region of South America, data interpretation and methodology, social relations, and early settled life. Her recent publications occur in the journals *American Antiquity, Journal of Anthropological Archaeology*, and *Economic Botany*, and in books such as *The Social Archaeology of Food, Histories of Maize, Time and Complexity in Historical Ecology: Studies in the Neotropical Lowlands, Handbook of South American Archaeology, Advances in Titicaca Basin Archaeology-I*, and *Archaeological Site Museums in Latin America*. Besides overseeing an archaeobotanical laboratory at UC Berkeley, she spends most summers in the field in Bolivia.